The Effect of Defined Benefit Liability on Firms' Valuations in Japan

Comparison of Japanese GAAP for Retirement Benefits with IAS19

Eriko Kasaoka

Kwansei Gakuin University Press

The Effect of Defined Benefit Liability on Firms' Valuations in Japan:

Comparison of Japanese GAAP for
Retirement Benefits with IAS19

Eriko Kasaoka

Kwansei Gakuin University Press

The Effect of Defined Benefit Liability
on Firms' Valuations in Japan:
Comparison of Japanese GAAP for
Retirement Benefits with IAS19

Copyright © 2014 by Eriko Kasaoka

All rights reserved.

No part of this book may be reproduced in any form or by
any means without permission in writing from the author.

Kwansei Gakuin University Press
1-1-155 Uegahara, Nishinomiya, Hyogo, 662-0891, Japan
ISBN: 978-4-86283-155-2

Contents

Preface *vii*

Chapter 1
Introduction   *1*

Chapter 2
Japanese Corporate Pension System   *7*
  2.1 Introduction   *7*
  2.2 Development of Retirement Lump Sum Grants and Corporate Pension Plans in Japan   *7*
  2.3 Structure of Retirement Lump Sum Grants   *9*
  2.4 Structure of Corporate Pension Plans   *11*
    2.4.1 Employees' Pension Fund   *12*
    2.4.2 Defined-Benefit Corporate Pension   *17*
    2.4.3 Tax-Qualified Pension Plan   *20*
    2.4.4 Defined-Contribution Pension   *22*
  2.5 Current Situation   *24*
  2.6 Summary and Conclusion   *27*

Chapter 3
Fair Value of Defined Benefit Obligations   *29*
  3.1 Introduction   *29*
  3.2 Components of Employee Benefits   *30*
  3.3 Definition of Pension in Accounting   *31*
  3.4 Recognition and Measurement for Defined Benefit Obligations   *32*
    3.4.1 Projected Benefit Methods and Accrued Benefit

Methods 32
3.4.2 Concepts for Defined Benefit Obligations 34
3.4.3 Recognition and Measurement of Contribution-based Promises in IAS19DP 37
3.5 Attribution Methods 40
3.6 Recognition of Unvested Benefits and Future Salary Increases 42
   3.6.1 Unvested Benefits 42
   3.6.2 Future Salary Increases 48
3.7 Summary and Conclusion 55

Chapter 4
Determinants of Actuarial Assumptions for Defined Benefit Pension Plans 57
4.1 Introduction 57
4.2 Categories of Actuarial Assumptions 58
   4.2.1 Mortality 59
   4.2.2 Rates of Employee Turnover 63
   4.2.3 Discount Rate 63
   4.2.4 Future Salary Increases 67
   4.2.5 Expected Rate of Return on Plan Assets 69
4.3 Actuarial Assumptions and Earnings Management 74
4.4 Summary and Conclusion 80

Chapter 5
Presentation of Defined Benefit Cost 83
5.1 Introduction 83
5.2 Components of Defined Benefit Cost 84
   5.2.1 Current Service Cost 85
   5.2.2 Interest Cost 85
   5.2.3 Past Service Cost 86
   5.2.4 Actuarial Gains and Losses 87
   5.2.5 Transitional Liability 90
   5.2.6 The Expected Return on Plan Assets 92
   5.2.7 Curtailments and Settlements 92
5.3 Transition of Defined Benefit Cost Presentation in IAS19 94

5.4 Categories of Defined Benefit Cost   *98*
  5.4.1 Service Cost   *98*
  5.4.2 Net Interest on the Net Defined Benefit Liability   *98*
  5.4.3 Remeasurements on the Net Defined Benefit Liability   *99*
5.5 Effects of Income Measurement Approaches and Concepts of Incomes   *100*
  5.5.1 Income Measurement Approaches and Concepts of Incomes   *100*
  5.5.2 Related Prior Research Studies   *104*
5.6 Summary and Conclusion   *107*

Chapter 6
Fair Value of Plan Assets   *109*
6.1 Introduction   *109*
6.2 Requirements of Plan Assets   *109*
6.3 Measurement of Plan Assets   *111*
6.4 Retirement Benefit Trusts   *112*
  6.4.1 The Structure of Retirement Benefit Trusts   *113*
  6.4.2 Requirements of Retirement Benefit Trusts Recognized as Plan Assets   *114*
  6.4.3 Recognition of Gain or Loss on Plan Assets in Retirement Benefit Trusts   *114*
6.5 Offset with Defined Benefit Obligations   *116*
  6.5.1 Measurement for Defined Benefit Liability   *117*
  6.5.2 Recognition of Defined Benefit Asset   *117*
  6.5.3 Net Approach and Gross Approach   *119*
6.6 Treatment for Multi-Employer Plans   *121*
6.7 Summary and Conclusion   *123*

Chapter 7
Disclosure of Defined Benefit Liability   *125*
7.1 Introduction   *125*
7.2 Definition and Recognition of a Liability   *126*
7.3 Recognition and Measurement of Defined Benefit Liability under Prior Accounting Standards   *131*

7.4 Unrecognized Obligations   *132*
   7.4.1 Unrecognized Past Service Cost   *132*
   7.4.2 Unrecognized Actuarial Gains or Losses   *133*
   7.4.3 Unrecognized Transitional Liability   *134*
7.5 Presentation of Defined Benefit Liability under the New Accounting Standard   *136*
7.6 The Significance of Unrecognized Obligations   *139*
7.7 Summary and Conclusion   *145*

Chapter 8
The Effect of Defined Benefit Liability on Firms' Valuations   *149*
   8.1 Introduction   *149*
   8.2 Prior Research   *150*
   8.3 Hypothesis Development   *154*
   8.4 Research Design   *158*
   8.5 Summary and Conclusion   *164*

Chapter 9
Discussion and Summary   *167*

References   *175*

Preface

The deficits which are commonly seen in company pension funds represent one of the most important issues facing Japanese firms today. Only a few percent of the Japanese companies listed on the first section of the Tokyo Stock Exchange have defined benefit plans that are overfunded. Until fiscal 1999, Japanese firms generally recognized only the pension cost on their profit and loss statement, and had to disclose in a footnote either the total amount of plan assets or the current amount of prior service cost. Therefore, a firm's pension funding status could not be known by its stakeholders.

However, recently, Japanese accounting standards have been revised to harmonize with other international accounting standards. There has also been a great change in accounting standards for retirement benefits. In fiscal 2000, the *Accounting Standard for Retirement Benefits* was introduced. The effect of this change in Japan's accounting rules was to reveal that most of the country's companies had huge deficits on their retirement benefits. Japan had been in a long recession after the so-called bubble economy burst. Retirement benefits were confined to lump sum grants and defined benefit plans. There were some restrictions on the asset allocation of corporate pension funds. Under these conditions, firms could not manage their pension assets efficiently. As a result, they had significant funding deficits on their retirement benefits, which was to become a serious social problem for Japan.

In accordance with a convergence project with the International Accounting Standards Board (IASB), a new accounting standard, ASBJ Statement No.26: *Accounting Standard for Retirement Benefits* (ASBJ Statement 26) was issued in May 2012. The important change in this standard is the required disclosure of a defined benefit liability on the balance sheet, which represents the firm's pension funding status. It is assumed that this accounting change will increase the presence and amount of the defined benefit liabilities on the balance sheet, and have a negative impact on Japanese firms' financial statements and their stock valuations.

In the U.S., both before and after Statement of Financial Accounting Standards No.158: *Employers' Accounting for Defined Benefit Pension and Other Postretirement Plans* (SFAS158) — which requires firms to disclose a defined benefit liability, i.e., the difference between defined benefit obligations and plan assets — was introduced in 2006, firms have been closing their plans to new hires or frozen their defined benefit plans owing to the significant negative effect on their balance sheets. Therefore, if the impact of the introduction of ASBJ Statement 26 on a firm's balance sheet is significant, firms might terminate their defined benefit plan, which would affect the financial security of employees in their retirement years.

The major purpose of this book is to examine and forecast the effect of the new accounting standard, ASBJ Statement 26, on firms' stock valuations. To examine and forecast the effect, this book has nine chapters. They comprise the following contents: the Japanese corporate pension system underlying accounting standards for retirement benefits; the recognition and measurement of defined benefit obligations and plan assets which are components in the calculation of a defined benefit liability; the presentation of defined benefit cost; the transition to the disclosure of a defined benefit liability on the balance sheet under prior and new accounting standards; and the effect of a defined benefit liability under the new accounting standard on firms' valuations.

This book is my doctoral thesis, which took several years to develop and write; it also includes a few changes and additions to account for the latest developments. I have obtained a lot of support, valuable comments, and helpful suggestions on my thesis from many people. First, I appreciate the significant support given by Professor Kazuo Hiramatsu, who has had a major effect on my thinking. I have studied under his supervision for more than 10 years, and he has always made room in his busy schedule to give me valuable advice on my study. Continually moving forward on my research is one small way I can repay my obligation to him.

I also acknowledge a great debt to Professor Akira Hamamura, who inspired me to go into research when I was at undergraduate. I am also indebted to Professors Akitomo Kajiura, Masanobu Kosuga, Yukio Fukui, Toshihiko Ishihara, Uichiro Nishio, Shinya Saito, Tatsuo Inoue, Keiichi Kimoto, Tokuei

Sugimoto, Noriaki Yamaji, Takatoshi Hayashi, Chika Saka, Koji Ueda, Toshiaki Nakajima, and Koji Kojima for their support. I appreciate the useful advice of the professors in the International Accounting Studies Group. And I wish to thank my best friend, Bob Schneider, for his helpful review.

I am also indebted to the director of Kwansei Gakuin University Press, Mrs. Kikuyo Tanaka, and its general manager, Mr. Naoya Tanaka, for their support of my publication.

Finally, I want to express my thanks to my husband, Toshio, and to my children, Himari and Haruto, for their love and support.

March 2014
Eriko Kasaoka

Chapter 1
Introduction

Japanese accounting standards for retirement benefits have been changed in accordance with a convergence project between Accounting Standards Board of Japan (ASBJ) and the International Accounting Standards Board (IASB). Until fiscal 1999, firms generally recognized only pension cost in the current fiscal year on the profit and loss statement. First Audit Committee Report No.33: *Accounting Procedures and Presentation, and Audit Treatment on Transition to a Tax-Qualified Pension Plan etc.* (First Audit Committee Report 33) required firms to disclose the total amount of plan assets or the current amount of prior service cost in the footnote (First Audit Committee Report 33, pars.12, 14). Therefore, the funding status of corporate pension plans could not be known under the prior accounting standards. However, in fiscal 2000, new accounting standards for retirement benefits, *Accounting Standard for Retirement Benefits* and *Statement on Establishing Accounting Standard for Retirement Benefits*, were introduced. They require firms to disclose defined benefit obligations, plan assets, defined benefit liability, and defined benefit cost on their financial statements. After these standards were introduced, it was revealed that many firms had huge deficits for their employees' corporate pension plans in the year. Most of them still have a serious problem with respect to their funding status.

In May 2012, the ASBJ revised these accounting standards for retirement benefits[1] by issuing ASBJ Statement No.26: *Accounting Standard for Retirement Benefits* (ASBJ Statement 26), which includes the change on disclosure of defined benefit liability. Before this accounting standard was issued, a defined benefit liability, which represents the firm's funding status, was calculated by

---

[1] There are also two other standards replaced in the new accounting standard: ASBJ Statement No.3: *Amendments to Accounting Standard for Retirement Benefits*, and ASBJ Statement No.19: *Amendments to Accounting Standard for Retirement Benefits (Part 3)*.

subtracting plan assets from defined benefit obligations with consideration of unrecognized obligations. Unrecognized obligations consist of unrecognized past service cost, unrecognized actuarial gains or losses, and unrecognized transitional liability. Deferred recognition was adopted to recognize these obligations due to the following characteristics they have: (1) past service cost might affect employees' incentives in the future, (2) actuarial gains and losses might be offset in the long run, and (3) transitional liability does not relate to firms' operation. Amounts which were not recognized as part of defined benefit cost in the period were disclosed as unrecognized obligations only in a footnote. The accounting procedure made it difficult for financial statement users to understand a firm's funding status. The new accounting standard requires disclosure of these unrecognized obligations on the balance sheet, and this treatment will be applied from fiscal 2013. This accounting change will affect levels of total assets, total liabilities, and net assets, and for most firms will have a significant negative effect on their financial statements.

The Securities Analysts Association of Japan (SAAJ) wrote a comment letter on Exposure Draft of Statement No.39: *Exposure Draft of Accounting Standard for Retirement Benefits* (ED39) which regulates the disclosure of a defined benefit liability to the ASBJ. The letter states that it is general practice for financial analysts to consider the effect of unrecognized obligations disclosed in the footnote, and include these amounts in the balance sheet when they evaluate firms. However, it would be helpful for them to recognize these obligations immediately on the balance sheet, thereby increasing the comparability with firms adopting other accounting standards, such as International Financial Reporting Standards (IFRS) or Statements of Financial Accounting Standards (SFAS) of the U.S.[2] From this point of view, unrecognized obligations in the footnote have been taken into consideration when financial analysts evaluate firms. Therefore, the accounting change might not have a significant effect on firms' valuations.

On the other hand, ASBJ has decided not to disclose unrecognized obligations on the balance sheet for non-consolidated financial statements. In a report, the ASBJ lists the following reasons not to recognize unrecognized

---

[2] The Securities Analysts Association of Japan, "Comment Letter on Exposure Draft of Statement No.39: *Exposure Draft of Accounting Standard for Retirement Benefits*," May 31, 2010, http://www.saa.or.jp/account/account/pdf/ikensho100531.pdf, p.1.

obligations on the balance sheet:[3]
 (a) Recognizing unrecognized obligations in the net assets on the balance sheet will affect firms' distributable amounts;
 (b) When firms transfer their defined benefit obligations or plan assets through organization restructuring, there are some cases in which firms have to recognize the difference between the obligations and assets measured under accounting standards for retirement benefits and under *Defined Benefit Corporate Pension Plan Act* as a liability; and
 (c) Recognizing unrecognized obligations on the balance sheet might conflict with financial covenants from financial institutions, which are imposed when firms obtain loans or procure funds by issuing their corporate bonds.

The report also notes that when unrecognized obligations are recognized on the balance sheet, procedures should be introduced to reduce the fluctuation in results caused by this accounting change. Therefore, this report assumes that recognizing unrecognized obligations on the balance sheet will have a significant impact on firms' financial statements and their valuations.

This thesis aims to examine and forecast the effect of the new accounting standard on firms' valuations. It includes the following chapters listed below.

Chapter 2 describes the Japanese corporate pension system underlying accounting standards for retirement benefits. Each country has a different pension system and pension law, which provide the framework for pension plans. Retirement benefits in Japan began with lump sum grants to reward employees who had worked for the firms for many years. With the development of the Japanese economy, some firms introduced corporate pension plans, which have the role of providing social security. The history and structure of retirement benefits are discussed, which affect the contents and implementation of the accounting standards for retirement benefits including ASBJ Statement 26, ASBJ Guidance No.25: *Guidance on Accounting Standard for Retirement Benefits* (ASBJ Guidance 25),[4] and other standards in Japan.

---
[3] Accounting Standards Board of Japan, "A Report on the Progress of Retirement Benefits (Step1)," January 19, 2012, https://www.asb.or.jp/asb/asb_j/minutes/20120119/20120119_02.pdf, p.2.
[4] JICPA Accounting Practice Committee Report No.13: *Practical Guidance on Accounting for Retirement Benefits (Interim Report)*, ASBJ Statement No.14: *Amendments to Accounting Standard for Retirement Benefits (Part 2)*, and *Questions and Answers on Accounting for Retirement Benefits* are replaced in the guidance.

Chapter 3 explains how to measure defined benefit obligations that occur at some future date. There are three concepts for the defined benefit formula. Currently, a concept of projected benefit obligation which reflects employees' future salary increases for all employees regardless of the possibility of acquisition of their vesting is adopted. However, there are two problems in the benefit formula: (1) the recognition of unvested benefits as a liability, and (2) the consideration of future salary increases in the projected unit credit method. These are treated as problems because employees' continuous activities in the future are assumed to recognize unvested benefits and future salary increases. To address these problems and propose solutions, this chapter explains the components of employee benefits, and recognition and measurement for defined benefit obligations. Also prior research examining the importance of unvested benefits and future salary increases are studied.

To estimate defined benefit obligations, several actuarial assumptions, including discount rates, rates of employees' turnover, and mortality, are used. These assumptions can be changed if necessary. Changes in actuarial assumptions have a significant effect on the calculation of defined benefit obligations and defined benefit cost. However, only a few actuarial assumptions are disclosed in footnotes. Several papers show that managers use their actuarial assumptions for earnings management. Chapter 4, therefore, explains how these actuarial assumptions are determined under Japanese accounting standards, and reviews prior research about the relationship between actuarial assumptions and earnings management.

Defined benefit obligations are estimated with consideration of future prospects, and attributed to each period as current service cost, which is a part of defined benefit cost. Because of the distinctive features of defined benefit obligations, defined benefit cost includes five other components: interest cost, past service cost, actuarial gains and losses, transitional liability, and the expected return on plan assets. In the Japanese accounting standards, all these components are included in a single item and disclosed as defined benefit cost in profit or loss. On the other hand, the IASB revised International Accounting Standard No.19: *Employee Benefits* (IAS19) in June 2011, and in so doing decided to disclose these defined benefit cost components depending on the feature. Chapter 5 clarifies the difference between the Japanese accounting standards for retirement benefits and IAS19, and considers the effect of the accounting change on IFRS.

To calculate a defined benefit liability, plan assets are deducted from defined benefit obligations. Under the accounting standards for retirement benefits, the net approach is adopted to recognize a defined benefit liability, because plan assets have different characteristics from other assets in the balance sheet. Chapter 6, therefore, explains requirements of plan assets and presentation of a defined benefit liability (asset), and discusses why different accounting procedures are allowed for recognition of plan assets.

A defined benefit liability was formerly calculated with consideration of unrecognized obligations. However, under ASBJ Statement 26, the difference between defined benefit obligations and plan assets will be recognized as a defined benefit liability on the balance sheet from fiscal 2013. Chapter 7 discusses whether the defined benefit liability meets the definition of a liability to determine if it is appropriate to recognize it on the balance sheet. It also estimates how the accounting change affects financial statements and some financial ratios.

Chapter 8 performs empirical research, and forecasts the effect of the new accounting standard, ASBJ Statement 26, on firms' valuations. Under the prior accounting standards, unrecognized obligations were disclosed only in the footnotes. To see the relationship between unrecognized obligations under the prior accounting standards and firms' stock prices, this chapter predicts whether recognizing these obligations on the balance sheet affect firms' stock prices.

Chapter 2
Japanese Corporate Pension System

2.1 Introduction

Pensions perform an important function in the social welfare system. Each country has a different pension system and pension law, which provide the framework for pension plans. For example, corporate pension plans are considered as complementary to public pension plans in Japan, whereas it is mandatory for firms to have corporate pension plans in Switzerland. Two types of public pension plans and one corporate pension plan are generally available to employees in Japan, while they have one public pension plan and two corporate pension plans in France. There are also differences in minimum funding standards, grant date of vesting, and the establishment of payment guarantee systems in each country. These differences stem largely from the history of the corporate pension plans, the structure of these pension plans, and national culture and business customs. Therefore, in this chapter, the history of retirement benefits in Japan, including retirement lump sum grants and corporate pension plans, is discussed first, while the structures of lump sum grants and corporate pension plans are subsequently explained.

Japanese accounting standards for retirement benefits treat mostly defined benefit pension plans, therefore, this chapter mainly discusses such plans. It is hoped that it will provide a better understanding of the Japanese pension system underlying accounting standards for retirement benefits.

2.2 Development of Retirement Lump Sum Grants and Corporate Pension Plans in Japan

The first Japanese retirement benefits were lump sum grants provided by the Kanegafuchi cotton-spinning firm in 1905.[5] The firm established a

---
[5] In some sense, the first pensions, if they may be considered as such, were benefits provided to employees in the Edo era. A business owner would allow employees who had worked for him faithfully ↗

mutual aid fund with the purpose of harmonious labor relations. Under the retirement lump sum grants system, employees paid 3% of their salaries to the firm's pension fund every year, and the firm would fund more than half of their retirement lump sum grants by their retirement.[6] The Mitsui general partnership firm, one of the largest *zaibatsu*, was the second firm to introduce retirement lump sum grants. Under its system, employees who worked for the firm over thirty years could acquire vesting rights, and twice a year they received post-retirement lump sum grants equal to four times their monthly salary at the time of retirement.[7] Some large firms introduced retirement lump sum grants to boost morale so that employees wouldn't quit their jobs due to poor working conditions, and trained workers wouldn't flee to other firms.[8] This movement formed a feature of current retirement benefit systems, i.e., merit rewards for employees who work for long periods for their firms.

After World War II, goods were in very short supply in Japan, and consequently there was high inflation. Setting the Tokyo wholesale price index in 1935-1937 as a benchmark 100, the index rose to 1,592 in 1945, 5,654 in 1946, and 14,448 in 1947. When the Japanese economy began to recover, Jujo Paper Industries Corporation and Mitsubishi Electric Corporation established corporate pension plans at their firms in 1952.[9] Jujo adopted a funding method which entailed contributions by both employees and the firm, based on the plan of American paper manufacturing firm, Crown Zellerbach. The firm contributed funds to the trust bank, and the bank made payments for pensions for the first 10 years after employees' retirement. Mitsubishi gave employees the option to receive their pension as a retirement lump sum grant (as previously) or as a lifelong annuity. In 1957, two other large firms also established corporate pension plans. Despite these developments, however, pension plans did not take firm root in Japan at the time because there was no tax benefit for

---

for many years to use the same shop name when they opened their own shops. The owner also gave financing help or consigned some goods. The Kanegafuchi cotton-spinning firm is treated as the first firm that provided a pension in the modern sense of monetary distributions following retirement.

[6] Utani, Ryoji, *History of Corporate Pensions -Trajectory of Failures*, Tokyo: Corporate Pension Research Institute Co., Ltd, 1993, pp.212-214.

[7] Chuo Audit Corp. and NLI Research Institute, *Accounting and Tax Practice for Corporate Pensions*, Tokyo: Nikkei Inc., 1999, pp.4-5.

[8] Nakakita, Toru, *The Future of Corporate Pension*, Tokyo: Chikumashobo Ltd., 2001, pp.42-43.

[9] Utani, Ryoji, *op.cit.*, pp.231-237.

using them.[10] To provide tax breaks to firms and encourage them to establish corporate pension plans, the tax-qualified pension plan was enacted in 1962, and the employees' pension fund was introduced in 1966.[11]

During this period of high economic growth in Japan, through both retirement lump sum grants and corporate pension plans, the number of pensioners and funding amount increased steadily. However, the burst of the bubble economy and the increase in retirement benefits due to employees' aging caused serious problems for firms' pension asset management. One of the solutions was a voluntary early retirement program. Under the program, a higher pension payment rate is used to calculate retirement benefits for employees who retire earlier than for those who retire at the mandatory age. As another solution, some firms used point-based retirement benefit plans that, rather than being calculated on the basis of employee salaries, instead consider employees' job grade, title, qualification acquisition, or working period. Several firms still use this plan. More recently, an increasing number of firms have adopted defined-contribution pension plans. Under these plans, firms have no risk for pension asset management after they pay for the pension contribution to employees. Employees who work for their firms over three years have vesting rights for their pension assets.

Japanese retirement benefits comprise both retirement lump sum grants and corporate pension plans. Under retirement lump sum grants, firms make a one-off payment of their retirement benefits for their employees at their retirement. Under corporate pension plans, firms pay retirement benefits in installments for their employees for a certain period after their retirement. Most corporate pension plans have shifted a part of their retirement lump sum grants to corporate pension plans to equalize the cost of retirement benefits, and prepare for employees' aging of their workforce.[12]

2.3 Structure of Retirement Lump Sum Grants

Table 2.1 shows the current status of retirement lump sum grants and corporate pension plans adopted by private corporate firms. In Japan, most

---

[10] Nakakita, Toru, *op.cit.,* pp.43-44.
[11] Murakami, Kiyoshi, *Corporate Pensions,* Tokyo: Nikkei Inc., 1999, pp.26-32.
[12] Labor Standards Bureau, *Current Situation and Issues for Retirement Benefits,* Tokyo: The Institute of Labour Administration, 2000, p.78.

Table 2.1   Presence or Absence of Retirement Benefit Plans

(Unit: %)

Number of Employees (Firm Size)	Total	Over 1,000	More Than 500, Less Than 1,000	More Than 100, Less Than 500	More Than 50, Less Than 100
Firms with Retirement Benefit Plans	93.5 (100.0)	98.8 (100.0)	97.5 (100.0)	93.6 (100.0)	91.4 (100.0)
Firms with Corporate Pension Plans	(59.9)	(88.1)	(80.8)	(63.9)	(42.8)
Firms with Only Corporate Pension Plans	(13.1)	(23.0)	(20.2)	(14.1)	(7.8)
Firms Using Corporate Pension Plans in Combination with Retirement Lump Sum Grants	(46.8)	(65.1)	(60.6)	(49.8)	(35.0)
Firms with Retirement Lump Sum Grants	(86.9)	(77.0)	(79.8)	(85.9)	(92.2)
Firms with Only Retirement Lump Sum Grants	(40.1)	(11.9)	(19.2)	(36.1)	(57.2)
Firms without Retirement Benefit Plans	5.4	1.0	1.8	5.2	7.5
Others	1.1	0.2	0.7	1.2	1.1
Total	100.0	100.0	100.0	100.0	100.0

Notes: Numbers in brackets indicate rates using only firms with retirement benefit plans.
Source: National Personnel Authority, "Table 2 Current Status of Corporate Pension Plans and Retirement Lump Sum Grants in Private Firms," http://www.jinji.go.jp/toukei/taisyokukyuufu/taisyoku_h23.htm.

firms provide retirement lump sum grants to employees. The smaller the size of the firm, the more likely it is to adopt only retirement lump sum grants. On the other hand, the larger the firm, the more it adopts corporate pension plans in combination with retirement lump sum grants. This tendency reflects the fact that corporate pension plans have more tax benefits, can secure the pension payment amount by funding it outside the firm, and can equalize the cost for pensions over time.

Most firms fund retirement lump sum grants within their firms. There are also two mutual aid systems to fund them outside the firm. One is for small and medium-sized firms. Generally it is difficult for small and medium-sized firms to establish retirement benefit plans by themselves. To expand adoption of retirement benefit plans and increase employees' welfare, this system was introduced and has encouraged firms to adopt retirement lump sum grants. The other system gives tax benefits in some specific cases to firms adopting retirement lump sum grants. They are for firms that hire employees retiring within a short period, and are in industries or areas that show different tendencies in employees' average working period or contingency rates. These firms cannot receive some tax benefits. Therefore, the system sets certain requirements and allows firms fulfilling these requirements to gain tax benefits.[13]

The amount of retirement lump sum grants is calculated based on employees' amount of labor during their employment period or the degree of contribution to their firms. There are the following three calculation methods.

(1) Proportion to salary method
   The amount is computed based on the salary at employee's retirement with consideration of service years or retirement reasons.
(2) Flat sum method
   The amount is fixed with consideration of retirement reasons.
(3) Point system
   Under this system, points are granted and accumulated depending on job grade, title, or qualification acquisition over service period, and multiplied by unit price to calculate the retirement lump sum grants.

Around 80% of firms with over 1,000 employees adopt the proportion to salary method.[14]

2.4 Structure of Corporate Pension Plans

There are three types of pension plans corporate employees can have: (1) national pension; (2) employees' pension insurance; and (3) corporate pension plans, including employees' pension fund, defined-benefit corporate pension, and defined-contribution pension. The tax-qualified pension plan was one of the corporate pension plans. However, it was abolished in March 2012 due to the lack of vesting protection.

National pension and employees' pension insurance are provided by the Japanese government. These public pensions are aimed at making up for the decrease in working income due to aging, disability, bereavement, or other reasons. They use a scheme for inter-generational support. With respect to the recent lower birth rate and aging population, the Japanese government is required to establish a sustainable pension system by law.[15]

---

[13] Hirano, Yoshiaki, *Tax Practice For 401(k) and Corporate Pensions -In Preparation for the Introduction of Japanese 401(k)-*, Tokyo: Zeimu Kenkyukai, 1999, pp.132-157.
[14] Yamaguchi, Osamu, *Retirement Benefit Plans*, Tokyo: Kindai-Sales Co., Ltd., 2001, p.98.
[15] Ministry of Health, Labour and Welfare, "Overview of Pension System1," http://www.mhlw.go.jp/english/org/policy/dl/p36-37p1-2.pdf, p.20.

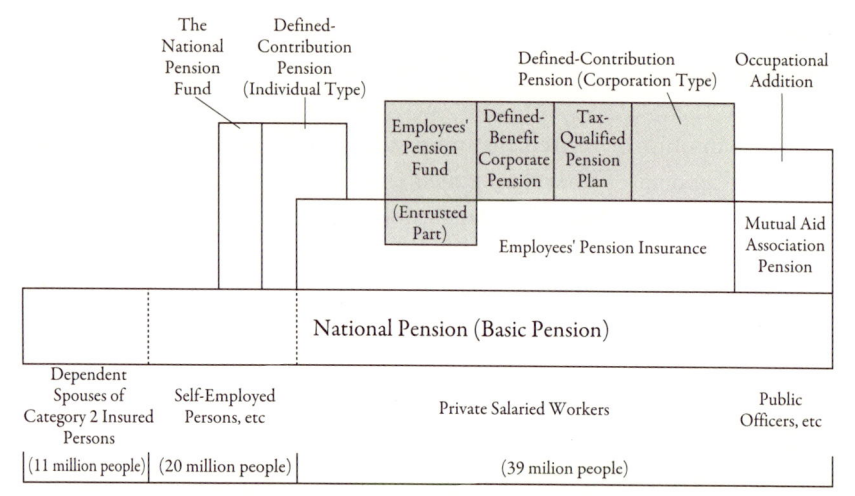

Figure 2.1 Structure of Japanese Pension System

Source: Ministry of Health, Labour and Welfare, "Overview of Pension System1," http://www.mhlw.go.jp/english/org/policy/dl/p36-37p1-2.pdf, p.13.

Corporate pension plans have the function of augmenting public pension plans. Employees' pension fund and defined-benefit corporate pension use a funding method in which assets are funded with the returns on pension asset management before employees' retirement for their future payments.[16]

The defined-contribution pension is also one of the corporate pension plans, and is funded (as opposed to pay-as-you-go). However, it is different from other pension plans in that employees bear investment and management risk. Private corporate firms can choose which corporate pension plan they provide to their employees. Some firms combine a defined-contribution pension with one of the other two defined benefit pension plans to reduce the risk component of pension asset management. The details of these corporate pension plans are explained below.

2.4.1 Employees' Pension Fund

The employees' pension fund was instituted in 1966. With the development of the Japanese economy, many firms adopted their own retirement lump sum grants or corporate pension plans for their employees.

---

[16] The tax-qualified pension plan also used the funding method.

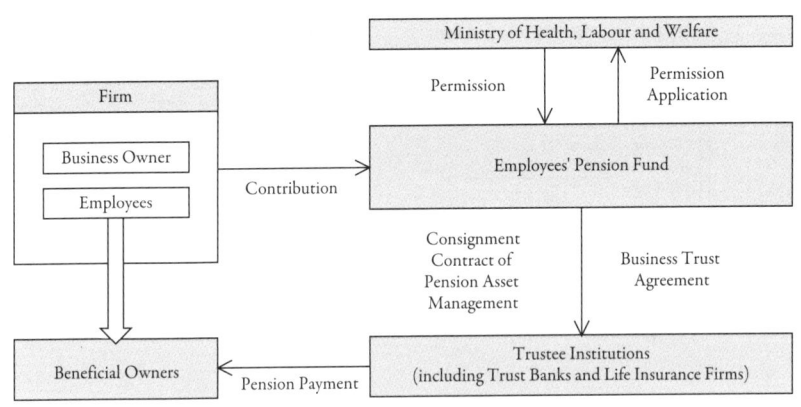

Figure 2.2 The Structure of Employees' Pension Fund

However, these retirement lump sum grants or corporate pension plans had overlapping functions and costs with government pension funds and employees' pension insurance. Therefore, the employees' pension fund was established to eliminate this overlap.

Figure 2.2 shows the structure of employees' pension fund. This fund is a corporation approved under *Employees' Pension Insurance Act*. A firm needs permission from the Ministry of Health, Labour and Welfare to establish this fund. The fund has several tasks: to collect contributions from firms, calculate employees' pension benefits, and consign management of pension assets to trust banks or life insurance firms. The fund is also allowed to manage pension assets itself.

The pension asset amount consists of the earnings-related part of employees' pension insurance which can be managed, at the firm's discretion, either by the government or the firm (entrusted part) and the firm-specific part. Figure 2.3 explains the structure of the entrusted part and firm-specific part. Employees' pension insurance provided by Japanese government includes old-age welfare annuity, survivor pension, disability pension, and the others. The employees' pension fund manages a part of the old-age welfare annuity, i.e., earnings-related part, provided by the government, which falls under the category of the entrusted part in employees' pension fund. Firms with employees' pension fund are exempted from the payment for the necessary insurance fee of the entrusted part. The exempt insurance fee is contributed to

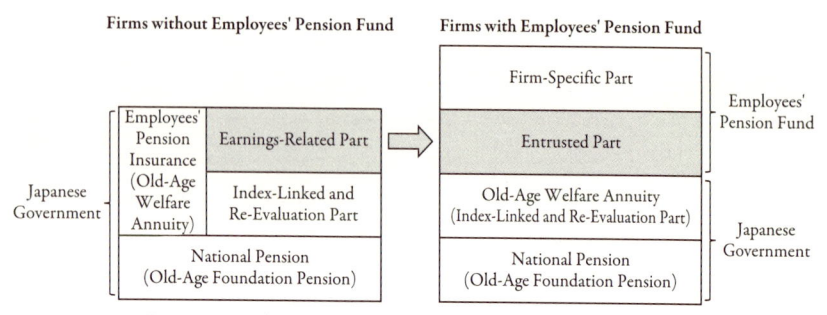

Figure 2.3 The Structure of Entrusted Part and Firm-specific Part

Firms without Employees' Pension Fund

Japanese Government — Employees' Pension Insurance (Old-Age Welfare Annuity):
- Earnings-Related Part
- Index-Linked and Re-Evaluation Part
- National Pension (Old-Age Foundation Pension)

Firms with Employees' Pension Fund

- Firm-Specific Part — Employees' Pension Fund
- Entrusted Part — Employees' Pension Fund
- Old-Age Welfare Annuity (Index-Linked and Re-Evaluation Part) — Japanese Government
- National Pension (Old-Age Foundation Pension) — Japanese Government

firms' employees' pension fund. Firms with employees' pension fund manage the entrusted part with their firm-specific part. The amount contributed by the firm to the pension fund is included in their expenses for the year.

The corporate tax system gives favorable treatment to firms that manage their pension funds. Another advantage in using an employees' pension fund is that firms can reduce their contribution to their funds when they manage their pension assets effectively. However, during the long recession, many firms have recorded significant pension deficits from their pension asset management, and they have accordingly changed their pension plans to others to reduce the risk associated with the entrusted part.

Figures 2.4 and 2.5 show that the number of pension funds and pensioners declines every year. An employees' pension fund can be organized in three ways: it can be instituted by a single institution, an associated institution, or an integrated institution. The single institution fund is formed by one firm. The associated institution is formed by parent and associated firms, business groups, and associations without parent firms. The integrated institution is formed by firms in the same or similar industries, or firms in the same region.

There was a significant decline in the number of pension funds from 2002 to 2004. About 750 pension funds formed by single and associated institutions went into liquidation. After the accounting standards for retirement benefits was introduced in fiscal 2000, firms started to reconsider their pension plans to reduce the tremendous pension deficits on their financial statements.

One way to reduce their pension deficits is returning their entrusted part of employees' pension funds to the government. When firms change their pension plans from employees' pension funds to defined-benefit corporate

Pension Funds

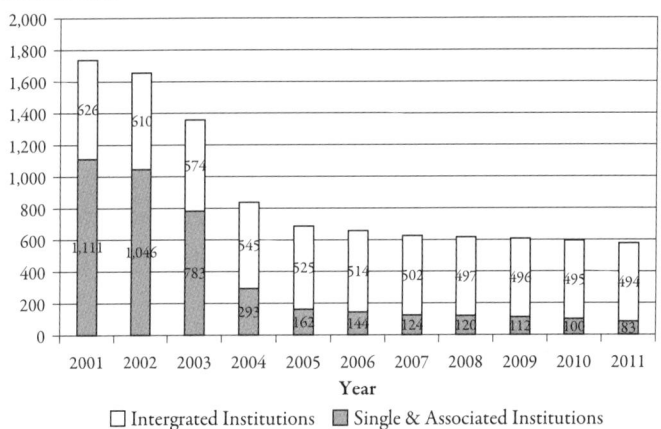

Figure 2.4 The Number of Pension Funds in Employees' Pension Fund

Source: Pension Fund Association, "Financial Condition on Employees' Pension Fund," http://www.pfa.or.jp/jigyo/tokei/zaisei/koseinenkin/index.html.

Pensioners (ten thousands)

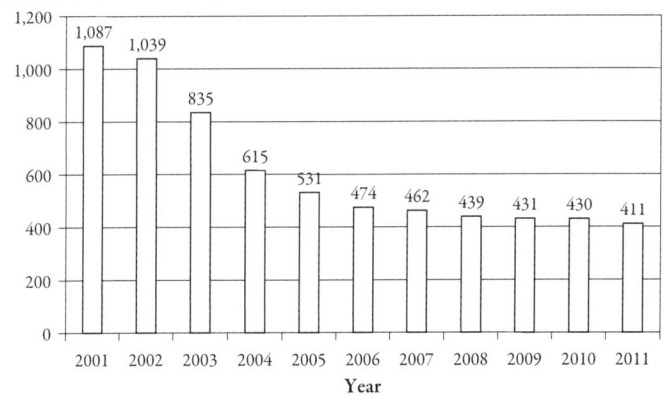

Figure 2.5 The Number of Pensioners in Employees' Pension Fund

Source: Pension Fund Association, "Financial Condition on Employees' Pension Fund," http://www.pfa.or.jp/jigyo/tokei/zaisei/koseinenkin/index.html.

pensions or defined-contribution pensions, they can return this part. Therefore, many firms change their pension plans from employees' pension funds to other pension plans. Most firms that still maintain this type of pension plan are small and medium-sized firms that have funding deficits for their entrusted part, which is a part of employees' pension insurance. Under the current act, firms are required to eliminate their funding deficits on their entrusted part before they dissolve their employees' pension funds.[17]

Pension contribution is calculated based on estimates of future factors, including predetermined mortality, salary increases, or expected rate of return set under a long-term plan. Therefore, there is a difference between the predicted amount of pension contribution and the actual amount. Under *Practical Standard for Defined-Benefit Corporate Pension* (Practical Standard for DB Pension), firms must examine their pension financing to judge whether a modification of their long-term plan is necessary using two standards: the going concern standard and the discontinued business standard (Practical Standard for DB Pension, pars.4.1, 4.2). The going concern standard determines whether firms have ensured that sufficient pension assets are available to make payments for employees' pension benefits in their future. The *Enforcement Regulation for Defined Benefit Corporate Pension Plan Act* (Enforcement Regulation for DB Pension Act) states that, when a firm does not have enough pension assets and the deficit exceeds a certain level, its pension contribution is to be reviewed (Enforcement Regulation for DB Pension Act, pars.56, 57).

On the other hand, the discontinued business standard reveals whether firms have enough money to make a payment for employees' pension if the firm's fund is terminated that same year. When pension assets are less than the amount of the minimum funding standard, (1) firms have to formulate their recovery plans, and need to secure the minimum funding level of pension assets in seven years, or (2) firms must reduce their contribution amount depending on their funding condition (Enforcement Regulation for DB Pension Act, pars.54, 55, 58, 59). Firms have to state which method they choose and continue to use it. *Standards for Fiscal Management of Employees' Pension Fund* issued by Ministry of Health, Labour and Welfare also state that firms must review their pension financing to ensure they have sufficient funds to pay for pensions once every five years (Standards for Fiscal Management of Employees'

---

[17] *Nihon Economic Newspaper (Morning)*, November 3, 2012, p.1.

Chapter 2   17

Pension Fund, par.4.1.(2)).

Japanese government investigated pension asset management conditions in all employees' pension funds in March 2012. The result showed that, for the most recent 10 years, the average rate of return from pension asset management was 1.2%, whereas over 90% funds set their expected rate of return as 5.5%. In fiscal 2011, over 50% of funds had paid more in pension benefits to employees who had already retired than they had received in contributions from their firms. Most funds whose pension benefits paid were more than their contributions received were of the integrated institution type, and were in manufacturing, construction, wholesale and retailing, and transport industries. Moreover, around 40% of funds had no fund for the firm-specific part and some deficit for the entrusted part.[18] These results indicate funds with employees' pension funds have much difficulty in their pension asset management.

2.4.2 Defined-Benefit Corporate Pension

In 2002, the defined-benefit corporate pension was established in consideration of the need for vesting protection. Under this pension plan, firms have to set rules on the funding standard, fiduciary responsibility, and disclosure system. They can contract with trust banks or insurance firms, or establish a foundation with corporate status to manage their funds based on their pension contract. The amount contributed to the fund is included in the firm's expense for the year.

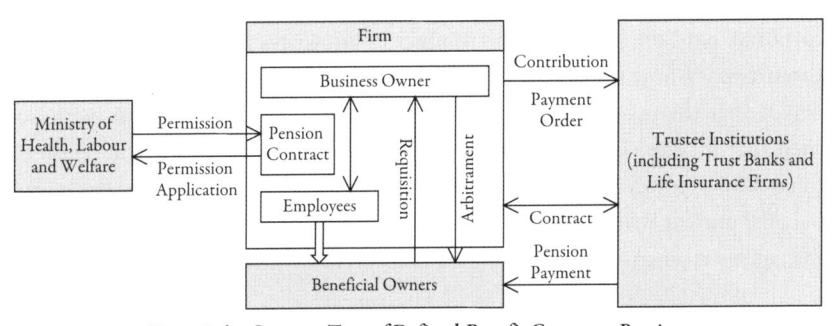

Figure 2.6   Contract Type of Defined-Benefit Corporate Pensions

---

[18] *Nihon Economic Newspaper (Morning)*, March 23, 2012, p.1.

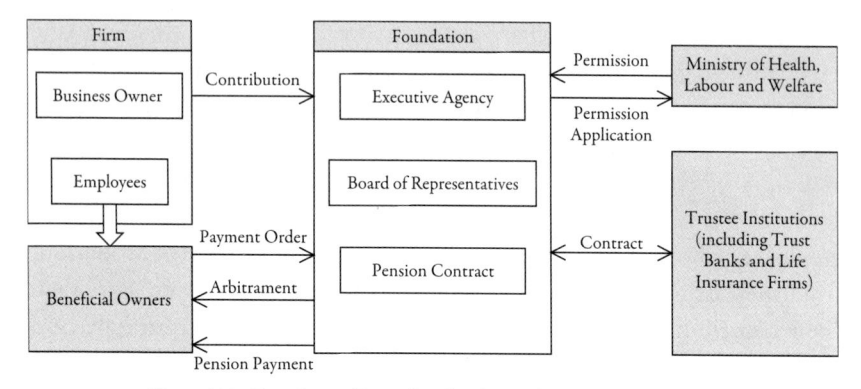

Figure 2.7 Foundation Type of Defined-Benefit Corporate Pensions

As Figures 2.6 and 2.7 show, there are two types of defined-benefit corporate pensions: contract and foundation.

In the contract type, the firm executes a pension contract with the consent of employees. The contract must be approved by the Ministry of Health, Labour and Welfare. The business owner makes a contract with a trustee institution, such as a trust bank or life insurance firm, to manage directly the pension fund, and provide pension credit to a person with vesting.

In the foundation type, a firm establishes a foundation to manage the pension fund with authorization from the labor union. As with the contract type, approval from the Ministry is required. The foundation makes a contract with a trustee institution, to provide pension credit to persons who are vested.[19]

Figure 2.8 shows the number of pension funds with defined-benefit corporate pensions. In 2011, the number of contract type pension funds was about twenty-four times that of foundation type pension funds. One reason why is that the management cost in foundation pension funds can be more than that for the contract type, due to the costs of establishing the pension foundation. However, there is a disadvantage in the contract type, in that it can become unclear who has a responsibility for decision-making in pension asset management when firms manage their pension funds with several other firms.[20]

---

[19] Hirano, Yoshiaki, *New Corporate Pension System -Legal Work, Tax Practice, and Accounting-*, Tokyo: Okura Zaimu Kyokai, 2002, pp.16-18.
[20] Kubo, Tomoyuki, *Defined Contribution Pension Plan Act & Defined Benefit Corporate Pension Plan Act*, Tokyo: Nippon Keidanren Publishing Department, 2001, p.73.

Pension Funds

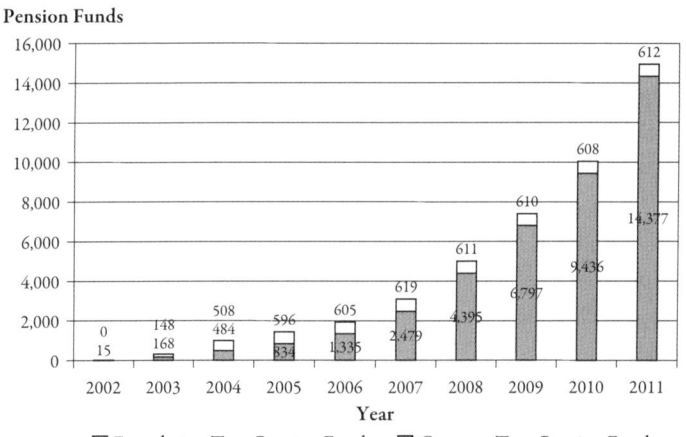

☐ Foundation Type Pension Funds ■ Contract Type Pension Funds

Figure 2.8 The Number of Pension Funds with Defined-Benefit Corporate Pension

Source: Pension Fund Association, "Financial Condition on Defined-Benefit Corporate Pension," http://www.pfa.or.jp/jigyo/tokei/zaisei/kakuteikyufu/index.html.

Pensioners (ten thousands)

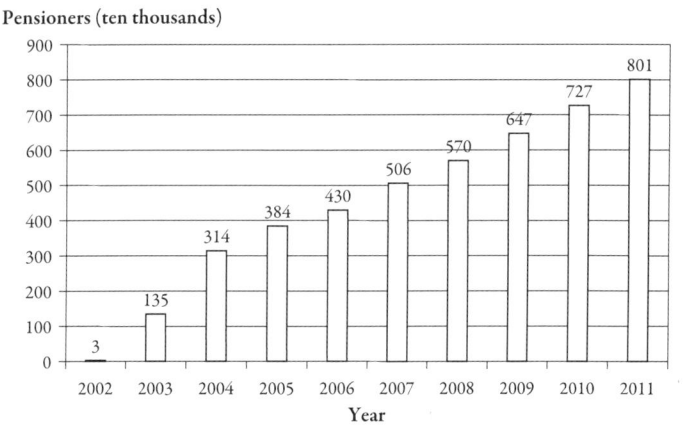

Figure 2.9 The Number of Pensioners in Defined-Benefit Corporate Pension

Source: Pension Fund Association, "Financial Condition on Defined-Benefit Corporate Pension," http://www.pfa.or.jp/jigyo/tokei/zaisei/kakuteikyufu/index.html.

With regard to vesting, it is defined more clearly in defined-benefit corporate pensions than in tax-qualified pension plans. Many firms did not provide pensions to their pensioners when they went bankrupt during the long recession after the bubble economy burst. Vesting was not protected by law. Therefore, the Defined Benefit Corporate Pension Plan Act stipulates the funding obligation, the fiduciary responsibility, and required disclosures to protect employees' vesting.[21] The funding obligations area seeks to ensure that the pension fund manages firms' pension assets as effectively as planned, and has no deficit. When the fund has funding deficits, the firm has to review its contributions (Defined Benefit Corporate Pension Plan Act, pars.55-64). The fiduciary responsibility rules state that business owners of foundation type pension funds, trustees of corporate pension funds, and institutions managing pension assets must follow rules and regulations related to pension asset management, and perform their activities for their members and pensioners faithfully (Defined Benefit Corporate Pension Plan Act, pars.69-73). The disclosure section specifies that business owners have a responsibility to disclose information on the content of their pension contracts, payment condition of their contributions, condition of pension asset management, and financial condition (Defined Benefit Corporate Pension Plan Act, pars.5, 73). These rules are in place to ensure that firms fund pension assets steadily and make pension payments for their employees, thereby implementing a social security system.

2.4.3 Tax-Qualified Pension Plan

The tax-qualified pension plan was based on the *Order for Enforcement of the Corporation Tax Act* and was mainly used by small and medium-sized firms because of their lenient establishment requirements. The amount contributed to the funds was included in expense for the year. However, this type of pension fund was abolished in March 2012.

Firms having this pension fund had to transfer the fund amount to one of the other pension plans before it was terminated. One reason it was abolished was that firms were unable to meet their defined benefit obligations under this plan during the long recession of the 1990s, and many employees lost their pensions. Vesting wasn't defined clearly in this plan, so employees' pension

---
[21] Hirano, Yoshiaki, *op.cit.*, 2002, pp.125-126.

Contracts

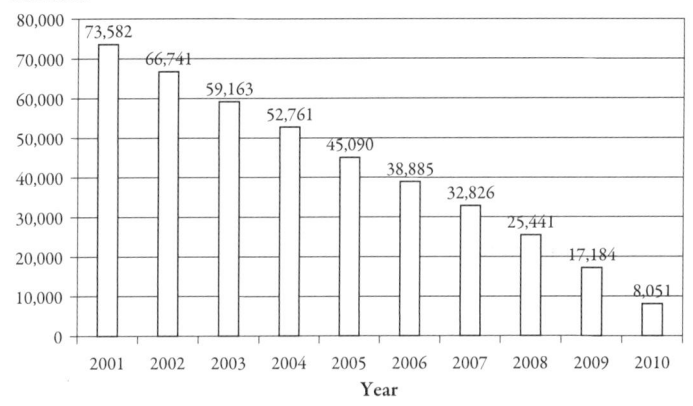

```
80,000 ┐
70,000 ┤ 73,582
60,000 ┤      66,741
50,000 ┤              59,163
40,000 ┤                      52,761
30,000 ┤                              45,090
20,000 ┤                                      38,885
10,000 ┤                                              32,826
    0 ┤                                                      25,441
                                                                      17,184
                                                                              8,051
       2001  2002  2003  2004  2005  2006  2007  2008  2009  2010
                                   Year
```

Figure 2.10   The Number of Contracts in Tax-Qualified Pension Plan

Source: Pension Fund Association, "Financial Condition on Tax-Qualified Pension Plan," http://www.pfa.or.jp/jigyo/tokei/zaisei/zaisei02.html.

Pensioners (ten thousands)

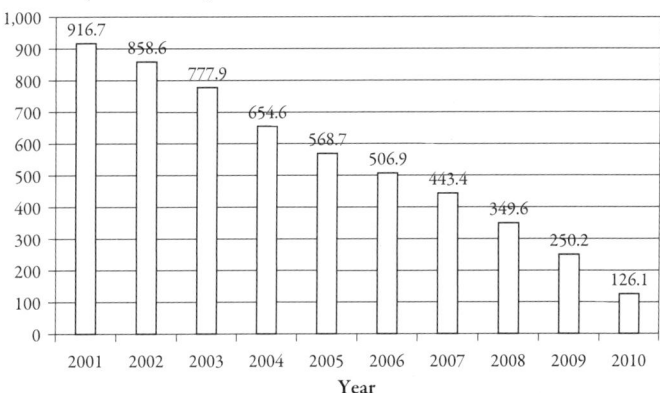

```
1,000 ┐ 916.7
  900 ┤         858.6
  800 ┤                 777.9
  700 ┤                         654.6
  600 ┤                                 568.7
  500 ┤                                         506.9
  400 ┤                                                 443.4
  300 ┤                                                         349.6
  200 ┤                                                                 250.2
  100 ┤                                                                         126.1
    0 ┤
       2001  2002  2003  2004  2005  2006  2007  2008  2009  2010
                                   Year
```

Figure 2.11   The Number of Pensioners in Tax-Qualified Pension Plan

Source: Pension Fund Association, "Financial Condition on Tax-Qualified Pension Plan," http://www.pfa.or.jp/jigyo/tokei/zaisei/zaisei02.html.

assets could not be protected by law. In consequence, the defined benefit obligation is now required to be recognized on financial statements under employees' pension fund and defined-benefit corporate pension.

As Figure 2.10 indicates, the number of contracts decreases every year. The decline is occurring because many firms could not manage their pension funds effectively under the long recession. In addition some firms went bankrupt. In 2001, it was determined that this pension plan would be abolished by 2012. Therefore, many firms have already transferred their pension plans to other plans.[22]

2.4.4 Defined-Contribution Pension

The defined-contribution pension was introduced in 2001, due to the more fluid nature of employment status, poor economic conditions for pension asset management, and the introduction of accounting standards for retirement benefits in fiscal 2000. Under this pension plan, employees have to manage their pension plans by themselves, and the amount of pension received is determined by the returns from their investments. Therefore, firms do not bear any risk for this type of pension management, and the defined benefit obligation is not recognized on the balance sheet. It is required that firms provide investment training programs to their employees. It was problematic to introduce this pension plan, because most Japanese tend to just save their money and do not invest in stocks or bonds. Therefore, most employees were somewhat hesitant and confused about investing in financial products. It took a long time to get employees to agree to this pension plan.

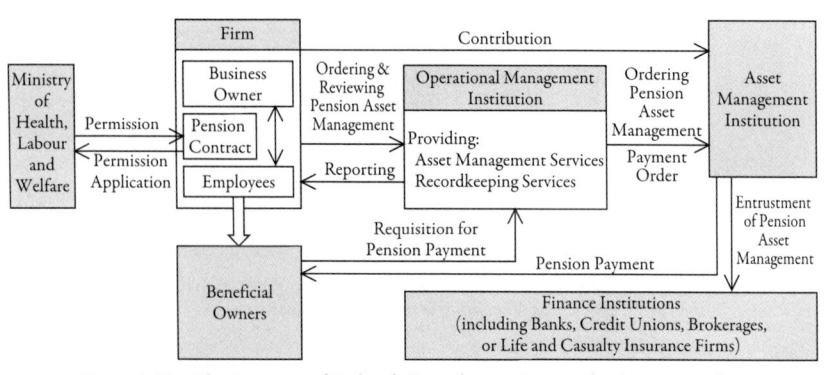

Figure 2.12 The Structure of Defined-Contribution Pension for Corporate Plans

---

[22] Izumi, Nobutoshi, *Corporate Pension Plans,* Tokyo : Productivity Center for Socio-Economic Development, 2007, p.54.

There are two types of defined-contribution pension: those for corporations, and those for individuals. Corporate plans are aimed at helping firms guarantee their employees' income after retirement. Individual plans aim at boosting individuals' savings. This paper focuses on pensions provided by firms, and therefore only corporate plans are discussed here.

Figure 2.12 shows the structure of defined-contribution pension for corporate plans. To establish a defined-contribution pension, a firm must make a corporation type defined-contribution pension contract with their employees, and the contract must be approved by the Ministry of Health, Labour and Welfare. The firm contributes a certain amount to the asset management institution every month, and the contribution is secured separately from the firm's assets. The asset management institution entrusts pension asset management to the finance institution it chooses, such as a bank, credit union, brokerage, or life and casualty insurance firm.

The employees determine how their pension assets should be managed and report their preferences to the operational management institution, which in turn reports this information to the asset management institution. The asset management institution contracts with the finance institution for asset management based on employees' determinations. When the beneficial owners

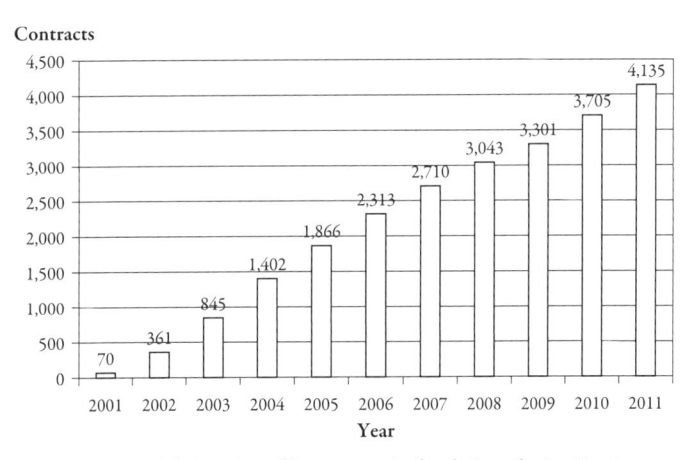

Figure 2.13 The Number of Contracts in Defined-Contribution Pension

Source: Ministry of Health, Labour and Welfare, "Defined-Contribution Pension," http://www.mhlw.go.jp/topics/bukyoku/nenkin/nenkin/kyoshutsu/kiyakusu.html.

Pensioners (ten thousands)

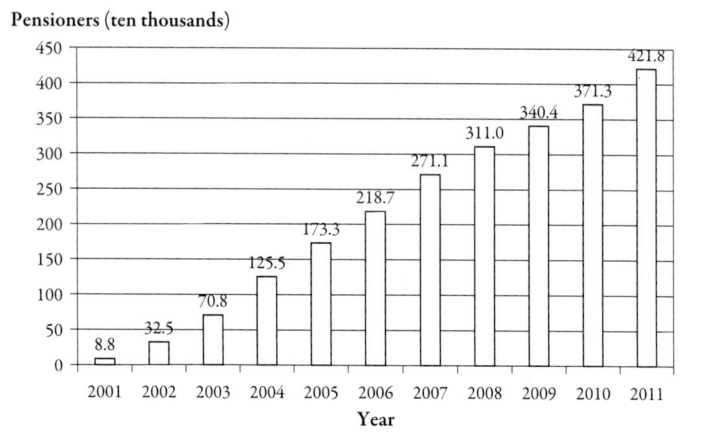

Figure 2.14 The Number of Pensioners in Defined-Contribution Pension

Source: Ministry of Health, Labour and Welfare, "Defined-Contribution Pension," http://www.mhlw.go.jp/topics/bukyoku/nenkin/nenkin/kyoshutsu/kiyakusu.html.

request to make their pension payment to their asset management institution, the institution starts to make the pension payment.

Figure 2.13 shows that the number of defined-contribution pension contracts (corporation type) has been increasing since it was introduced in 2001. The advantage of this pension plan for firms is, as noted earlier, they do not bear any risk for their pension asset management. However, they cannot reduce their pension premiums even where pension assets are managed effectively and make profits.

Employees also have some advantages. This pension plan is portable, therefore they can move their pension funds to their new firms when they change their jobs. Also, if they manage their pension funds effectively, there is a potential to make profits and increase their retirement monies. However, they also bear investment management risk, and there is no guarantee they will receive at least the same amount of money firms provided at retirement.

2.5 Current Situation

In fiscal 2000, new Japanese accounting standards for retirement benefits were introduced to harmonize with other standards, such as IFRS and SFAS in the U.S. Before this accounting change, only pension cost in the current fiscal year was recognized on the profit and loss statement, and the unfunded status of pension plan was not shown on the balance sheet. Only one of the following amounts had to be noted in the footnote: total amount of plan assets, or current amount of prior service cost. Disclosing just one of these amounts did not provide sufficient information to determine the funding status of corporate pension plans.[23] In fiscal 2000, many firms had huge pension deficits, because business conditions had been bad for so long. Therefore, after these accounting standards were adopted, pension accounting became a serious problem for firms.

Beyond poor business conditions, there were several reasons Japanese firms had significant deficits on their pension plans:

(a) Firms had to use a high, 5.5% fixed expected rate of return on plan assets in their calculations. Given the long recession, Japanese firms could not achieve this high expected rate of return;[24]

(b) Japanese pensions comprised only defined benefit plans, employees' pension funds and tax-qualified pension plans before 2001. Under a defined benefit plan, firms incur risks in managing their pension assets; and

(c) There were restrictions on the asset allocation of corporate pension funds. Firms had to invest at least 50% of pension assets in bonds and less than 30% of pension assets in stocks or assets of a foreign currency. The balance could be in other assets like real estate.

As a result of these problems, firms had to recognize huge pension deficits on the balance sheet when the accounting standards were introduced in fiscal 2000. Therefore, the Japanese government abolished these restrictions, i.e., the fixed expected rate of return and the asset allocation, to encourage firms to manage pension assets efficiently. In the past five years, firms have, on average, invested 26% of their assets in domestic bonds, 20% in domestic stocks, 12% in foreign bonds, and 16% in foreign stocks. The government also introduced the

---

[23] Sekine, Aiko, "Accounting Procedure for Pensions," *JICPA Journal*, Vol.10 No.3, March 1998, pp.39-40.

[24] Actual rates of return on plan assets in employees' pension fund from 1991 to 2000 are as follows;

	1991	1992	1993	1994	1995	1996	1997	1998	1999	2000
Actual Rate of Return (%)	1.98	5.21	5.21	0.74	10.27	3.65	5.65	2.56	13.09	-9.83

Source: Pension Fund Association, "Management Condition on Pension Assets," http://www.pfa.or.jp/jigyo/tokei/shisanunyo/shisanunyo01.html.

defined-contribution pension to reduce pension asset management risks.

After the accounting standards for retirement benefits were introduced, many firms changed their pension plans to reduce pension asset management risks. Some firms with employees' pension funds returned their entrusted part to the government. Most small and medium-sized firms with tax-qualified pension plans changed their pension plans to others before the pension plan was abolished in 2012. In some cases, firms just closed their pension funds.[25] More than 16,000 firms have introduced a defined-contribution pension plan since it was introduced. The number of defined-contribution pensioners is 4.4 million people while the number of defined benefit pensioners is 12 million people.[26] This high increase in defined-contribution pension plans reflects the low investment yield. A large retailing firm, AEON, has decided to raise the age for pension issuance from 60 to 65 for their defined benefit pension plans and to increase use of defined-contribution pension to reduce their risk of pension management.[27] On the other hand, Hitachi and Panasonic have introduced a cash balance plan which has the characteristics of both defined benefit plans and defined contribution plans with a floating interest rate. Under the plan, a firm guarantees a certain amount of benefits for their employees; however, employees have their own individual accounts. Toshiba has decided to adopt a floating interest rate for the fixed-term annuity that is a part of the retirement benefits of employees to stabilize the financial condition and reduce their defined benefit obligations.[28] In these scenarios, firms take into account their employees' income after retirement, and try to achieve a balance between giving employees' more income during retirement and managing their pension risk under financial pressure.

While firms seek to find ways to manage their pension assets efficiently, it was revealed that a money management firm in Tokyo, AIJ Investment Advisors Co., lost the better part of two hundred billion yen in clients' pension

---

[25] Yamaguchi, Osamu, "Transition of Japanese Corporate Pension Plans and Accounting," *Kigyo Kaikei*, Vol.62 No.7, July 2010, p.956.

[26] Ministry of Health, Labour and Welfare, "Enforcement Status of Defined-Contribution Pension," http://www.mhlw.go.jp/topics/bukyoku/nenkin/nenkin/kyoshutsu/sekou.html.

[27] *Nihon Economic Newspaper (Evening)*, March 18, 2010, p.1.

[28] The Asahi Shimbun Company, "20 Toshiba Group Companies Introduced a Floating Interest Rate for a Part of Their Corporate Pension," http://www.asahi.com/money/pension/news/TKY200310180278.html.

assets in 2012.[29] There were 84 pension funds that entrusted their pension asset management to the firm. Eight of these funds delegated over 30% of their pension assets to AIJ. These funds lost all of their pension assets entrusted to this firm. Therefore, the Japanese government has discussed reviewing the pension asset management regulations on employees' pension fund to facilitate diversified investment for firms. The government has restricted firms from entrusting a high proportion of their pension assets to one trustee institution.[30]

This development represents how difficult it is to manage pension assets efficiently under the current worldwide economic downturn. It also clarifies regulatory and systemic problems Japan's financial regulator has in dealing with the challenges of pension management, given that it overlooked AIJ's financial condition for several years. Therefore, it is also important for firms to confirm that their employees' pension assets are well-managed by their trustee institutions.

2.6 Summary and Conclusion

Retirement benefits in Japan began with lump sum grants. They were intended to reward employees who had worked for the firm for many years, as well as encourage existing employees to stay with the firm. Therefore, one feature of retirement lump sum grants was as a reward to employees, specifically for longevity at the firm. With the development of the Japanese economy, retirement benefits assumed the role of social security, and some firms introduced corporate pension plans. After tax-qualified pension plans and employees' pension funds were introduced to provide tax benefits to firms having corporate pension plans, these plans spread throughout the economy. The tax-qualified pension plan was abolished in March 2012, because vesting was not defined clearly under the plan, and there were some cases where firms that had gone bankrupt did not make payments for their employees' pension. Corporate pension plans derived from retirement lump sum grants, and Japanese corporate pension plans still reflect the sense that a pension is a reward for meritorious behavior, such as longevity at the firm. Therefore, some requirements, such as those for vesting, are less onerous than those in other countries.

---

[29] *Nihon Economic Newspaper (Morning)*, February 26, 2012, p.1.
[30] *Nihon Economic Newspaper (Morning)*, May 16, 2012, p.1.

Currently there are three corporate pension plans: employees' pension fund, defined-benefit corporate pension, and defined-contribution pension. With the long recession after the collapse of the bubble economy, many firms were unable to manage their employees' pension assets effectively. After the accounting standards for retirement benefits were introduced, firms had to recognize their funding deficits on the balance sheet. Therefore, firms have worked to cut costs for pension fund operations and the risk of pension management to reduce the negative impact on financial statements, which explains the increase in the number of contracts in defined-benefit corporate pensions and in defined-contribution pensions.

These features of Japanese corporate pension plans affect the contents and implementation of the accounting standards for retirement benefits in Japan, as will be explained in following chapters.

Chapter 3
Fair Value of Defined Benefit Obligations

3.1 Introduction

A common topic of discussion is how to measure defined benefit obligations, because employee benefits, especially the pensions employees receive when they retire, occur at some future date. To calculate defined benefit obligations, firms (1) estimate the future amount of defined benefit obligations at employee retirement, and (2) discount the amount to its present value. Many assumptions are included in the calculation of defined benefit obligations, including mortality, rates of employee turnover, discount rates, and rates of future salary increases. There are three concepts for defined benefit obligations. These concepts are different depending on the inclusion of unvested benefits, i.e., benefits for employees who have not had their vesting rights granted for their employee benefits, and the consideration of future salary increases in the calculation of defined benefit obligations.

The IASB adopts a method that includes both unvested benefits and future salary increases to calculate defined benefit obligations. However, the IASB suggests using alternative methods for measuring defined benefit obligations, and it will discuss this topic in the next step of the IASB project. Because these unvested benefits and future salary increases are related to future events, their recognition leads to inconsistencies with other accounting standards. Japanese accounting standards also adopt the same accounting procedures to recognize defined benefit obligations as IASB does.

To address the various problems on recognition of unvested benefits and future salary increases and propose solutions, this chapter will first explain the components of employee benefits, the definition of pension in accounting, and recognition and measurement for defined benefit obligations. Second, prior research examining the importance of unvested benefits and future salary increases are studied. With regard to unvested benefits, vesting is not defined clearly under Japanese defined benefit plans. Therefore, requirements of vesting in Japan are compared to those in the U.S., which are stated under the requirements of federal law, and it is considered whether the difference in these requirements for vesting gives rise to any problem in the recognition of unvested benefits.

3.2 Components of Employee Benefits

The Japanese accounting standards for employee benefits regulate only accounting procedures for retirement benefits. Statement on Establishing Accounting Standard for Retirement Benefits defines retirement benefits as benefits paid to firms' employees after their retirement due to the services they provided to their firms in the past. Retirement benefits comprise retirement lump sum grants and retirement pensions including defined benefit plans and defined contribution plans (Statement on Establishing Accounting Standard for Retirement Benefits, par.3.1). Basically, the accounting standards for retirement benefits indicate accounting procedures for defined benefit plans.[31] They also state an accounting procedure for defined contribution plans which, put briefly, is that pension plan contributions are recognized as expenses (Statement on Establishing Accounting Standard for Retirement Benefits, par.3.3.(2)).

IAS19 states that "employee benefits are all forms of consideration given by a firm in exchange for service rendered by employees or for the termination of employment" (IAS19, par.8). Employee benefits include the following components (IAS19, par.5):

(a) Short-term employee benefits, such as wages, salaries and social security contributions, paid annual leave and paid sick leave,

---

[31] There are two kinds of accounting procedures to be considered in recognition of defined benefit obligations, plan assets, and defined benefit cost, i.e., (1) those for an entrusted part of employees' pension fund, and (2) those for contributions from employees. With regard to an entrusted part of the employees' pension fund, the fund has a distinctive system in which the fund amount consists of the earnings-related part of employees' pension insurance (entrusted part) and the firm-specific part. The pension benefit levels and calculation methods are different for each part. However, firms manage both parts in a lump. It is difficult to recognize these parts separately, therefore, firms adopt the same accounting procedure for both the entrusted part and the firm-specific part. As for contributions from employees, firms include the contributions from their employees to their pension funds in the calculation of defined benefit obligations and defined benefit cost. The contributions are deducted from defined benefit cost after the total amount of defined benefit cost including the contributions is calculated (Statement on Establishing Accounting Standard for Retirement Benefits, par.3.3.(1)).

profit-sharing and bonuses, and non-monetary benefits (such as medical care, housing, cars and free or subsidized goods or services) for current employees;

(b) Post-employment benefits, such as retirement benefits including pensions and lump sum payments on retirement, and other post-employment benefits, such as post-employment life insurance and post-employment medical care;

(c) Other long-term employee benefits including long-term paid absences, such as long-service leave or sabbatical leave, jubilee or other long-service benefits, and long-term disability benefits; and

(d) Termination benefits.

Retirement benefits including pensions are categorized in (b), and IAS19 mentions that "post-employment benefit plans are classified as either defined benefit plans or defined contribution plans, depending on the economic substance of the plan as derived from its principal terms and conditions" (IAS19, par.27). Therefore, the range of employee benefits in IAS19 is wider than that in Japanese accounting standards. Retirement benefits defined in Japanese accounting standards can apply to post-employment benefits in IAS19.

3.3 Definition of Pension in Accounting

"Pension" has three characteristics: future payment of employees' salary, employees' merit rewards, and income security for employees. In general, Japanese firms make payments for their employees' pension as compensation for their work after their retirement (Statement on Establishing Accounting Standard for Retirement Benefits, pars.3.1, 3.2). Defined benefit cost for the period is recognized based on employees' work period. Therefore, basically "pension" is defined as future payment of employees' salary.[32]

Under IAS19, pension is treated as a part of post-employment benefits. The IASB states "IAS19 requires a firm to recognize a liability when an employee has provided service in exchange for employee benefits to be paid in the future. An expense has to be recognized when the firm consumes the

---
[32] However, there is a condition that firms have some discretion for reducing or cutting off their employees' pension amount. This condition applies to merit rewards.

economic benefit arising from service provided by an employee in exchange for employee benefits" (IAS19, Objective). Therefore, IASB also defines pension as future payment of employees' salary.

3.4 Recognition and Measurement for Defined Benefit Obligations
3.4.1 Projected Benefit Methods and Accrued Benefit Methods

There are several actuarial valuation methods to measure defined benefit obligations. Methods including time value in their calculations are categorized into projected benefit methods or accrued benefit methods. These methods are subdivided further depending on the consideration of future salary increases in their calculations.

```
Time Value                              Future Salary Increases
not including ─────────────┬─────────── including
                           └─────────── not including

including ──┬── Projected Benefit Methods ──┬── including
            │                                └── not including
            │
            └── Accrued Benefit Methods ─────┬── including
                                             │   (Projected Unit Credit Method)
                                             └── not including
```

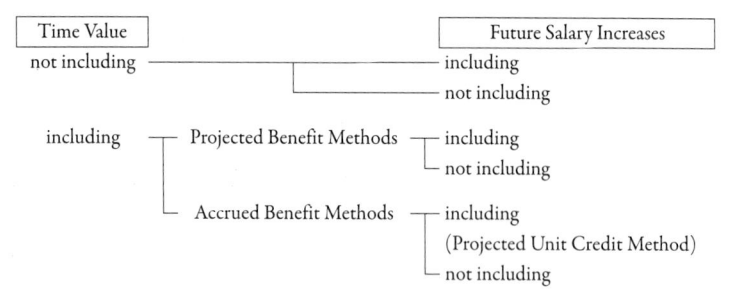

Figure 3.1   Categories of Actuarial Valuation Methods

Source: KPMG Azusa LLC, *Q&A for Japanese Accounting Standards*, Tokyo: Seibunsha Co. Ltd, 2010, p.82.

Projected benefit methods are based on the premise that employee benefits occur equally throughout the employee's entire service period. Therefore, under these methods, the estimated total amount of defined benefit obligations at retirement is calculated, discounted, and attributed to each period. The cost is equalized in each period, and these methods are not calculated on accrual basis.

Accrued benefit methods accrue on the basis that employee benefits occur when employees provide their services. Under these methods, the estimated total amount of defined benefit obligations at retirement is calculated, attributed to each period, and discounted. One of these methods that includes time value and future salary increases in the calculation is the projected unit credit method, which is adopted under Japanese accounting standards and

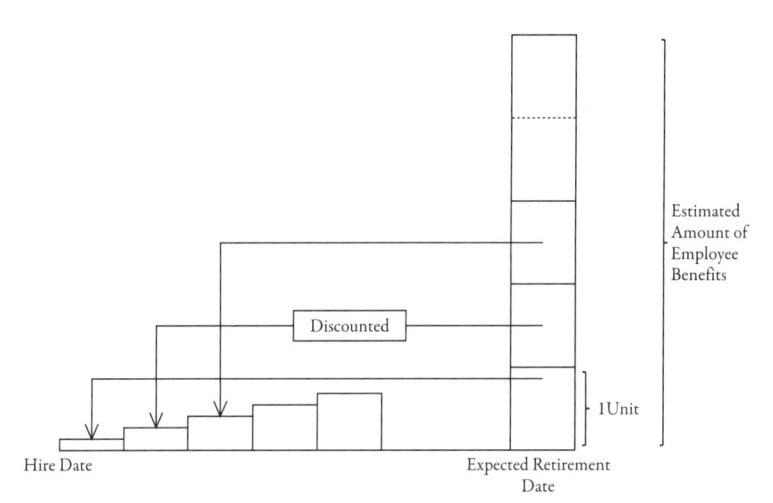

Figure 3.2 Projected Unit Credit Method

IAS19. The projected unit credit method assumes each period of service as adding a unit of benefit entitlement, and measures each unit separately to accumulate the final obligation (IAS19, par.68).

Prior Japanese accounting standards did not state which method should be adopted. Most firms adopted projected benefit methods because of the following reasons:[33]

(a) They meet the going concern assumption in accounting convention, in that defined benefit cost occurring from a significant amount of defined benefit obligations is amortized throughout employee's lifetime service period. Notably, it can reduce firm's arbitrariness in making accounting assumptions;

(b) Employee's salary properly represents the value of the service provided to the firm by the employee. It is preferable to recognize a certain percentage of salary as defined benefit cost in the period; and

(c) In essence, accrued benefit methods are based on the fair value approach. However, deferred recognition for actuarial gains and losses and past service cost is inconsistent with this

---

[33] Sawa, Etsuo, "Reporting (No.2) and Comment on IASC "Retirement Benefits and Other Costs for Employee Benefits" from Drafting Committee," *JICPA Journal*, Vol.8 No.8, August 1996, pp.25-26.

approach.

Japanese accounting standards introduced in fiscal 2000 state that the projected unit credit method, one of the accrued benefit methods, must be adopted. It appears that Japanese accounting standards eventually adopted this method to harmonize with other international accounting standards, such as IFRS, SFAS in the U.S. or Financial Reporting Standards (FRS) in the U.K.

At one point, IAS19 permitted firms to choose projected benefit methods or accrued benefit methods. However, projected benefit methods were eliminated, because such methods (IAS19, par.BC110):

(a) focus on future events (future service) as well as past events, whereas accrued benefit methods focus only on past events;

(b) generate a liability which does not represent a measure of any real amount and can be described only as the result of cost allocations; and

(c) do not attempt to measure fair value and cannot, therefore, be used in a business combination, as required by International Accounting Standard No.22: *Business Combinations*.

Currently IAS19 adopts the projected unit credit method, which is the most widely used accrued benefit method (IAS19, par.BC111). However, Discussion Paper: *Preliminary Views on Amendments to IAS19 Employee Benefits* (IAS19DP) suggests considering alternative measurement methods, including projected benefit, accumulated benefit, fair value, and settlement value, because the projected unit credit method in IAS19 is fundamentally different from the measurement models in other accounting standards (IAS19DP, par.1.11).

3.4.2 Concepts for Defined Benefit Obligations

There are three concepts to calculate defined benefit obligations: vested benefit obligation (VBO), accumulated benefit obligation (ABO), and projected benefit obligation (PBO). These are different owing to the recognition of unvested benefits as a liability and the consideration of future salary increases.

(1) VBO

VBO is the present value of legal obligations for employees who have had their vesting for employee benefits.

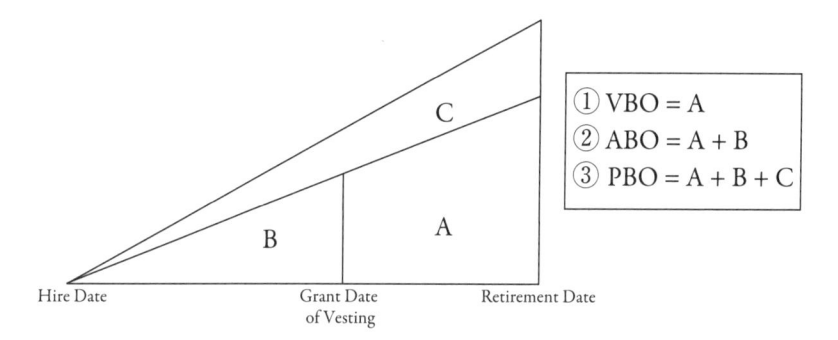

Figure 3.3 Concepts of Defined Benefit Obligations

① VBO = A
② ABO = A + B
③ PBO = A + B + C

(Hire Date — Grant Date of Vesting — Retirement Date)

(2) ABO

ABO is the present value of legal obligations for all employees regardless of the possibility of acquisition of their vesting.

(3) PBO

PBO is the present value of legal obligations reflected by employees' future salary increases for all employees regardless of the possibility of acquisition of their vesting.

Japanese accounting standards state that defined benefit obligations occur from employees' services in the past, and the benefits funded by their firms are provided to employees after their retirement. There is a long time lag between when employees provided their services to their firms and when their salaries are paid as pensions. Therefore, estimated defined benefit obligations at employees' retirement are discounted to measure the present value of the obligation (ASBJ Statement 26, par.6). ASBJ Guidance 25 states that the calculation includes employees' future salary increases which can be estimated in the future (ASBJ Guidance 25, par.99). Thus, Japanese accounting standards adopt PBO to calculate defined benefit obligations. However, there are some voices against the adoption of PBO, because of the inconsistency with provisioning. *Corporate Accounting Principles* state a provision is recognized when the obligation is related to a certain cost or loss in the future, results from a past event, is probable, and can be estimated reliably (Corporate Accounting Principles, footnote18). The concept of PBO includes future salary increases, which are expected future events. It is not appropriate to recognize obligations that do not result from past events, because it is inconsistent with the definition of a provision.[34] However, PBO is adopted to harmonize with other international accounting standards.

IAS19 also adopts PBO to calculate defined benefit obligations. IAS19 states defined benefit obligations reflect estimated future salary increases (IAS19, par.87). Some arguments have been made that estimated future salary increases should not be included in the measurement of defined benefit obligations, because they are related to future events and such estimates are too subjective (IAS19, par.BC140). The IASB believes that a firm should use the assumptions to measure an existing obligation based on a method which represents the most relevant measure of the estimated outflow of resources. It would be misleading to assume no change if a firm expects a change (IAS19, par.BC141). Therefore, IAS19 includes future salary increases in the calculation of defined benefit obligations.

Statement of Financial Accounting Standards No.87: *Employers' Accounting for Pensions* (SFAS87) required firms to recognize an additional minimum liability. In principle, firms have to measure their defined benefit obligations based on PBO. However, the additional minimum liability was recognized when an unfunded ABO existed and (SFAS87, par.36):

(a) an asset had been recognized as prepaid pension cost;

(b) the liability already recognized as unfunded accrued pension cost was less than the unfunded ABO; or

(c) no accrued or prepaid pension cost had been recognized.

SFAS87 adopted ABO for recognition in order to be consistent with the method adopted in the *Employee Retirement Income Security Act* (ERISA). ERISA is "a U.S. federal law that sets minimum standards for most voluntarily established pension and health plans in private industry to protect employee benefits for individuals in these plans."[35] It states that, when a fund is dissolved, the obligations are measured based on ABO. However, Statement of Financial Accounting Standards No.158: *Employers' Accounting for Defined Benefit Pension and Other Postretirement Plans* (SFAS158) eliminated the requirement under SFAS87. Both Japanese accounting standards and IAS19 have not

---

[34] Daigo, Satoshi, *Coursework for Accounting,* Tokyo: University of Tokyo Press, 1998, pp.213-214.
[35] United States Department of Labor, "Employee Retirement Income Security Act - ERISA," http://www.dol.gov/dol/topic/health-plans/erisa.htm.

adopted this additional minimum approach. IAS19 states that the reason for non-adoption is that the approach is potentially confusing and does not provide relevant information (IAS19, par.BC105).

3.4.3 Recognition and Measurement of Contribution-based Promises in IAS19DP

IAS19DP notes two problems in the benefit formula in IAS19: (1) the recognition of unvested benefits as a liability, and (2) the consideration of future salary increases in the projected unit credit method. These problems lead to inconsistency with other accounting standards (IAS19DP, par.1.11). It suggests using alternative measurement methods to calculate defined benefit obligations.

Under current IAS19, post-employment benefits are classified into two categories, defined benefit plans and defined contribution plans. IAS19 prescribes accounting procedures for both plans. IAS19DP suggests abolishing these categories and introducing new categories which consist of contribution-based promises and defined benefit promises.[36] IAS19DP states accounting procedures for post-employment benefit *promises*, because sometimes pension funds provide several different promises in one plan.[37] A contribution-based promise is defined as a post-employment benefit promise in which, during the accumulation phase, the benefit can be expressed as (IAS19DP, par.5.3):

(a) The accumulation of actual or notional contributions that, for any reporting period, would be known at the end of that period, except for the effect of any vesting or demographic risk; and

(b) Any promised return on the actual or notional contributions is linked to the return from an asset, group of assets, or an index. A contribution-based promise need not include a promised return.

The following promises are examples of contribution-based promises (IAS19DP, par.5.10):

---

[36] The IASB suggested that this issue should not be addressed in the amendments made in IAS19 in June 2011, and it will be reviewed in a possible future project (IAS19, pars.BC7, BC120).
[37] Nakata, Tadashi, "Review of Discussion Paper: Preliminary Views on Amendments to IAS19 Employee Benefits," *NFI Research Review*, July 2008, http://www.nikko-fi.co.jp/uploads/photos1/648.pdf, p.1.

(a) promises that IAS19 classifies as defined contribution plans;
(b) promises of a return based on notional contributions;
(c) promises that guarantee a fixed return on contributions;
(d) promises expressed as a fixed lump sum at retirement that is not dependent on service; and
(e) career average promises (i.e., promises based on the average of the employee's salary over his or her entire service period).

On the other hand, the following promises are excluded from contribution-based promises (IAS19DP, par.5.11):

(a) any promise that includes salary risk; and
(b) other post-employment benefit promises, such as typical post-employment life insurance and medical care.

A defined contribution plan treated in IAS19 is included in contribution-based promises. However, the same accounting treatment as in IAS19 is adopted for this plan. A significant effect of this accounting change is on *cash balance plans*.[38] They are included in defined benefit plans under IAS19 and are categorized into contribution-based promises under IAS19DP. A defined benefit promise is specified as a post-employment benefit that is not a contribution-based promise (IAS19DP, par.5.3).

Changes treated in IAS19DP are part of the IASB project on the accounting for post-employment benefit promises as a first step. This project is limited in scope to certain issues, including the deferred recognition of some gains and losses arising from defined benefit plans, presentation of defined benefit liabilities, accounting for benefits that are based on contributions and a promised return, and accounting for benefit promises with a higher of option (IAS19DP, par.IN4). Recognition and measurement of defined benefit promises will be discussed in the next step. Therefore, the projected unit credit method will be adopted for defined benefit promises until the discussion for the recognition and measurement of defined benefit promises is completed. On the other hand, IAS19DP suggests measuring contribution-based promises at

---

[38] A cash balance plan is a defined benefit plan that has some characteristics of a defined contribution plan. In a typical cash balance plan, a pension participant's account is credited each year with a pay credit (monthly standard salary multiplied by a certain rate) and an interest credit (the virtual balance of participant's account at the balance sheet data in a previous year multiplied by the reassessment rate). A participant does not acquire the risk of the plan's investments. Therefore, he can have the benefit amounts promised by the employer.

fair value (IAS19DP, par.ITC11). All changes in any plan assets are presented in profit or loss (IAS19DP, par.9.11). The objective of the IASB is to select a measurement attribute for a contribution-based promise that provides useful information about the amount, timing, and uncertainty of future cash flows regarding the promise to financial statement users. The IASB believes that the measurement approach that includes the following characteristics would meet this objective (IAS19DP, par.7.7):

(a) an estimate of the future cash flows;
(b) the effect of the time value of money; and
(c) the effect of risk.

With respect to estimating future cash flows, there are four views that a firm should consider to make the estimation, including explicit estimates, consistency with observed market prices, unbiased use of all available information, and current estimates (IAS19DP, par.7.9). As for unbiased use of all available information, a contribution-based promise liability is measured based on an expected value approach. The expected present value is stated as "the probability-weighted average of the present value of the cash flows" (IAS19DP, par.7.16). Therefore, the liability is calculated with consideration of expected variability such as under the cash balance plan or reassessment rate using a certain assumption.[39]

With regard to the effect of the time value of money, IAS19 requires discounting for defined benefit liabilities and defined contribution liabilities. IAS19DP also states that a current measure of the time value of money should be included in the measurement of contribution-based promises (IAS19DP, par.7.19).

The effect of risk comprises asset-based risk, demographic risk, credit risk, and risk that the terms of the benefit promise change. Asset-based risk includes changes in the value of the assets or indices, and it is similar to market risk for financial instruments. Market risk is defined as "the risk that the fair value or future cash flows of a financial instrument will fluctuate because of changes in market prices" (IAS19DP, par.7.22). The IASB believes inclusion of this asset-based risk is one of the main improvements in measuring contribution-based

---

[39] Inoue, Masahiko, "Current Condition and Future Prospects of Accounting Standard for Employee Benefits -Summary of IASB Discussion Paper and the Effect-," *Weekly Keiei Zaimu*, No.2897, December 8, 2008, p.37.

promises (IAS19DP, par.7.23). Demographic risk is longevity risk in particular. Credit risk is "the risk that a firm will be unable to make the necessary payments" (IAS19DP, par.7.22). The IASB recognizes this is a significant change, and it could be difficult to include credit risk in the calculation of contribution-based promises, because there is no readily observable price to calculate the risk for the initial exchange of service for post-employment (IAS19DP, par.7.28).

This measurement for contribution-based promises does not include future salary increases which are related to a future event. The definition of fair value in the measurement of contribution-based promises might serve as a useful reference for considering the alternative measurement for defined benefit promises, because it eliminates one of the problems of the benefit formula the IASB states in IAS19DP, namely, the consideration of future salary increases in the projected unit credit method.

From another point of view, Exposure Draft: *Defined Benefit Plans-Proposed Amendments to IAS19* (IAS19ED) requires firms to disclose the present value of defined benefit obligations, adjusted to exclude the effect of future salary increases as an alternative measure of the long-term employee benefit liability (sometimes referred to as ABO) (IAS19ED, par.125H). The amount is similar to the amount of the firm's defined benefit obligation if the plan were to be terminated (IAS19ED, par.BC60.(f)). These two measurement methods treated in IAS19DP for contribution-based promises and in IAS19ED might be a way to solve the two problems described above in the projected unit credit method.

3.5 Attribution Methods

Attribution methods are methods that attribute the present value of defined benefit obligations to employees' service periods as service cost. There are several attribution methods as follows.[40]

(1) Straight-line basis

This method allocates defined benefit obligations and service cost in direct proportion to service periods.

(2) Salary amount basis

---

[40] JP Actuary Consulting Co., Ltd., "Glossary of Pension Terms," http://www.jpac.co.jp/english/glossary/.

This method allocates defined benefit obligations and service cost in direct proportion to total salary. In most Japanese firms, employees' salaries increase along with their length of service years. Therefore, the service cost is higher in later years.

(3) Benefit multiplier basis

This method allocates defined benefit obligations and service cost in direct proportion to the multiplier of salary.

(4) Point basis

Under this basis, points are granted monthly or annually, accumulated depending on employees' service periods, job grade, title, qualification acquisition, etc. over service period, and multiplied by unit price to calculate the terminal benefits. This method cannot be stated clearly, because the definition of *point* is different in each firm.

In principle, straight-line basis was adopted in the prior accounting standards for retirement benefits. Other methods could also be adopted under certain conditions.[41] The characteristic of merit rewards that Japanese firms display had facilitated adoption of the straight-line method, which equalizes current service costs throughout the entire employees' service period. However, firms will be allowed to choose straight-line basis or the plan's benefit formula from fiscal 2013 (ASBJ Statement 26, par.19). The plan's benefit formula includes a method similar to benefit multiplier basis, or to point basis (ASBJ Guidance 25, par.76). In ED39, the ASBJ states that the plan's benefit formula is more accurate and precise than straight-line basis, because it represents increases of current service cost according to employees' length of service (ED39, par.59).

IAS19 states a firm attributes benefit to periods of service under the plan's benefit formula (IAS19, par.70). However, it also states that, if an employee's service in later years will lead to a materially higher level of benefit than in earlier years, which is called *back-loading*, straight-line basis is adopted to attribute benefit (IAS19, par.70). The ASBJ also states that firms must adopt a plan's benefit formula which is adjusted to recognize service cost equally if a firm's pension payment is back-loading (ED39, par.19.(2)). Therefore, these

---

[41] The method based on proportion to salary could be adopted only when the labor value rationally reflected the pensionable salary used in the calculation. With regard to point basis, it could be adopted only when the increase in points rationally reflected the value of labor in each period.

accounting standards provide some attribution methods whereby firms can equalize their service cost in each period.

3.6 Recognition of Unvested Benefits and Future Salary Increases

There are several research studies concerning the importance of defined benefit obligations. Landsman (1986) examines whether defined benefit obligations and plan assets associated with defined benefit plans are valued by the securities markets as corporate assets and liabilities in the same way as other assets and liabilities. He concludes that defined benefit obligations measured by ABO[42] and plan assets are statistically significant. Therefore, the market values pension information. Barth et al. (1993) examine the effect of pension earnings and balance sheet disclosures on the structure of share prices from 1987 to 1990. Their results show that the coefficients of PBO have the correct sign for all four years and are significant in three of the four years. The t-values in three of the four years range from -3.47 to -1.76, and the coefficients run from -5.47 to -1.13. They are volatile from year to year. They conclude that defined benefit obligation is an important factor for investors to evaluate firms.

As mentioned above, there are two problems in the benefit formula for defined benefit obligations that the IASB describes: (1) the recognition of unvested benefits as a liability, and (2) the consideration of future salary increases in the projected unit credit method. With respect to the recognition of unvested benefits as a liability, there is the issue that Japan's defined benefit plan acts do not define requirements of vesting clearly. On the other hand, in the U.S., the requirements of vesting are defined in specific terms and vesting is treated as a nonforfeitable right. In comparing these requirements of vesting in Japan and the U.S., problems in Japan's defined benefit plan acts arise, which will be discussed below. Regarding the consideration of future salary increases in the projected unit credit method, there are several prior research studies examining the importance of future salary increases. Therefore, these studies are referred to in order to consider if future salary increases should be included in the measurement of defined benefit obligations.

3.6.1 Unvested Benefits

Japan's retirement benefit plans started with a retirement lump sum

---

[42] It was not required for firms to measure defined benefit obligations at PBO at the time.

grant to employees to encourage them to work longer for their firms. The first retirement lump sum grant as a monetary allocation was introduced in 1905 by a cotton-spinning firm.[43] Until tax-qualified pension plans were introduced by the Japanese government, some firms adopted their own defined benefit plans to address the social need of providing income security to their employees after retirement. However, because tax treatments for defined benefit plans were inconsistent and inadequate, these pension plans were not widely implemented. To meet the need for a uniform tax system for defined benefit plans, the tax-qualified pension plan was introduced in 1962, and subsequently the employees' pension fund was established in 1966.[44] Thereupon many firms transferred their funding from retirement lump sum grants to defined benefit plans. In consequence, Japanese defined benefit plans have characteristics of both merit rewards, which retirement lump sum grants have, and income security after employees' retirement. Requirements for vesting are not established because, given the merit reward component, the pension might not be provided to employees under certain conditions such as punitive dismissal.

There are two defined benefit plans in Japan: employees' pension fund and defined-benefit corporate pension.[45] There is no unified act for these pension plans in Japan, i.e., each pension plan operates under a different law. Defined-benefit corporate pension is regulated by the Defined Benefit Corporate Pension Plan Act, and the employees' pension fund is regulated by the Employees' Pension Insurance Act. To assure employees' pension payment, the following requirements should be considered: grants of vesting in accordance with employees' length of service, funding obligations, and payment guarantee institutions.

With regard to grants of vesting in accordance with employees' length of service, vesting is granted to employees while in their firms, and it is not possible for firms to seize employees' vesting or reduce their pension amounts after the grant date of vesting. In Japan, under both employees' pension fund and defined-benefit corporate pension, there is no requirement for grants of vesting, and it is possible to seize or reduce employees' pensions when there

---

[43] Utani, Ryoji, *History of Corporate Pensions -Trajectory of Failures*, Tokyo: Corporate Pension Research Institute Co., Ltd, 1993, pp.212-214.
[44] Nakakita, Toru, *The Future of Corporate Pension*, Tokyo: Chikumashobo Ltd., 2001, pp.43-44.
[45] There were three defined benefit plans: employees' pension fund, defined-benefit corporate pension, and tax-qualified pension plan. However, tax-qualified pension plans were abolished in March 2012.

Table 3.1 Requirements for Vesting Protection

	Defined-Benefit Corporate Pension	Employees' Pension Fund	ERISA (U.S.)
Grants of Vesting	Not defined	Not defined	Defined
Funding Obligations	Defined	Defined	Defined
Institution Guaranteeing Payment	Not established	Established	Established (PBGC)

are serious infractions by employees, such as criminal acts, leakage of firm's secrets, or long absence without any legal excuse (Defined Benefit Corporate Pension Plan Act, par.54). The absence of this regulation for grants of vesting in accordance with employees' length of service is related to a problem on portability of defined benefits. It is difficult for employees under both employees' pension fund and defined-benefit corporate pension to transfer their pension funds when they change their jobs, because grants of vesting are not defined distinctly and the possession of their funds is not clear at their retirement. It also creates a problem for labor liquidity.

As for funding obligations, defined-benefit corporate pension has requirements for funding obligations, actuarial review, verification of funding status, and elimination of pension deficits to ensure firms' pension payment for their employees.[46] Employees' pension fund also requires firms to disclose their actuarial verification of funding status. In terms of the institution guaranteeing payment, only employees' pension fund has the institutional machinery that assures a certain amount of pension payment for beneficiaries when their funds go into liquidation or there is a funding shortage. To calculate the contribution amount to pension funds, firms have to consider the payment guarantee limit in the calculation. When firms' funding does not meet the level their funds require, fund management experts must consult or advise their firms' financial reorganization.[47]

In addition, the Defined Benefit Corporate Pension Plan Act states two other rules to protect vesting rights, namely, the responsibility of fiduciaries

---

[46] Ministry of Health, Labour and Welfare, "Outline of Defined-Benefit Corporate Pension Plan Act," http://www.mhlw.go.jp/topics/0102/tp0208-1a.html.

[47] Employees' Pension Fund Association, *Pension Systems in Other Countries,* Tokyo: Toyo Keizai, Inc., 1999, p.112.

and information disclosure requirements for their beneficiaries. Fiduciaries have some responsibilities regulated under the Defined Benefit Corporate Pension Plan Act, such as the fiduciary's duty of loyalty to beneficiaries and diversification in investment, and a code for their conduct, including conflict of interest actions. Employers have to disseminate their pension contracts to their employees, and also disclose contribution payments, asset management, and financial conditions to their beneficiaries, and also report them to the Minister of Health, Labour and Welfare.[48] These regulations also facilitate the protection of vesting.

In the U.S., vesting is defined more clearly. All pension plans are regulated under ERISA, which is a unified basic act in the *United States Code* (USC). ERISA states vesting is a nonforfeitable right. In the case of a defined benefit plan, a plan has to satisfy the requirements of either of the following clauses (USC29, §1053):

(a) An employee who has completed at least five years of service has a nonforfeitable right to 100 percent of the employee's accrued benefit derived from employer contributions; or

(b) An employee has a nonforfeitable right to a percentage of the employee's accrued benefit derived from employer contributions, determined under the following table:

Years of Service	3	4	5	6	7 or More
The Nonforfeitable Percentage	20	40	60	80	100

ERISA forbids changing a defined benefit plan to reduce employee benefits that have already accrued. It also states benefit accrual requirements to restrict occurrences where the rate of pension paid increases sharply at or near the end of employees' retirement date (USC29, §1054).[49] These benefit accrual

---

[48] Ministry of Health, Labour and Welfare, *op.cit.*.
[49] Benefit accrual requirements are as follows (USC29, §1054):
(a) The accrued benefit should not be less than 3 percent of the normal retirement benefit to which he would be entitled at the normal retirement age if he commenced participation at the earliest possible entry age under the plan and served continuously until the earlier of age 65 or the normal retirement age specified under the plan, multiplied by the number of years of his participation in the plan;
(b) The annual rate at which any individual who is or could be a participant can accrue the retirement benefits payable at normal retirement age under the plan for any later plan year should not be more than 133 1/3 percent of the annual rate at which he can accrue benefits for any plan year beginning on or after such particular plan year and before such later plan year; and

requirements ensure a certain amount of employee benefits for employees who retire before their normal retirement age and protect vesting effectively.[50] With regard to funding obligations, the *Pension Protection Act of 2006* was signed into law to enhance and protect pension savings, and it affects ERISA. The Act states that, as a funding requirement, a plan has to stay fully funded. If the plan is not fully funded, the contribution to the pension fund also includes the amount necessary to amortize the pension funding deficits over seven years. There is also an institution established within the Department of Labor to guarantee employees' pension payment, known as the Pension Benefit Guaranty Corporation (PBGC). The PBGC has specific powers to encourage the continuation and maintenance of voluntary private pension plans, and to provide for the timely and uninterrupted payment of pension benefits (USC29, §1302). These include the power:[51]

(a) to obligate firms which have pension funding deficits to report the details of their pension plans;

(b) to have an executive right granted to the corporation to make firms adhere strictly to the minimum funding requirement; and

(c) to attach its security right to employers who fall behind their plan termination insurance fee.

ERISA was enacted to protect employees' vesting and establish an institution guaranteeing payment to prepare for the bankruptcy of pension plans. It creates a system whereby employees can receive the benefits stemming from their services in the past. Therefore, it is based on the concept that a pension is a future payment of employees' salary. Compared to requirements for vesting protection in Japan, those in ERISA define vesting more clearly and protect payments for employees after their retirement.

(c) The accrued benefit should not be less than a fraction of the annual benefit commencing at normal retirement age to which he would be entitled under the plan as in effect on the date of his separation if he continued to earn annually until normal retirement age the same rate of compensation upon which his normal retirement benefit would be computed under the plan, determined as if he had attained normal retirement age on the date any such determination is made.

[50] Yamaguchi, Osamu,"A Study on the Present Value of Defined Benefit Obligations in Japan," *Yokohama Business Review*, The Society for Business Administration of Yokohama National University, Vol.25 No.2/3, December 2004, p.40.

[51] Employees' Pension Fund Association, *op.cit.*, p.203.

The following two research studies observe whether unvested benefit obligations should be included in defined benefit obligations. Lorensen and Rosenfield (1983) compare the VBO method with the projected unit credit method. In their study, they discuss when a defined benefit obligation is incurred, and indicate two conditions to determine whether a defined benefit obligation exists at a particular date as follows:

(a) There is at present an obligation to make a future sacrifice to another entity, that is, an obligation that is a result of past transactions or events; and

(b) It is at present probable that a sacrifice will be made in the future.

They mention that the VBO method satisfies these two conditions, whereas the projected unit credit method satisfies only the second condition, because it includes unvested benefit obligations and future salary increases which are related to future events. Regarding unvested benefit obligations, there is no defined benefit obligation to employees before vesting, because they have to work additional time to become entitled to receive pension payments until their vesting is granted. Therefore, the authors conclude that the VBO method is more suitable for measuring defined benefit obligations.

Gopalakrishnan and Sugrue (1993) divide PBO into its three components — vested benefits, non-vested benefits, and future salary increases — and adopt cross-sectional valuation models to regress market value of equity on these components of defined benefit obligations. The following model is adopted to examine whether investors perceive future salary increases as a liability of the firm, and whether investors regard the three components of PBO to assess a firm's market value:

$$MVE_i = b_0 + b_1 ASSET_i + b_2 LIABY_i + b_3 PASSET_i + b_4 VBO_i + b_5 NONVEST_i + b_6 SALARY_i + e_i$$

The sample years are 1987 and 1988, which represent mandatory disclosure years of SFAS87. In the result on non-vested benefits (NONVEST), the component is highly significant for 1987, and significant only at the six percent level for 1988. They conclude that investors regard non-vested benefits as corporate liabilities, but the unstable magnitude of the component means that investors might not perceive it as similar to VBO.

As explained above, there are several alternative measurement methods IAS19DP suggests for defined benefit obligations. If unvested benefit obligations are not included in the calculation of defined benefit obligations due to the fact that they are not accrued, grants of vesting must be defined to enhance the comparability of financial statements. Establishing requirements for grants of vesting and a payment guarantee institution is important for the measurement of defined benefit obligations in accounting standards, and for social security to protect employees' livelihoods after their retirement. However, in Japan employees generally work longer for their firms than those in other countries. If vesting is granted five to seven years after employees work for their firms as ERISA states, it will be highly possible that their unvested benefit obligations are realized. It might be better not to include unvested benefit obligations for all employees. However, as IAS19DP suggests "providing more useful information about the amounts, timing, and uncertainty of the cash flows generated by those obligations and rights to financial statement users" (IAS19DP, par.7.18), the probability that unvested benefit obligations will be realized in each firm should be included in the calculation of defined benefit obligations as a faithful representation of the firm's obligations. With regard to IFRS, many countries adopt this accounting standard. The legal structure, work environment, or social system is different in each country. Also, the requirements of vesting must be different. Therefore, the measurement methods suggested in IAS19DP would be useful to reflect the distinctive characteristics each country has, and including the probability in the calculation would provide a more faithful representation of the defined benefit obligations on a firm's financial statements.

3.6.2 Future Salary Increases

Most financial accounting standards concern recognition of items resulting from past events. However, the measurement of defined benefit obligations includes future events, i.e., discount rate, expected rate of return on plan assets, future salary increases, and so on. An important issue is whether future salary increases are included in the measurement of defined benefit obligations, which affects the concept of defined benefit obligations. Beaver (1991) mentions that "uncertain future events are inherently multidimensional because they have a probabilistic nature. Given this multidimensional quality, it is difficult to characterize the probabilistic nature of future events within the deterministic format of current financial statements." It might give firms an opportunity to apply arbitrary treatment of future events. The probabilistic quality of future events is generally considered as subjective or judgmental, because what information people use to condition their beliefs is an important factor in assessing probability.

There are several papers that examine the importance of future salary increases. Lorensen and Rosenfield (1983) indicate two conditions to determine the amount of a liability at a particular date, as listed in Section 3.6.1 above. They mention that future salary increases are not a result of past transactions or events, which leads to the conclusion that the amount of a defined benefit obligation at a particular date should be the VBO at that date. Barth (1991) studies which measures of defined benefit obligations it appears investors implicitly use in valuing a firm. The result indicates that ABO is the defined benefit obligation measure that appears to be most relevant and reliable to investors for the full sample. When the sample is partitioned to compare the effects of defined benefit measurements, i.e. PBO and ABO, on stock prices, these results show that the PBO has less measurement errors than the ABO on the subsample incorporating expected productivity changes. This means investors recognize future salary increases as part of the firm's defined benefit obligations.

As explained in Section 3.6.1, Gopalakrishnan and Sugrue (1993) disaggregate PBO into its three components, vested benefits, non-vested benefits, and future salary increases, and examine the relationship between equity and these components of defined benefit obligations, using firms' data in 1987 and 1988. In the results of the regression analysis, the component of future salary increases (SALARY) is highly significant only for 1988. In 1987, it is significant at only the seven percent level. They also conduct an F-test to test the equality of regression coefficients of these three components and conclude that investors regard these components as liabilities of the firm. Nakano (2000) adopts two methods to compare the importance of the information in PBO to that in ABO, namely, the incremental information content test and relative information content test. Biddle et al. (1995) state that "incremental information content focuses on whether one accounting measure or set of measures provides information content beyond that provided by another. It applies when one measure is viewed as given and an assessment is desired regarding the incremental contribution of another. Relative information content asks which measure has greater information content, and it applies when making mutually exclusive choices among alternatives, or when rankings by information content are desired." In the incremental information content test, he disaggregates PBO into ABO and future salary increases, and treats the information of future salary increases as incremental information content. He examines the relationship between PBO (broken down into ABO and future salary increases) and market value of equity. The result shows that the information of future salary increases is significant, therefore, PBO is more useful for investor's decision-making than ABO. With regard to the relative information content test, the following hypotheses are adopted:

H0:
$$MVE_i = \beta_0 + \beta_1(BVA_i - BVL_i) + \beta_2(PA_i - ABO_i) + \beta_3 NONPEN_i + \beta_4 PENX_i + e_i \quad (1)$$

H1:
$$MVE_i = \beta_0 + \beta_1(BVA_i - BVL_i) + \beta_2(PA_i - PBO_i) + \beta_3 NONPEN_i + \beta_4 PENX_i + e_i \quad (2)$$

MVE (Market Value of Equity)
BVA (Book Value of Asset)
BVL (Book Value of Liability)
PA (Plan Asset)
ABO (Accumulated Benefit Obligation)
PBO (Projected Benefit Obligation)
NONPEN (Non-Pension Flow)
PENX (Pension Expense)

To test these hypotheses mutually, the following equations are given:
$$MVE_i = \beta_0 + \beta_1(BVA_i - BVL_i) + \beta_2(PA_i - ABO_i) + \beta_3 NONPEN_i + \beta_4 PENX_i + \beta_5 [\text{Predicted Metric from Equation (2)}] + e_i \quad (3)$$
$$MVE_i = \beta_0 + \beta_1(BVA_i - BVL_i) + \beta_2(PA_i - PBO_i) + \beta_3 NONPEN_i + \beta_4 PENX_i + \beta_5 [\text{Predicted Metric from Equation (1)}] + e_i \quad (4)$$

As for the equation (3), first, H1 is regressed, and the predicted metric from the H1 is added to the H0 as the fifth regression coefficient. If the hypothesis of equation (3) is not rejected, H0 is not rejected by H1. If it is rejected, H0 is rejected by H1. Equation (4) is tested in the same way as equation (3). The result also shows that PBO has greater information content than ABO.

Picconi (2006) explores the ability of investors and analysts to establish prices and make earnings forecasts through available pension information. In a part of this study, he examines whether various pension plan parameters make it difficult for investors and analysts to estimate the long-run earnings and cash flow implications, and whether the magnitude of these parameters is useful information to predict firms' short and long-run returns. The parameters are the firm's funded status, the firm's PBO, and the levels of the three disclosed pension rate assumptions, including expected rate of return on plan assets, discount rate, and rate of future salary increases. He adopts a regression analysis of future returns on pension rate assumptions. The result of the analysis on future salary increases shows that firms adopting low rates of future salary increases tend to experience significantly lower cumulative returns than firms adopting high rates. The cumulative return is statistically significant for four out of five years. Therefore, the research indicates investors consider information on future salary increases when making earnings forecasts. A rate of future salary increases firms' management chose might show their expectation for future firm performance.

Hann et al. (2007b) study whether the discretion in the choice of actuarial assumptions including the discount rate and future salary increases improves or impairs the value relevance of the PBO. They develop a measure of nondiscretionary PBO by replacing the firms' discount rate and future salary increases assumptions with their respective industry medians, and compare the nondiscretionary PBO with PBO as stated in the footnotes to the financial statements. They suggest that discretionary choices in actuarial assumptions made by managers provide useful information to the market about the underlying economics of PBO. They provide no results related only to future salary increases. However, they indicate the discretionary choices in actuarial assumptions in each firm improve the communication of value-relevant information through the PBO.

Rue and Tosh (1987) study the importance of future salary increases from a different standpoint, namely, the unit problem that Devine (1985) defines. Devine (1985) explains the unit problem: "whether to select small units and aggregate them so long as they prove to be useful, or to select a large unit and use imputation devices until interest wanes. Many of the arguments and controversies in accounting result from undisclosed differences in points of view with regard to the accountability units selected."[52] Rue and Tosh (1987) apply this idea for the recognition of future salary increases, and mention that if the question is limited to the defined benefit obligation for a particular employee, the obligation may not be sufficiently probable to merit recognition. However, if it is viewed from the perspective of the total number of employees in a firm, the uncertainty related to individual cases in future salary increases is diversified away, and the conclusion would be different. Therefore, if the unit is defined as the total number of employees, employees' future salary increases can be predicted based on past experience, and the uncertainty in the prediction will be reduced. They suggest adopting PBO to measure defined benefit obligations.

Reiter (1991) has a different result from the research cited above. This paper examines the relationship between bond risk measures and unfunded defined benefit obligations. Some 209 new-issue electric utility bonds, debentures, and long-term notes issued from 1981 to 1984 are selected as the sample. The risk premium model includes several factors such as year to maturity, level of treasury yields, debt to equity ratio, or property funding ratio, and adds unfunded pension variables. Pension variables are accumulated net assets (liabilities), projected net assets (liabilities), and economic net assets (liabilities) which are calculated based on Economic Benefit Obligations (EBO) that assume all benefits are adjusted for inflation. The result shows that when economic net assets (liabilities) or projected net assets (liabilities) are added to the model including the accumulated net assets (liabilities), there is no significant increase in explanatory power. Therefore, ABO measures provide adequate information to bond market participants to determine the default risk related to defined benefit promises. The study finds no evidence on the importance of future salary increases. Bader (2003) suggests adopting

---

[52] Devine, Carl Thomas, "The Unit Problem," *Essays in Accounting Theory*, Sarasota, Fla.: American Accounting Association, 1985, p.2.

ABO, which does not include future salary increases. The study mentions that future salary increases are not a corporate liability, nor should defined benefit obligations occurring from those increases be included in a liability. PBO overstates the economic reality of the defined benefit plan.

There are two main reasons that some people support PBO rather than ABO: (1) the premise of a going concern, and (2) estimation of future cash flow. With respect to the premise of a going concern, if a firm has no plan to terminate the pension fund, the amount of ABO is not adequate to measure the firm's defined benefit obligation at a practical level. As for estimation of future cash flow, PBO reflects future cash outflow based on a premise of a going concern. On the other hand, some people support ABO rather than PBO, because ABO is consistent with the definition of a liability, and the uncertainty in PBO is higher than ABO.[53]

Table 3.2 shows funding status from 2006 to 2011 calculated by PBO and ABO of Japanese firms adopting SFAS87, which requires disclosing ABO in a footnote. The difference between average funding status under PBO compared with ABO is about 5 to 10%. Firms which disclose larger amounts of PBO or ABO, such as Hitachi, Panasonic, or Toyota, have 200,000 to 300,000 consolidated employees. On the other hand, firms which disclose smaller amounts of PBO or ABO, such as Advantest, Makita, or Konami, have 5,000 to 20,000 consolidated employees. The date of the firm's foundation affects the difference between the amount of PBO and ABO in a firm. The later the firm was established, the wider the difference between the amount of PBO and ABO is. The average of employees' service years is not related to the amount of PBO or ABO in this result. Even though a firm has a small amount of PBO or ABO, employees in these firms work as long as in firms with a large amount of PBO or ABO.

There is no consistent result with respect to determining whether future salary increases should be included in the calculation of defined benefit obligations. Conceptually, future salary increases should not be included in the calculation, because in Discussion Paper: *Conceptual Framework for Financial Accounting* (Conceptual Framework), ASBJ states that "a liability

---

[53] Nakano, Makoto, "Measurement of Defined Benefit Obligations under Corporate Pension Accounting -ABO and PBO-," *The Japan Industrial Management & Accounting*, Vol.56 No.3, October 1996, pp.95-96.

Table 3.2 Funding Status under PBO and ABO

		PBO (million yen)	ABO (million yen)	Plan Assets/PBO	Plan Assets/ABO
2006	Average	798,519	750,576	87.40%	97.24%
	Maximum	4,465,837	4,174,391	166.39%	197.42%
	Minimum	1,329	751	40.79%	43.51%
	Std. dev.	1,069,830	1,008,283	28.58%	33.77%
	No. of Firms	23			
2007	Average	801,478	755,750	89.34%	97.03%
	Maximum	4,328,191	4,050,525	179.49%	212.03%
	Minimum	1,636	938	35.40%	37.82%
	Std. dev.	1,052,934	991,146	30.32%	34.16%
	No. of Firms	23			
2008	Average	755,206	713,736	84.69%	91.89%
	Maximum	3,521,711	3,301,475	161.64%	192.85%
	Minimum	2,044	1,145	36.40%	38.99%
	Std. dev.	933,154	880,610	29.59%	32.70%
	No. of Firms	23			
2009	Average	772,558	738,628	68.52%	73.79%
	Maximum	3,506,972	3,295,027	129.81%	154.04%
	Minimum	2,189	1,247	31.81%	34.67%
	Std. dev.	934,639	888,644	21.79%	24.95%
	No. of Firms	22			
2010	Average	803,367	764,493	75.45%	81.28%
	Maximum	3,505,512	3,293,193	152.45%	168.28%
	Minimum	2,346	1,242	35.11%	38.47%
	Std. dev.	960,705	909,929	25.05%	27.44%
	No. of Firms	22			
2011	Average	856,707	820,525	73.50%	77.30%
	Maximum	2,241,669	2,155,066	145.75%	162.04%
	Minimum	3,246	3,048	39.69%	40.94%
	Std. dev.	860,256	825,604	24.86%	27.86%
	No. of Firms	19			

Source: Nikkei Economic Electrionic Databank System (2011).

is recognized when it is probable that the event will occur in the future" (Conceptual Framework, Introduction). Future salary increases are based on future events which require employees' continuous work in the future. These amounts of ABO and PBO can be equal at employees' retirement. However, they are different depending on the inclusion of future salary increases in the calculation of defined benefit obligations until their retirement. Under PBO, defined benefit obligations are divided over employees' entire service period more equally than under ABO, and reduces the volatility in the calculation of defined benefit obligations. Future salary increases might be predictable if firms build employees' salary structure systematically. However, employees' salaries are affected by economic conditions, which cannot be predicted based on past experience. Therefore, only liabilities resulting from past events do not bring much uncertainty into the calculation of defined benefit obligations.

3.7 Summary and Conclusion

There are three concepts to measure defined benefit obligations: VBO, ABO and PBO. These are different due to the recognition of unvested benefits and future salary increases as a liability. Currently, both Japanese accounting standards and IAS19 adopt PBO. However, there are various debates concerning the recognition of these items, which are related to future events.

With regard to unvested benefits, Japan's Defined Benefit Corporate Pension Plan Act and Employees' Pension Insurance Act do not state requirements of vesting clearly. The grant date of vesting is different depending on each firm. Vesting is not defined as a nonforfeitable right, therefore firms can reduce retirement benefits that have already accrued. Moreover, an institution guaranteeing payment is not established under defined-benefit corporate pensions. Under these conditions, retirement benefits are not protected by these acts. Before entering upon a discussion of the recognition of unvested benefits, requirements of vesting should be established to provide retirement benefits to employees with certainty. It will improve the comparability among firms in their accounting. In Japan, employees tend to work longer for their firms than those in other countries. If vesting is granted five to seven years after employees' hire date as ERISA states, a high proportion of unvested benefit obligations might be realized. Therefore, to provide more useful information about the amounts, timing, and uncertainty of the cash flows generated by those obligations and rights in financial statements, the probability that unvested benefit obligations will be realized in each firm can be included in the calculation of defined benefit obligations.

As for future salary increases, most research conclude that future salary increases are recognized as liabilities of the firm by investors. A liability is defined as a present obligation of the firm arising from past events. Therefore, conceptually future salary increases should not be included in the calculation of defined benefit obligations, because they result from future events. However, there are two main reasons that some people support PBO rather than ABO: the premise of a going concern, and estimation of future cash flow. Table 3.2 shows the difference between the average funding status under PBO and that under ABO of Japanese firms adopting SFAS87 is from 5 to 10%. Future salary increases have a significant effect on the calculation of defined benefit obligations. These amounts of PBO and ABO can be equal when employees retire. They are different before their retirement. PBO includes future salary increases in the calculation, and seems to equalize the periodic service cost to reduce volatility. On the other hand, ABO reduces the uncertainty in the calculation of defined benefit obligations, because the obligation is recognized when it is accrued. It is more consistent with other standards. Therefore, only liabilities resulting from past events should be recognized.

The measurement of defined benefit obligations includes many assumptions, and it makes financial statements difficult for users to understand. To provide useful information and clear understanding for those users, accounting standards for employee benefits should be consistent with other standards, and have less uncertainty in their calculation. It should be determined whether unvested benefits and future salary increases are included in the calculation of defined benefit obligations with consideration of these points.

Chapter 4
Determinants of Actuarial Assumptions for Defined Benefit Pension Plans

4.1 Introduction

International Accounting Standard No.37: *Provisions, Contingent Liabilities and Contingent Assets* (IAS37) states that "a provision should be recognized when a firm has a present obligation as a result of a past event, it is probable that an outflow of resources embodying economic benefits will be required to settle the obligation, and a reliable estimate can be made of the amount of the obligation" (IAS37, par.IN2). Pension is defined as future payment of employees' salary. The future payment has to be discounted and recognized as "present obligations." Firms use some actuarial assumptions to estimate the present obligations. The accounting method makes pension accounting difficult to understand for financial statement users.

Changes in actuarial assumptions have a significant effect on the calculation of defined benefit obligations and defined benefit cost. However, only a few actuarial assumptions are disclosed in footnotes. Several papers show that managers change their actuarial assumptions to reduce their defined benefit obligations and manage their earnings. There are also some differences in setting actuarial assumptions in each accounting standard. In Japan, discount rates might be determined with consideration of the movement in bond yields over a preceding time-period, less than five years until fiscal 2008, whereas IFRS and SFAS require firms to review their discount rates annually. Japanese accounting standards include the expected rate of return on plan assets in actuarial assumptions, whereas IFRS does not. It can be assumed that these differences would have an effect on the amount of defined benefit obligations and defined benefit cost.

This chapter will explain, first, how these actuarial assumptions are determined under Japanese accounting standards. Second, prior research about the relationship between actuarial assumptions and earnings management are reviewed to discuss what elements, especially financial factors, affect the determination of actuarial assumptions; and third, it considers the impact on the pension financing valuation.

4.2 Categories of Actuarial Assumptions

There are several assumptions made to determine the firm's defined benefit obligations and defined benefit cost. ASBJ Guidance 25 states these assumptions include the discount rate, the expected rate of return on plan assets, rates of employee turnover, mortality, and expected future salary increases (ASBJ Guidance 25, pars.22-28). IAS19 states that these assumptions must be unbiased and mutually compatible (IAS19, par.75). IAS19 classifies them according to their characteristics as follows (IAS19, par.76):

(a) Demographic assumptions
   (i) mortality;
   (ii) rates of employee turnover, disability and early retirement;
   (iii) the proportion of plan members with dependants who will be eligible for benefits;
   (iv) the proportion of plan members who will select each form of payment option available under the plan terms; and
   (v) claim rates under medical plans.

(b) Financial assumptions
   (i) the discount rate;
   (ii) benefit levels, excluding any cost of the benefits to be met by employees, and future salary;
   (iii) in the case of medical benefits, future medical costs, including claim handling costs; and
   (iv) taxes payable by the plan on contributions relating to service before the reporting date or on benefits resulting from that service.

IAS19 eliminated the requirement that firms disclose the expected rate of return on plan assets to calculate defined benefit cost, because it might allow firms to manipulate profit or loss (IAS19ED, par.BC41).

In pension financing, actuarial assumptions including mortality, rates of employee turnover, the discount rate, future salary increases, and the expected rate of return on plan assets are mainly used to estimate defined benefit obligations.[54] There are some differences in these assumptions between the Japanese accounting standards related to employee benefits and those of other international accounting standards. Therefore, the details of these five assumptions are discussed below.

4.2.1 Mortality

A mortality rate is a death rate at each age during employees' tenure of office and after their retirement. It is calculated based on the population mortality table of each country a firm operates. Mortality rates in each country are different, but it is not well-known that this has a significant effect on the amount of defined benefit liability within pension funding valuations. Only a quarter of the firms provide mortality assumptions in their financial statements.[55]

Verrall et al. (2011) examine current practice on mortality assumptions in the EU. Their paper consists of two analyses, in-country analysis and cross-border analysis. In in-country analysis, they focus on the probability of death; the expected future lifetime for an individual aged x years; probabilities of survival conditional on reaching ages 50, 60, 65 and 70; and the expected present value of annuities at a reference rate of interest. Regarding cross-border analysis, they show observed and assumed future life expectancy based on mortality tables of the population as a whole, the ratio of typically assumed probability of death for a male or female member aged 65, the expected present value of annuity at a rate of discount of 3%. They compare these data in each country, and conclude that current practice varies considerably across the EU, and the mortality assumption can have a significant effect on the liabilities in firm balance sheets. Collinson (2001) also examines how firms across the EU use different actuarial methods and assumptions. He mentions how some countries, such as Denmark and Portugal, use a single mortality rate at each age while most countries including Ireland, the U.K., and Luxembourg apply different mortality rates to actives, pensioners, and disability pensioners.

There are two pension funds in Japan based on defined benefit pension

---

[54] Kobayashi, Nobuyuki and Satoru Fujiwara, *Accounting Practice on Retirement Benefits*, Tokyo: Toyo Keizai, Inc., 1999, p.81.
[55] Ernst & Young, *IFRS -Observations on the Implementation of IFRS-*, September 2006, http://www2.eycom.ch/publications/items/ifrs/single/200609_observations_on_ifrs/200609_EY_Observations_on_IFRS.pdf, p.68.

plans, employees' pension fund and defined-benefit corporate pension. Firms that have employees' pension fund rely partly on the mortality rates indicated in a notification provided by the Ministry of Health, Labour and Welfare. Firms having defined-benefit corporate pension use the mortality rates regulated by the enforcement ordinance of defined-benefit corporate pension.[56] They both provide that assumptions including mortality rate shall be the same rate as the one used in the last funding valuations when there is no significant effect on pension funding valuations (ASBJ Guidance 25, par.32). However, when the rate is revised, the change has to be reflected in the valuations.

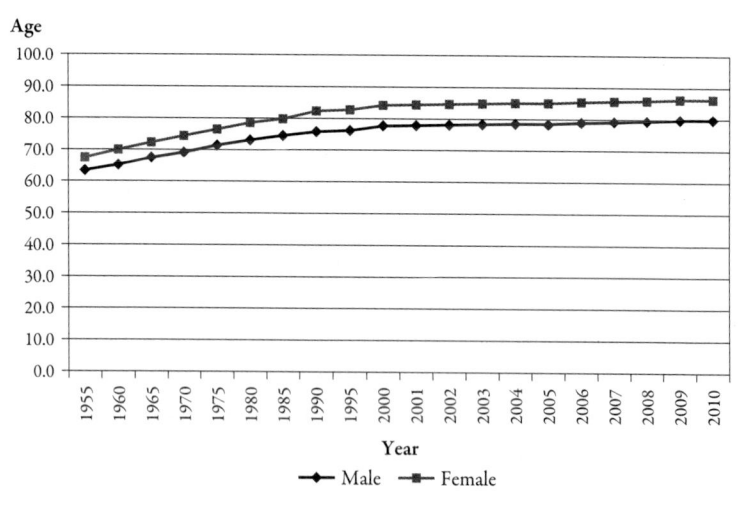

Figure 4.1 Average Lifetime in Japan

Source: Ministry of Health, Labour and Welfare, "Average Lifetime," http://www.mhlw.go.jp/toukei/saikin/hw/life/life10/01.html.

In general, when people live longer, the mortality rate becomes lower, and as a result, the estimated amount of defined benefit obligation increases. With the improvement of medical care quality and hygiene, mortality rates all over the world are getting lower. As shown in Figure 4.1, average lifetime is increasing every year in Japan. It can be predicted that the mortality rate used in pension funding valuations must be getting lower.

Because of the increase in the average lifetime, the Ministry of Health, Labour and Welfare revised the mortality rate tables for employees' pension

---

[56] Pension Fund Association, "Glossary," http://www.pfa.or.jp/yogoshu/yo/yo06.html.

Table 4.1 Tables of Mortality Rates on Employees' Pension Fund

Age	Employees Male Present	Employees Male Previous	Employees Female Present	Employees Female Previous	Post-Employees, Bereaved Family, and Disabilities Male Present	Post-Employees, Bereaved Family, and Disabilities Male Previous	Post-Employees, Bereaved Family, and Disabilities Female Present	Post-Employees, Bereaved Family, and Disabilities Female Previous
15	0.00025	0.00028	0.00007	0.00009	0.00020	0.00028	0.00011	0.00009
20	0.00054	0.00060	0.00015	0.00017	0.00053	0.00060	0.00024	0.00017
25	0.00039	0.00048	0.00011	0.00022	0.00066	0.00048	0.00031	0.00022
30	0.00041	0.00055	0.00023	0.00024	0.00071	0.00055	0.00034	0.00024
35	0.00044	0.00071	0.00022	0.00054	0.00091	0.00071	0.00047	0.00046
40	0.00084	0.00103	0.00027	0.00048	0.00131	0.00130	0.00065	0.00068
45	0.00131	0.00164	0.00047	0.00111	0.00204	0.00208	0.00094	0.00106
50	0.00214	0.00288	0.00111	0.00125	0.00318	0.00349	0.00143	0.00168
55	0.00288	0.00468	0.00142	0.00178	0.00510	0.00548	0.00209	0.00234
60	0.00483	0.00670	0.00194	0.00235	0.00778	0.00791	0.00284	0.00321
65	0.00709	0.01289	0.00293	0.00497	0.01082	0.01281	0.00381	0.00496
70	0.01178	0.01640	0.00486	0.00562	0.01660	0.01988	0.00570	0.00792
75	0.01973	0.02532	0.00859	0.00940	0.03077	0.03102	0.01229	0.01350
80	0.03329	0.04162	0.01582	0.01743	0.05338	0.05393	0.02393	0.02671
85	0.05588	0.06718	0.03110	0.03158	0.09043	0.09540	0.04833	0.05256
90	0.09132	0.10419	0.05767	0.05775	0.14668	0.14959	0.09164	0.09386
95	0.13742	0.14711	0.09798	0.09531	0.21861	0.20594	0.15838	0.14437
100	0.19354	0.19438	0.15334	0.13658	0.30860	0.27996	0.24820	0.20734
105	0.25874	0.24444	0.22548	0.18105	0.41453	0.36405	0.36710	0.27485
110	0.32977	0.29478	0.31147	0.22777	0.53078	0.45450	0.51029	0.34578

Source: Ministry of Health, Labour and Welfare, *Amendments of Financial Administration Policy on Employees' Pension Fund*, Tokyo: MHLW, September 30, 2009.

fund in 2009. In Table 4.1, most of the rates under age 90 in the current tables are lower than the previous one, except in the case of female post-employees, bereaved family, and disabilities. Because of the longer average lifetime for females, all rates for women are lower than those for males.

Table 4.2 shows comparisons of the average lifetime in each country. Japan has the third highest lifetime for men and the highest for women. This means that the mortality rates used in pension funding valuations for Japan must be lower than other countries. This will not be a big problem if investors compare firms within Japan. However, the method of setting the rate and the rate itself must be different in each country, and the rate has a significant effect on pension funding valuations. Therefore, the rate should be required to be disclosed on financial statements.

Table 4.2 Average Lifetime in Each Country

(Unit: Years)

Country		Year Calculated	Male	Female	Population (millions)
	Japan	2010	79.6	86.4	126.0
AFRICA	Algeria	2008	74.9	76.6	34.8
	Egypt	2007	69.5	74.0	75.2
	South Africa	2008	53.3	57.2	48.7
	Tunisia	2009	72.5	76.5	10.3
NORTH AMERICA	Canada	2005	78.0	82.7	33.3
	Mexico	2010	73.1	77.8	106.7
	United States	2007	75.4	80.4	304.1
SOUTH AMERICA	Argentina	2006-2010	72.5	80.0	39.8
	Brazil	2009	69.4	77.0	189.6
	Chile	2005-2010	75.5	81.5	16.8
	Colombia	2005-2010	70.7	77.5	44.5
	Peru	1995-2000	65.9	70.9	28.8
ASIA	Bangladesh	2007	65.4	67.9	144.5
	China	2000	69.6	73.3	1,324.7
	India	2002-2006	62.6	64.2	1,150.2
	Iran	2006	71.1	73.1	72.6
	Israel	2009	79.7	83.5	7.3
	Korea, Republic of	2009	77.0	83.8	48.6
	Malaysia	2010	71.7	76.6	27.7
	Pakistan	2007	63.6	67.6	162.4
	Qatar	2008	77.9	78.1	1.5
	Singapore	2010	79.3	84.1	3.6
	Thailand	2005-2006	69.9	77.6	66.5
	Turkey	2008	71.4	75.8	71.1
EUROPE	Austria	2010	77.7	83.2	8.3
	Belgium	2006	77.0	82.7	10.7
	Czech Republic	2009	74.2	80.1	10.4
	Denmark	2009-2010	77.1	81.2	5.5
	Finland	2010	76.7	83.2	5.3
	France	2010	78.1	84.8	62.3
	Germany	2007-2009	77.3	82.5	82.1
	Iceland	2010	79.5	83.5	0.3
	Italy	2008	78.8	84.1	59.8
	Netherlands	2010	78.8	82.7	16.5
	Norway	2010	78.9	83.2	4.8
	Poland	2009	71.5	80.1	38.1
	Russian Federation	2008	61.8	74.2	142.0
	Spain	2009	78.6	84.6	45.6
	Sweden	2010	79.5	83.5	9.2
	Switzerland	2009	79.8	84.4	7.7
	United Kingdom	2007-2009	77.7	81.9	61.4
OCEANIA	Australia	2007-2009	79.3	83.9	21.5
	NewZealand	2007-2009	78.4	82.4	4.3

Source: Ministry of Health, Labour and Welfare, "Average Lifetime in Each Country," http://www.mhlw.go. jp/toukei/saikin/hw/life/life10/03.html.
Note: The population is a mid-year estimate of 2008. For Japan, it is estimated as of October 1, 2010.

4.2.2 Rates of Employee Turnover

The rate of employee turnover is an estimated rate of the number of employees who retire at each age in relation to the average number of employees. Generally speaking, it is calculated based on the past record, excluding abnormal values on mass layoffs or retirement in each firm. The rate varies for industry segments and individual firms. In general, the ratio is high around 20's, it becomes stable after 30 years of age, and it gets very high around retirement age. When the rate of employee turnover is high, the estimated amount of defined benefit obligations becomes smaller.[57]

The formula to calculate defined benefit obligations is as follows. The first three factors calculate the estimated total amount of employee benefits at the retirement. A rate of employee turnover is a factor to indicate the probability that employees receive their employee benefits.[58]

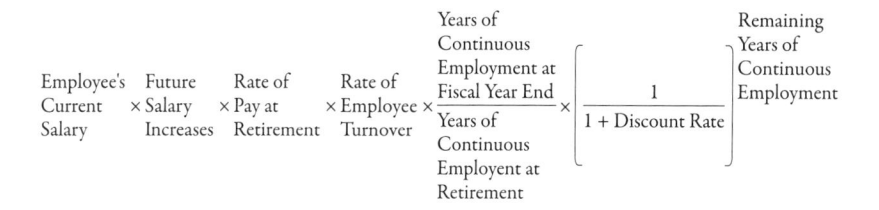

$$\text{Employee's Current Salary} \times \text{Future Salary Increases} \times \text{Rate of Pay at Retirement} \times \text{Rate of Employee Turnover} \times \frac{\text{Years of Continuous Employment at Fiscal Year End}}{\text{Years of Continuous Employent at Retirement}} \times \left[\frac{1}{1 + \text{Discount Rate}} \right]^{\text{Remaining Years of Continuous Employment}}$$

From a different point of view, Ippolito (1997) studies the relation between pensions and quit rates. The study proves that wage increase and pensions are important factors for employees to decide to stay at their firms. Therefore, if firms provide good salaries and pensions to employees, it affects three factors in the formula above, employee's current salary, future salary increases, and rate of employee turnover, and as a result, increases defined benefit obligations.

4.2.3 Discount Rate

The IASB requires a firm to use the discount rate determined by reference

---

[57] Chuo Audit Corp. and NLI Research Institute, *Accounting and Tax Practice on Corporate Pensions*, Tokyo: Nikkei Inc., 1999, p.62.
[58] Emura, Hiroshi and Masahiko Inoue, *The New Retirement Benefit Scheme and the Practical Accounting*, Tokyo: Nikkei Inc., 2002, p.27.

to market yields on high quality corporate bonds at the end of the reporting period, and if there is no deep market for these bonds, the firm have to use the market yields on government bonds (IAS19, par.83). As a result of the recent global financial crisis, the difference between yields on corporate bonds and yields on government bonds has a significant effect on the amount of defined benefit obligations. Therefore, in Exposure Draft: *Discount Rate for Employee Benefits -Proposed Amendments to IAS19* (ED for Discount Rate), IASB states not to use the market yields on government bonds. If there is no deep market for such bonds, it requires a firm to apply the principles and approach in International Accounting Standard No.39: *Financial Instruments: Recognition and Measurement*. IASB believes that "this accounting change will improve comparability in financial statements across firms and through time for the same firm" (ED for Discount Rate, pars.78, BC4).

Japanese accounting standards provide that a firm shall determine the discount rate based on yields on safe and secure long bonds. The safe and secure long bonds include government bonds, government agency securities, and high-grade corporate bonds (ASBJ Statement 26, par.20). High-grade corporate bonds mean bonds with better than AA grades assigned by several credit-rating agencies, Standard & Poor's, Rating and Investment Information Inc., or Japan Credit Rating Agency, Ltd. (ASBJ Guidance 25, par.24). Basically, yields of these corporate bonds are set higher than government bonds because of their lower credit capability.

The discount rate might be determined with consideration of the movement in bond yields over a preceding time-period, less than five years in each firm until fiscal 2008 (Accounting Standard for Retirement Benefits, par.footnote6). With the ongoing convergence project with IASB, Japanese accounting standards eliminated the rule to consider the movement in bond yields, because ASBJ Statement No.19: *Amendments to Accounting Standard for Retirement Benefits (Part 3)* (ASBJ Statement 19) states there is no adequate reason that can explain why this discount rate is more reliable than the one calculated by a market yield at the balance sheet date (ASBJ Statement 19, par. Appendix11). Therefore, now Japanese accounting standards require firms to review the discount rate annually.

Figure 4.2 compares average discount rates with government bond rates from 2001 to 2011. The data were collected from Nikkei Economic Electronic

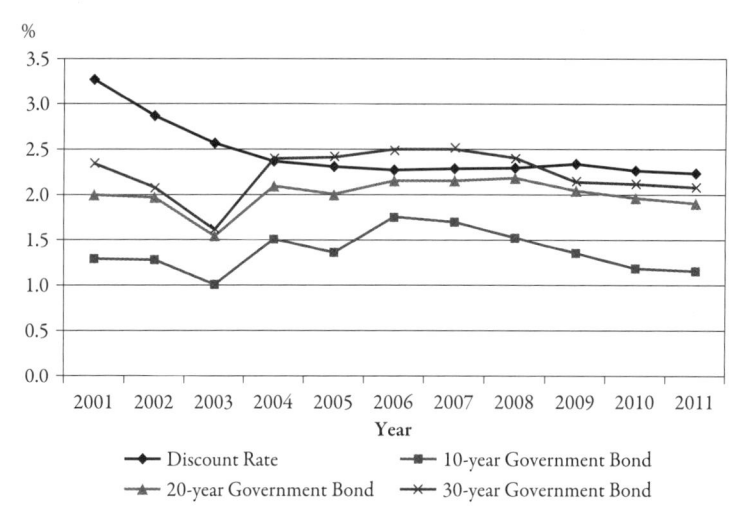

%

3.5
3.0
2.5
2.0
1.5
1.0
0.5
0.0
         2001 2002 2003 2004 2005 2006 2007 2008 2009 2010 2011
                                      Year

—♦— Discount Rate   —■— 10-year Government Bond
—▲— 20-year Government Bond   —✕— 30-year Government Bond

(%)

	2001	2002	2003	2004	2005	2006	2007	2008	2009	2010	2011
Discount Rate	3.26	2.87	2.55	2.38	2.31	2.28	2.29	2.29	2.34	2.27	2.24
10-year Government Bond	1.29	1.28	0.99	1.50	1.36	1.75	1.70	1.52	1.36	1.19	1.15
20-year Government Bond	2.00	1.96	1.53	2.10	2.02	2.16	2.15	2.19	2.05	1.97	1.90
30-year Government Bond	2.34	2.07	1.60	2.41	2.42	2.50	2.50	2.41	2.14	2.12	2.08

Figure 4.2   Average Discount Rates and Yields of Government Bonds

Sources: Nikkei Economic Electronic Databank System (2011)
Ministry of Finance, "Auction Announcement and Result," http://www.mof.go.jp/jgbs/auction/past_auction_schedule/index.html.

Databank System (2011), which is provided by the Nikkei Digital Media, Inc. Firms (excluding banks and insurance firms) were selected which are listed on the first section of the Tokyo Stock Exchange, and set both discount rates and expected rates of return on plan assets for accounting standards for retirement benefits, because it is possible that firms do not have pension plans if they do not set these rates.[59]

For the first three years, there is a significant difference between average discount rates and yields on government bonds. The accounting standards for retirement benefits were introduced in fiscal 2000. Firms were not required to recognize defined benefit obligations and plan assets on their financial

---

[59] Suda, Kazuyuki, *Empirical Analysis of Accounting Reform,* Tokyo: Dobunkan Shuppan, Co. Ltd., 2004, p.58.

Table 4.3 Range of Discount Rates Firms Adopt

	2001	2002	2003	2004	2005	2006	2007	2008	2009	2010	2011
Under 1%	0	0	0	0	0	0	0	0	0	2	4
1.0% to 1.99%	2	12	35	60	82	94	97	100	122	163	186
2.0% to 2.99%	75	564	966	1,022	1,019	1,010	1,020	1,023	982	907	875
3.0% to 3.99%	914	622	171	50	25	13	13	10	10	2	2
4.0% to 4.99%	18	12	5	3	1	4	5	5	1	2	5
5.0% to 5.99%	1	1	1	2	12	19	20	14	3	27	30
6.0% to 6.99%	0	2	15	19	16	9	12	21	34	13	7
7.0% to 7.99%	14	19	6	3	0	0	0	1	4	2	1
8.0% to 8.99%	3	1	1	1	0	0	1	0	3	3	8
9.0% to 9.99%	0	0	0	0	2	0	0	0	0	2	3
10.0% to 10.99%	0	0	0	0	0	0	2	3	4	2	2
11.0% to 11.99%	0	0	1	0	0	2	1	0	2	2	0
12.0% to 12.99%	0	0	0	0	0	1	0	0	1	1	0
Number of Firms	1,027	1,233	1,201	1,160	1,157	1,152	1,171	1,177	1,166	1,128	1,123
Mean	3.26	2.87	2.55	2.38	2.31	2.28	2.29	2.29	2.34	2.27	2.24
Standard Deviation	0.67	0.72	0.75	0.71	0.72	0.79	0.81	0.86	1.12	1.07	1.02

Source: Nikkei Economic Electronic Databank System (2011)

statements before the accounting change. Therefore, they might have some difficulties in estimating the best discount rates for them according to the accounting standards. From 2004 to 2011, the movement of average discount rates was similar to the movement on yields of 20- and 30-year government bonds. From 2004 to 2008, firms tended to choose discount rates between those for 20-year government bonds and 30-year government bonds. For the recent three-year period, the average rates they chose were higher than those for 30-year government bonds.

Table 4.3 shows the range of discount rates Japanese firms adopt. The chart indicates that firms tended to adopt rates around 3.0 to 3.99% in 2001 and 2002, and 2.0 to 2.99% from 2003 to 2011. Firms adopting SFAS, such as Toyota, Honda, Sony, or Nissan, tended to set higher discount rates. From 2009 to 2011, these standard deviations were higher than those from 2001 to 2008 because, while most firms chose discount rates between 2.0 and 2.99%, there were increasing number of firms that chose rates from 1.0 to 1.99% and over 50 firms that assumed rates of more than 5.0% in each year. The discount rates firms adopted varied more widely than those from 2001 to 2008.

Table 4.4 Frequency and Level of Changes in Discount Rates

	Increased	Decreased	No Change	Min.	Max.	Mean	Std.	No. of Firms
2001-2002	4	601	413	-4.45	4.25	-0.384	0.452	1,018
2002-2003	5	678	501	-2.50	4.25	-0.345	0.398	1,184
2003-2004	10	393	732	-9.30	4.50	-0.178	0.432	1,135
2004-2005	13	188	925	-1.00	3.75	-0.068	0.275	1,126
2005-2006	20	136	969	-3.70	9.00	-0.040	0.478	1,125
2006-2007	49	40	1,047	-2.70	7.50	0.010	0.359	1,136
2007-2008	54	38	1,061	-6.00	3.65	0.011	0.309	1,153
2008-2009	66	90	995	-3.90	9.50	0.026	0.553	1,151
2009-2010	37	172	919	-10.10	6.00	-0.077	0.472	1,128
2010-2011	24	139	939	-4.70	6.50	-0.046	0.419	1,102

Source: Nikkei Economic Electronic Databank System (2011)

Table 4.4 reports the frequency and level of changes in the discount rates. For the first three years, the frequency of changes on discount rates is high. After 2004, over 80% of firms did not change their discount rates. Figure 4.2 also indicates that discount rates and yields of 20- and 30-year government bonds became stable after 2004. As mentioned above, prior Japanese accounting standards prescribed that the discount rate might be determined with consideration of the movement in bond yields for the past five years in each firm. However, Table 4.4 shows that over 35% of firms changed their discount rates from 2001 to 2004. Over 90% of firms had no change on discount rates from 2005 to 2011, even though there was a big economic slump starting from the bankruptcy of Lehman Brothers in 2008. Thus it was difficult for firms to set appropriate discount rates owing to the introduction of the accounting standards for retirement benefits from 2001 to 2004. After the accounting standards required firms to review their discount rates annually, the number of firms that changed their discount rates increased. The accounting change might affect firms' discretionary behavior on determining discount rates.

4.2.4 Future Salary Increases

Future salary increases are based on employee wage administration in each firm, average salary, salary raise in the past, and so on.[60] It consists of

---
[60] Yamaguchi, Osamu, *Practice of Defined Benefit Obligations*, Tokyo: Chuokeizai-Sha, Inc., 2000, p.130.

two categories: a mandatory pay raise and an across-the-board pay increase. A mandatory pay raise is affected by age-related procession on employees' salaries. According to the Japanese accounting standard, *Practices on Accounting for Retirement Benefits*, the mandatory pay raise should be calculated based on age-specific average salaries according to the statistical data on current employees. An across-the-board pay increase determines movement of future salary levels (Practices on Accounting for Retirement Benefits, par.Appendix.2). These rates are included in the future salary increases when these are expected in the future (ASBJ Statement 26, par.57). As for IAS19, IASB states that estimates of future salary increases take account of inflation, seniority, promotion, and other relevant factors (IAS19, par.90). It also states that a firm should consider both a mandatory pay raise and an across-the-board pay increase to determine the future salary increases. Under the prior Japanese accounting standard, Accounting Standard for Retirement Benefits, the across-the-board pay increase was included in the future salary increases only when it was estimated for certain. However, the standard was revised to consider the expected across-the-board pay increase in determining future salary increases in order to maintain harmony with other international accounting standards, and consistent with the calculation basis for other actuarial assumptions (ASBJ Statement 26, par.57).

Japanese accounting standards do not require firms to disclose the rates of future salary increases. However, SFAS87 requires the disclosure of the rates on financial statements (SFAS87, par.54d). There were 18 Japanese firms listed on the New York Stock Exchange from 2006 to 2011 continuously. The rates of future salary increases used to determine defined benefit obligations for these firms are shown in Table 4.5.

The level of the rate each firm chooses depends on the firm's management condition, salary increase scheme, and economic situation it is in. Most of firms in Table 4.5 chose rates from 2.0 to 4.0%. Firms tend not to change their rates significantly every year. As mentioned above, there was the bankruptcy of a big investment bank in 2008, and worldwide recession spread after that. However, most firms still keep their rates level, and some firms even assume higher rates. This rate might be easier to predict than other assumptions, such as a discount rate or an expected rate of return on plan assets, since there are fewer uncertainties.

Table 4.5   Rates of Future Salary Increases

(%)

	2006	2007	2008	2009	2010	2011
Advantest Corporation	3.1	3.0	3.0	3.0	3.0	3.0
Canon Inc.	3.3	3.4	2.9	3.0	3.0	3.0
Hitachi Ltd.	2.5	2.7	2.7	2.7	2.7	2.6
Honda Motor Co. Ltd.	2.2	2.3	2.3	2.3	2.3	2.3
Konami Corporation	1.7	2.0	1.9	1.9	1.9	1.8
Kubota Corporation	N/A	N/A	N/A	N/A	N/A	N/A
Kyocera Corporation	N/A	N/A	N/A	N/A	N/A	N/A
Mitsubishi UFJ Financial Group Inc.	2.95	2.98	3.10	3.07	3.06	3.23
Mizuho Financial Group Inc.	1.37-5.67	1.51-5.76	1.61-5.62	1.93-6.27	2.13-6.12	2.28-6.15
Nidec Corporation	0.0-3.5	1.0-3.5	1.0-3.2	1.0-3.2	2.5	2.9
Nomura Holdings Inc.	3.6	3.7	3.7	2.5	2.5	2.5
NTT Corporation	1.5-3.4	1.5-3.4	1.9-3.2	1.9-3.2	1.9-3.2	2.5-3.4
NTT DOCOMO INC.	2.1	2.1	2.2	2.2	2.2	2.9
Orix Corporation	6.0	6.2	6.2	5.8	5.9	6.1
Panasonic Corporation	1.6	1.7	1.7	1.7	1.8	1.8
RICOH	5.4	5.3	6.5	6.5	6.5	3.3
Sony Corporation	3.2	2.5	2.5	2.7	N/A	N/A
Toyota Motor Corporation	0.1-10.0	0.1-10.0	0.1-10.0	0.1-10.0	0.5-10.0	0.8-11.0

Note: Kubota and Kyocera corporations use a point system. Sony corporation also adopts a point system in 2010 and 2011.

4.2.5 Expected Rate of Return on Plan Assets

Japanese accounting standards state that the expected rate of return on plan assets is assumed with consideration of investment portfolio, management performance in the past, management policy, and the market for plan assets that firms hold (ASBJ Guidance 25, par.25). Imafuku (2000) states the reasons why expected rate of return on plan assets is set based on different information from that of the discount rate:[61]

(a) Expected rate of return on plan assets is an expected rate rather than a realized rate. The amount of defined benefit obligations calculated by the expected rate is not based on present value;

(b) It shall impair comparability if the amount of defined benefit obligations is influenced by management of plan assets; and

(c) Risks and uncertainty on future cash flows of defined benefit obligations are not related to expected yield rates of plan assets.

---
[61] Imafuku, Aishi, *Accounting for Retirement Benefits,* Tokyo: Shinsei-Sha Co. Ltd., 2000, pp.71-73.

In accounting standards, the definition of defined benefit obligations is different from that of plan assets. Therefore, the method of setting expected rate of return on plan assets should be different from the one for the discount rate.

There are many papers examining the relationship between earnings manipulation and expected rate of return on plan assets. Bergstresser et al. (2006) find three reasons firms adopt higher assumed expected rates of return on plan assets. They are (1) when they prepare to take over other firms, (2) when they are near critical earnings thresholds, and (3) when their managers exercise stock options. Managers can use pension accounting to raise reported profits on financial statements, and as a result, to influence stock prices. Li and Klumpes (2007) suggest that highly leveraged firms and underfunded firms systematically report higher expected rates of return on plan assets. They also show that sample firms with higher leverage have a greater propensity to increase reported expected rates of return on plan assets.[62] These results support the premise that U.K. managers increase reported expected rates of return on plan assets when they confront a higher probability of technical default. Yoshida (2009) finds that unprofitable firms tend to choose higher expected rates of return on plan assets. In a limited way, if firms can achieve their return on assets (ROA) in the previous fiscal year, they increase their expected rates of return on plan assets.

In light of this situation, additional information on expected rate of return on plan assets might be useful to investors. There are some firms that disclose the expected rate of return on plan assets, such as equities, bonds, property, etc. The IASB could not mandate this information to be on financial statements, because there was resistance from those who commented on the exposure draft.[63] Also, Amir and Benartzi (1998) suggest considering enforcement of disclosure requirements regarding plan asset composition, because their study shows plan asset composition information is positively correlated with the future actual return on plan assets.[64] Such accounting standards might improve the comparability among firms in different countries.

---

[62] However, they suggest that there is no evidence on the expected rate of return on plan assets being used to smooth earnings under Financial Reporting Standard No.17: *Retirement Benefits*.
[63] Ernst & Young, *op.cit.*, pp.68-69.
[64] Their study also indicates that the expected rate of return on plan assets is not significantly associated with the future actual return on plan assets.

%

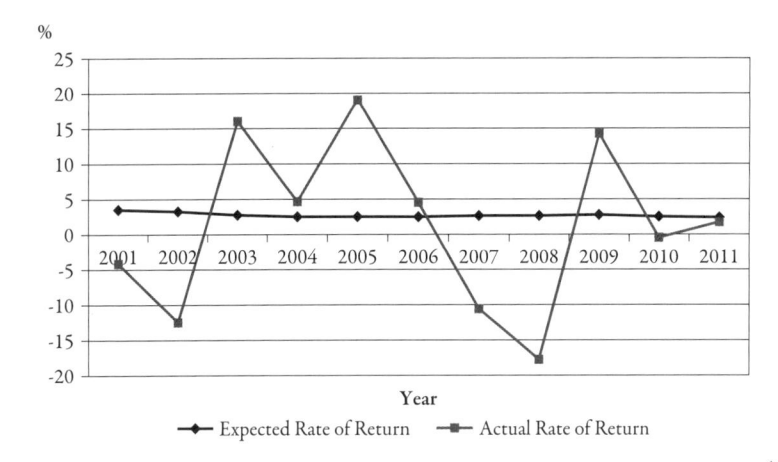

	2001	2002	2003	2004	2005	2006	2007	2008	2009	2010	2011
Expected Rate of Return	3.55	3.27	2.87	2.54	2.47	2.47	2.57	2.65	2.65	2.47	2.45
Actual Rate of Return	-4.16	-12.46	16.17	4.59	19.16	4.50	-10.58	-17.80	14.29	-0.54	1.82

Figure 4.3 Average Expected Rates of Return and Actual Rates of Return on Plan Assets

Sources: Nikkei Economic Electronic Databank System (2011)
 Pension Fund Association, "Annual Report 2011," http://www.pfa.or.jp/jigyo/tokei/shisanunyo/jittai/files/AnnualReport 2011.pdf, p.5

Figure 4.3 presents average expected rates and actual rates of return on employees' pension fund and defined-benefit corporate pension. JICPA Accounting Practice Committee Report No.13: *Practical Guidance on Accounting for Retirement Benefits (Interim Report)* (JICPA Report 13) states that the expected rate of return on plan assets is reviewed annually in principle (JICPA Report 13, par.19). It is apparent from the graph that the average expected rate in each year is always different from the actual rate of return. The movement of the actual rate of return has rapid swings, whereas the expected rate of return is stable.

Table 4.6 reports the range of expected rates of return on plan assets firms adopt. Most of firms choose expected rates of return from 1.0 to 4.99%. The standard deviation in each year is higher than that for discount rates. It means that the range of expected rates of return firms select is wider than that for discount rates.

Tables 4.7 and 4.8 explain the movement of actual rates of return in

Table 4.6 Range of Expected Rates of Return on Plan Assets Firms Adopt

	2001	2002	2003	2004	2005	2006	2007	2008	2009	2010	2011
Under 0%	0	0	2	2	2	2	0	0	0	1	1
0.0% to 0.99%	4	13	38	70	69	63	52	37	35	52	49
1.0% to 1.99%	76	136	174	207	206	202	195	185	177	222	229
2.0% to 2.99%	115	219	382	496	547	552	550	552	567	555	553
3.0% to 3.99%	467	513	376	247	219	221	242	256	243	195	195
4.0% to 4.99%	235	243	163	92	72	69	78	84	72	43	36
5.0% to 5.99%	96	73	36	14	13	9	15	21	22	10	12
6.0% to 6.99%	15	15	7	3	2	3	6	9	14	17	17
7.0% to 7.99%	3	3	4	6	5	12	11	12	15	15	15
8.0% to 8.99%	5	5	9	14	16	14	16	16	16	14	14
9.0% to 9.99%	9	11	8	9	6	5	5	4	4	2	1
10.0% to 10.99%	2	2	2	0	0	0	0	0	1	1	0
11.0% to 11.99%	0	0	0	0	0	0	0	0	0	0	0
12.0% to 12.99%	0	0	0	0	0	0	0	1	0	1	1
Over 13.0%	0	0	0	0	0	0	1	0	0	0	0
Number of Firms	1,027	1,233	1,201	1,160	1,157	1,152	1,171	1,177	1,166	1,128	1,123
Mean	3.55	3.27	2.87	2.54	2.47	2.47	2.57	2.65	2.65	2.47	2.45
Standard Deviation	1.28	1.31	1.36	1.39	1.31	1.31	1.39	1.36	1.38	1.40	1.38

Source: Nikkei Economic Electonic Databank System (2011)

Figure 4.3. From 2001 to 2006, employees' pension funds and defined-benefit corporate pensions invested 40 to 50% of their assets in domestic and foreign stocks. After 2007, the proportion of plan assets invested in these stocks decreases to 30 to 40% because of the worldwide economic downturn beginning with the defaults on sub-prime mortgage loans in the U.S.

In 2002, the Nikkei Stock Average tumbled to a new low after the Japanese economic bubble burst. The recession in the U.S. and the bankruptcy of WorldCom made foreign stock prices decline further. In 2003, worldwide monetary policy relaxation increased domestic and foreign stock prices. In 2004, the decrease of GDP in Japan, the increase in crude oil prices, and monetary tightening in China decreased domestic stock prices. In 2006, there was a worldwide decline in stock values, stock prices in China declined, and the financial crisis in the U.S. was triggered by defaults on sub-prime mortgage loans. However, strong corporate performance in both Japan and other countries increased domestic and foreign stock prices in the end of

Table 4.7   Rates of Return Categorized by Assets

(%)

	Domestic Bonds	Domestic Stocks	Foreign Bonds	Foreign Stocks
2001	0.97	-16.41	7.48	2.62
2002	4.31	-25.25	14.25	-32.18
2003	-1.55	50.04	0.62	22.72
2004	2.04	2.58	10.36	14.23
2005	-1.52	50.37	7.15	28.45
2006	2.12	-0.32	9.29	16.91
2007	2.37	-27.75	0.43	-17.02
2008	0.21	-35.98	-7.00	-42.82
2009	2.63	30.01	1.55	45.01
2010	2.02	-7.95	-6.18	2.13
2011	2.82	0.44	4.76	-0.79

Source: Pension Fund Association, "The Survey and Comment on Pension Asset Management," http://www.pfa.or.jp/jigyo/tokei/shisanunyo/jittai/index.html.

Table 4.8   Plan Asset Structure

(%)

	Domestic Bonds	Domestic Stocks	Foreign Bonds	Foreign Stocks	General Account Assets	Others	Short-Term Fund
2001	21.97	31.98	10.24	19.61	12.05	1.49	2.66
2002	23.51	25.92	11.90	16.01	13.95	4.26	4.44
2003	20.20	28.20	10.30	15.10	10.50	5.30	10.40
2004	22.12	26.75	11.99	16.53	8.50	7.01	7.11
2005	20.87	30.81	11.67	18.32	7.46	7.41	3.47
2006	21.80	28.04	12.52	18.80	8.24	7.70	2.90
2007	24.94	23.49	13.09	16.23	10.10	8.66	3.48
2008	26.99	20.34	13.31	13.30	12.59	9.03	4.44
2009	26.11	21.33	12.17	16.65	4.69	3.16	4.19
2010	26.84	18.89	11.49	17.53	12.97	8.58	3.70
2011	27.16	17.43	12.04	16.33	14.00	8.81	4.22

Source: Pension Fund Association, "The Survey and Comment on Pension Asset Management," http://www.pfa.or.jp/jigyo/tokei/shisanunyo/jittai/index.html.

the period. In 2007, sub-prime mortgage loans grew into a serious problem, and they affected all domestic and foreign bond and stock prices. In 2008, the bankruptcy of the big investment bank, Lehman Brothers led to a global economic slowdown.[65] The Japanese yen has trended upward against foreign

---

[65] Pension Fund Association, "The Survey and Comment on Pension Asset Management," http://www.pfa.or.jp/jigyo/tokei/shisanunyo/jittai/index.html.

Table 4.9 Frequency and Level of Change in Expected Rates of Return on Plan Assets

	Increased	Decreased	No Change	Min.	Max.	Mean	Std.	No. of Firms
2001-2002	31	260	727	-4.31	8.00	-0.274	0.779	1,018
2002-2003	13	503	668	-4.45	3.50	-0.441	0.716	1,184
2003-2004	22	452	661	-8.40	6.00	-0.356	0.757	1,135
2004-2005	75	184	867	-6.72	7.25	-0.061	0.663	1,126
2005-2006	89	120	916	-6.00	6.00	0.000	0.554	1,125
2006-2007	136	80	920	-5.00	13.10	0.100	0.766	1,136
2007-2008	134	54	965	-3.90	4.50	0.077	0.481	1,153
2008-2009	97	122	932	-7.00	5.70	-0.021	0.598	1,151
2009-2010	48	241	839	-6.20	6.00	-0.183	0.755	1,128
2010-2011	76	142	883	-7.22	5.00	-0.036	0.641	1,102

Source: Nikkei Economic Electrionic Databank System (2011)

currencies since 2008, and at the end of 2010 the exchange rate to the U.S. dollar was about 82 yen (compared with 90 yen in 2009); to the Euro, 107 yen (130 yen in 2009); and to the British pound, 125 yen (145 yen in 2009). The strong yen decreased the investment return in foreign stocks and bonds from firm's plan asset management.

Table 4.9 reports how often and how much firms change their expected rates of return on plan assets. Comparing the data to that in Table 4.4, firms change their expected rates of return more than their discount rates, except in 2001 and 2002. Similar to the tendency of changes in discount rates, many firms changed their expected rates of return from 2001 to 2004, and had no change in expected rates of return after 2005.

Many factors affect the determination of expected rates of return on plan assets. These factors include much uncertainty concerning economic movement all over the world. The average expected rates of return are stable, however, average actual rates of return moves up and down every year. It means that volatility on expected rates of return is quite high.

4.3 Actuarial Assumptions and Earnings Management

These results above indicate how different actuarial assumptions selected by each firm are. All actuarial assumptions are not disclosed on financial statements. Okumura (2005) states that if a firm's discount rate is increased 1% from 3 to 4% under certain conditions, employees' average age is 40 year-old, retirement age is 60 year-old, and period of benefit is for 15 years, the PBO will drop by 23%. Therefore, these rates have a significant effect on the calculation of defined benefit obligations and defined benefit cost. Several studies show there is a possibility that managers in firms control these assumptions to make their financial statements look better.

Morris et al. (1983) discuss why firms change actuarial assumptions. They indicate that firms change their assumptions due to a decrease of defined benefit cost and an increase in the reported income figure, an advantage in tax status of pension contributions and plan earnings, and a decrease of defined benefit obligations. They conclude that corporate managers change their actuarial assumptions with consideration given to the extent of a plan's overfunding or underfunding. Bodie et al. (1987) find a defined benefit liability on financial statements is strongly related to firms' profitability through the choice of a discount rate. More profitable firms tend to choose lower discount rates, which leads to a greater amount of defined benefit liabilities. They also find a relationship between the level of pension funding and firms' long-run profitability. Ghicas (1990) shows when firms have lower working capital, higher debt, and a lower rate of undertaking new investments, they switch their actuarial cost methods, and reduce their pension funding. Gopalakrishnan and Sugrue (1995) find that leverage and pension plan funding status are related to the choice of actuarial assumptions, the discount rate and the rate of future salary increases. In their study, firms with higher leverage and lower pension plan funding choose higher discount rates and lower rates of future salary increases. They suggest that firms might set these rates in a manner that is favorable to them.

Godwin et al. (1996) examine whether six factors — including changes in cash flows, earnings per share, tax status, leverage, dividends, and the market interest rate — affect the choice of actuarial assumptions or not. Their study provides evidence that managers are likely to increase actuarial assumptions to deal with tighter dividend restrictions, lower earnings, higher leverage, and reductions in the tax benefits of plan funding. Asthana (1999) examines if firms' financial and pension profiles have some effects on their funding strategies and actuarial choices, using factors similar to those of Godwin et al. (1996). This paper's results indicate that when firms have greater profitability, greater cash flows from operating activities, lower tax liability, and smaller debt, they tend to choose conservative actuarial choices to maximize contributions. Conversely, when firms have smaller profitability, smaller cash flows from operating activities, higher tax liability, and larger debt, they tend to select liberal actuarial choices to minimize contributions. Funding status also affects firms' actuarial choices. Firms overfunded make conservative actuarial choices, and those underfunded make liberal actuarial choices to avoid defined benefit costs. Obinata (2000) examines what factors have an effect on firms' discount rate choices, and reports that profitability has a significant impact on firms' choices. This paper also studies if stock prices reflect the size of pension discount rate. It indicates that firms choosing lower pension discount rates are valued higher.

Blankley and Swanson (1995) examine whether firms manipulate actuarial assumptions while still remaining consistent with the requirements of SFAS87 as a tool of earnings management. Among the various studies, only their research concludes that there is no evidence of systematic manipulation of actuarial assumptions in order to manage earnings or pension funding.

Most studies suggest that managers tend to manipulate pension transactions as an earnings management tool. As explained above, firms' profitability, leverage, pension funding status, cash flows from operating activities, tax-paying status, and firm size can be primary factors to determine actuarial assumptions. Most Japanese firms disclose only discount rates and expected rates of return on plan assets. Therefore, the effects of these factors on actuarial assumptions, mainly discount rates and expected rates of return are discussed as follows.

Profitability: Several papers demonstrate that managers at firms change their actuarial assumptions for earnings management. With regard to discount rates, increases in these rates decrease defined benefit obligations and defined benefit cost, and the resulting increase in earnings would yield a better valuation from investors. Therefore, firms whose profitability decreases adopt higher discount rates. Bodie et al. (1987), Asthana (1999), Gopalakrishnan and Sugrue (1995), Godwin et al. (1996), and Obinata (2000) include profitability in their models to examine the effect of financial ratios on firm's changes in actuarial assumptions, and all of them[66] present profitability as significant in their

---

[66] Obinata (2000) states earnings before income taxes deflated by equity have the most significant effect on the changes in discount rate.

models.

Leverage: The Japanese accounting standards for retirement benefits will require disclosing unfunded defined benefit liabilities including unrecognized obligations on the balance sheet since fiscal 2013. SFAS158 and IAS19 also require disclosing them on the balance sheet. The defined benefit liabilities are added to total liabilities, and a part of the unrecognized obligations are subtracted from net assets. Therefore, the effect of defined benefit liabilities on firms' capital structure is significant. In particular, defined benefit liabilities have a negative impact on debt to equity ratio, which is one of the most important financial ratios for determining firms' leverage and capital risk. The ratio has an effect on the cost of capital, which essentially is the rate of return a firm is expected to earn, because stakeholders invest at the same level of risk as the rate of return. It is often used when stakeholders evaluate, invest, or finance the firm. The cost of capital is an important factor in financing and business decisions, and thus the debt to equity ratio is also an important factor.

Under the prior Japanese accounting standards, prior IAS19, and SFAS87, unrecognized obligations were disclosed only in footnotes. They were amortized over several years and affected future earnings. Defined benefit liabilities including unrecognized obligations could be regarded as long-term liabilities. Gopalakrishnan and Sugrue (1995), Godwin et al. (1996), and Obinata (2000) include the debt to equity ratio in their models, and recognize firms tend to change their actuarial assumptions in response to higher leverage. Therefore, when a firm's leverage became higher, there was a possibility that the firm used actuarial assumptions to avoid the cost over several years.

Pension Funding Status: When the Japanese accounting standards for retirement benefits were introduced, it became apparent that firms had a considerable amount of pension deficits, and there was a lot of public attention on their pension funding status. Defined benefit liabilities provide the greatest share of their total liabilities. Li and Klumpes (2007) indicate that higher expected rates of return on plan assets have a positive impact on both the existence and magnitude of defined benefit liability amount actuarially determined for financial reporting and funding purposes. Gopalakrishnan and Sugrue (1995) suggest that there is a positive correlation between the discount rate and the size of the defined benefit liability, because a large unfunded defined benefit liability could mean a lower credit rating and higher cost of debt for the firms. The levels and changes of actuarial assumptions directly affect the amount of defined benefit obligations. Therefore, firms that have an underfunded pension status might adopt higher discount rates, expected rates of return on plan assets, and lower future salary increases.

Cash Flows from Operating Activities: Increases in discount rates and expected rates of return on plan assets reduce the defined benefit cost and the cash contribution to the pension plans. As a result, cash flows increase for several years after the assumption change. Statement on Establishing Accounting Standard for Retirement Benefits states, in general, Japanese firms make payments for their employees' pension as compensation for their work after their retirement (Statement on Establishing Accounting Standard for Retirement Benefits, par.3.1). Pension is defined as future payment of employees' salary. Therefore, the increases of cash flows are included in cash flows from operating activities on statements of cash flows. Obinata (2000) uses both operating cash flows and investing cash flows in his model to see what factors affect firms' choice of pension discount rates. The result shows that only operating cash flows are significant.

International Accounting Standard No.7: *Statement of Cash Flows* (IAS7) states that "firms need cash and cash equivalents to conduct their operations, to pay their obligations, and to provide returns to their investors. A statement of cash flows enhances the comparability of the reporting of operating performance by different firms, because it eliminates the effects of using different accounting treatments for the same transactions and prices" (IAS7, pars.3, 4). Therefore, cash and cash equivalents are important factors for users of financial statements to evaluate firms. Firms might change their actuarial assumptions to increase their cash and cash equivalents if cash decreases.

Tax-Paying Status: Tax deduction is one of the most important reasons firms provide pension plans to their employees. All pension premiums made can be recognized as expense in that year in Japan. When firms make additional contributions to make up for the shortage of pension funding, it is also recognized as expense. Feldstein and Morck (1983) note that the tax law gives firms a strong incentive to assume a low discount rate. Their analysis shows that firms with large defined benefit liabilities tend to choose high discount rate assumptions, and firms with overfunded status increase their defined benefit liability amount to enjoy the tax benefits. The assumed discount rate is related to the firm's unfunded pension status. Most Japanese firms have underfunded pension status. Therefore, it might be difficult to see the effect of tax-paying status on actuarial assumption changes for Japanese firms.

Firm Size: Firm size can be an important factor to affect the choice of actuarial assumptions. Larger firms have more employees, therefore, they have larger defined benefit obligations. If firms can manage their plan assets effectively, they can make use of economies of scale. However, as mentioned above, in Japan most firms have underfunded pension status, and they do not manage their plan assets effectively. Therefore, it is assumed that larger firms will choose higher discount rates and expected rates of return on plan assets to reduce their large amount of defined benefit obligations.

The prior Japanese accounting standards for retirement benefits were introduced in fiscal 2000. Before the accounting change, Japanese accounting rules required disclosing only the content of the pension plan and the transition method when firms change their pension plans. It did not require firms to recognize defined benefit obligations, plan assets, defined benefit liability, and defined benefit cost on financial statements. When the accounting standards were changed, most firms had to recognize significant amounts of defined benefit liabilities on their financial statements. Tables 4.4 and 4.9 show that from 2001 to 2004, many firms decreased their discount rates and expected rates of return on plan assets, which increased their defined benefit obligation and defined benefit cost amounts, and after 2005, firms tended not to change these assumptions. From 2001 to 2004, firms might have sought proper discount rates for their best estimation of defined benefit obligations and defined benefit cost. More firms changed discount rates than expected rates of return on plan assets, which have to be reviewed annually. From 2005 to 2008, which is five years after the introduction of the accounting standards, firms might have been able to decide their discount rates with consideration of the movement in bond yields over a preceding time-period. After fiscal 2009, Japanese accounting standards required firms to review their discount rates annually, and the number of firms that change their discount rates has been increasing. Most of the firms that changed their discount rates after the accounting change decreased their discounts rates linked to the movement of 20- to 30-year government bond yields.

Most of the papers described above prove managers change their actuarial assumptions in response to reduce defined benefit obligations and defined benefit cost. Japanese firms were allowed to decide their discount rates with consideration of the movement in bond yields over a preceding time-period, less than five years under the prior accounting standards. Under this condition, it seemed to be difficult for Japanese firms to use pension accounting to manipulate their earnings until fiscal 2008. After fiscal 2009, firms have to review all of their actuarial assumptions annually. Firms have more opportunities to use actuarial assumptions for earnings management. However, most firms changing their discount rates decreased their rates, which increased their amount of defined benefit obligations and defined benefit cost. Therefore, firms might not be able to solve their problems on their pension funding by choosing favorable actuarial assumptions.

4.4 Summary and Conclusion

The prior Japanese accounting standards for retirement benefits were introduced in fiscal 2000. The accounting change revealed that Japanese firms had considerable amounts of pension deficits. Pension is defined as future payment of employees' salary, and future prospects must be considered to calculate defined benefit obligations and defined benefit cost. This chapter mainly explained how actuarial assumptions — including mortality, rates of employee turnover, discount rates, future salary increases, and expected rates of return on plan assets — are determined under Japanese accounting standards. These rates are set differently in each firm and under each accounting standard. Mortality rates in Japanese firms must be lower than in other countries due to the high average life-span in Japan. Rates of employee turnover also can be assumed to be lower in Japan, because of the lower labor liquidity than in other countries. Japanese accounting standards require disclosing only discount rates and expected rates of return on plan assets. Discount rates are likely to be determined in reference to the movement of 20- or 30-year government bond yield. Expected rates of return on plan assets are set in consideration of firms' investment portfolio, management performance in the past, or management policy. Firms' decision-making on plan asset management and economic situation as a whole affect the determination of expected rates of return on plan assets. Therefore, the expected rates of return firms adopt vary more widely than discount rates.

Several prior studies prove that, in pursuit of earnings management, firms change the discount rates and expected rates of return needed for predictions. This chapter selected profitability, leverage, pension funding status, cash flows from operating activities, tax-paying status, and firm size as important factors in determining actuarial assumptions, and explained these effects on setting actuarial assumptions in prior research. As explained in Section 4.3, actuarial assumptions have a significant impact on the amount of defined benefit obligations and defined benefit cost. Most prior research reviewed in this chapter proved there is a relationship between changes in, or levels of, actuarial assumptions and other financial factors on financial statements.

Until fiscal 2008, the Japanese accounting standards allowed firms to determine their discount rates with consideration of the movement in bond yields over a preceding time-period, less than five years. Under this condition, it seemed to be difficult for Japanese firms to change their discount rates for earnings management. Table 4.4 indicates that the number of firms that change their discount rates has been increasing from 2009, when the discount rate was required to be reviewed annually. However, most firms decreased their discount rates, which increased amounts of their defined benefit obligations and defined benefit cost.

After the accounting change, firms have more opportunities to change or choose favorable actuarial assumptions to decrease their defined benefit obligations and defined benefit cost, and reduce the negative effect of these amounts on financial statements. However, it cannot be an ultimate solution for firms seeking to decrease their pension deficits. Changing actuarial assumptions for earning management is just a way for firms to avoid a problem on defined benefit pension plans temporarily, and it overstates their financial condition and operating results on their financial statements. Therefore, Table 4.4 shows most firms are likely to use their best estimates for their discount rates, which is linked to the movement of yields of Japanese government bonds. Only a small percentage of firms increased their discount rates. However, it might be useful to examine this issue further if it appears firms are increasing their discount rates for earnings management.

Chapter 5
Presentation of Defined Benefit Cost

5.1 Introduction

The Japanese accounting standards for retirement benefits were introduced in fiscal 2000 to harmonize with other international accounting standards. Most Japanese firms experienced a significant negative effect on their financial statements from this accounting standard change owing to their underfunding of retirement benefits. Moreover, because employees in Japan tend to work for the same firms for longer periods than in other countries, Japanese firms have a higher proportion of pension components, including defined benefit obligations, plan assets, defined benefit liability, and defined benefit cost, in their financial statements than firms in other countries.[67]

The IASB revised IAS19 in June 2011. The revised IAS19 has made a significant change in defined benefit cost presentation that will classify defined benefit cost components into three categories: service cost, net interest on the net defined benefit liability, and remeasurements of the net defined benefit liability. The IASB has also decided to adopt immediate recognition for actuarial gains and losses and past service cost.

In the Japanese accounting standards, all defined benefit cost components are included in a single item and disclosed as defined benefit cost in profit or loss. Deferred recognition is adopted for the recognition of actuarial gains and losses, past service cost, and transitional liability. Currently, Japan is making progress toward convergence with, and adoption of IFRS. Therefore, it is important for Japanese firms to understand the accounting change in IAS19 and the effect it will have on their financial statements.

This chapter will clarify the difference between the Japanese accounting

---

[67] Kagaya, Tetsuyuki, "Does the Convergence of the Pension Cost Presentation Affect Earnings Attributes?," *PIE/CIS Discussion Paper,* No. 438, Tokyo: Institute of Economic Research, Hitotsubashi University, August 2009, pp.4,5.

standards for retirement benefits and IAS19, and consider the effect of the accounting change to IFRS.

5.2 Components of Defined Benefit Cost

Defined benefit cost consists of six components: current service cost, interest cost, past service cost, actuarial gains and losses, transitional liability, and the expected return on plan assets.[68] Under Japanese accounting standards, the total of these components is recognized as defined benefit cost in operating income or expense.

IAS19 before the amendments made in 2011 (Prior IAS19) required disclosing one more cost, namely, gains or losses for the effect of any curtailments or settlements of a defined benefit plan (Prior IAS19, par.109), which is not currently required under accounting standards for retirement benefits in Japan. In addition, Prior IAS19 did not specify whether a firm should present current service cost, interest cost, and the expected return on plan assets as components of a single item of income or expense on the comprehensive income statement (Prior IAS19, par.119). Therefore, it allowed firms to recognize these components in items that did not affect operating income or expense. In fact, there were some firms that included interest cost and the expected return on plan assets in financial income or expense, due to the characteristics of these components that stem from financial activities for the payment of employee benefits after employees' retirement.[69]

① Current Service Cost	⑥ The Expected Return on Plan Assets
② Interest Cost	Defined Benefit Cost
③ Past Service Cost	
④ Actuarial Gains and Losses	
⑤ Transitional Liability	

Figure 5.1 Components of Defined Benefit Cost

---

[68] In accordance with past service cost, actuarial gains and losses, and transitional liability, deferred recognition is applied for these costs. Therefore, these amortization costs in the fiscal year are included in the defined benefit cost.

[69] Accounting Standards Board of Japan, *Issues on Accounting Standards for Employee Benefits*, Tokyo: ASBJ, January 2009, p.30.

5.2.1 Current Service Cost

Current service cost is a retirement benefit resulting from employee service in the current period, and is measured at the present value of defined benefit obligations (ASBJ Statement 26, par.8). The defined benefit obligations are calculated based on the accrued benefit method, which "recognizes each period of service as giving rise to an additional unit of benefit entitlement and measures each unit separately to build up the final obligations" (IAS19, par.68). Under the accounting standards for retirement benefits introduced in fiscal 2000, Japanese firms attributed benefits to periods of service on a straight-line basis over the average employees' remaining service period (Accounting Standard for Retirement Benefits, par.2.(3)). However, the new accounting standard allows firms to choose straight-line basis or the plan's benefit formula (ASBJ Statement 26, par.19). In support of the use of the plan's benefit formula, the ASBJ states that this method, by representing current service cost increases according to employees' length of service, is more accurate and precise than straight-line basis (ED39, par.59). However, ASBJ offers firms the option to choose either straight-line basis or the plan's benefit formula, because some other accounting standard regimes state the plan's benefit formula cannot be applied for some plans, such as cash balance plan (ED39, par.60).

With regard to IAS19, in principle firms attribute benefits to periods of service under the plan's benefit formula. If an employee's service in later years leads to a materially higher level of benefit than in earlier years, a firm will adopt the straight-line basis to allocate benefits (IAS19, par.70). In Japan, many firms state their employees' salaries for all service periods systematically, and the labor market is not as fluid as those in the U.S. or in Europe. The prevailing economic situation in each area might have allowed Japanese firms to adopt the straight-line basis.

5.2.2 Interest Cost

Interest cost is the cost that occurs from the passage of time because employees are one year closer to retirement, based on the calculation of the present value of the defined benefit obligations at the beginning period (ASBJ Statement 26, par.9). With regard to IAS19, interest cost can be categorized into financial expenses, whereas all defined benefit cost components are included in operating income or expense in Japanese accounting standards. It can be assumed that interest cost occurs from financial activities to manage employees' pension fund.

5.2.3 Past Service Cost

Past service cost is recognized when a firm changes the benefits payable under an existing defined benefit plan (ASBJ Statement 26, par.12).

In Japan, past service cost is recognized over the average remaining service lives of the firm's employees. Past service cost for employees that have already retired can be recognized immediately. When negative past service cost arises, it is also recognized over the average remaining service lives of the employees. The amount of past service cost that has not been recognized as a part of net periodic defined benefit cost is unrecognized past service cost. The unrecognized past service cost will be shown on the balance sheet as a component of accumulated other comprehensive income for fiscal years beginning on or after April 1, 2013 (ASBJ Statement 26, par.25).

IASB previously stated that past service cost should be recognized as an expense using a straight-line basis over the average period until the benefits became vested. When the benefits were already vested at the time firms introduced, or changed to, a defined benefit plan, the past service cost was recognized immediately (Prior IAS19, par.96). Therefore, this accounting procedure depended on whether vesting had occurred or not.[70] IASB recognized the amount of past service cost for former employees as already having been realized, because the transaction between a firm and its former employees had occurred. When negative past service cost arose because of the reduction in the defined benefit liability, it was recognized in the same way as when positive past service cost was recognized (Prior IAS19, par.100).

IASB adopted deferred recognition, because in IAS19DP, it states immediate recognition produces too much volatility in profit or loss (IAS19DP, par.2.5). However, under IAS19, it adopts recognition of unvested past service cost in the period of plan amendment, because "past service cost can be assumed as increasing the present obligation that arises from employees' past service" (IAS19DP, par.2.17).

Vesting is an important factor for the calculation of past service cost. In

---

[70] IASB defined vested employee benefits as employee benefits that were not conditional on future employment (Prior IAS19, par.7).

the U.S., the ERISA was enacted in 1974. The major purpose of the law is to protect the right of vesting. The law defines minimum vesting standards to guarantee pension payments. In the U.K., vesting can be provided immediately. When there are not enough funds to pay for guaranteed minimum pensions in a firm, the pension plan is transferred to the State Earnings-Related Pension Scheme (SERPS), a public entity, and this entity pays the guaranteed minimum pension.[71]

In Japan, the Defined Benefit Corporate Pension Plan Act was enacted in 2002 to encourage the protection of vesting. However, the Act has some problems in its requirements for vesting. First, it does not regulate the grant date of vesting. Second, it allows firms to reduce their employees' pension payment when their operating situation becomes worse and, in addition, two-thirds of their post-employment and current employees agree with the reduction of their pensions.[72] Third, it does not provide for a pension benefit guarantee system.[73] With these provisions, it seems to be difficult for the Act to guarantee firms' pension payments to their employees and protect employees' vesting. The grant date of vesting is different in each firm, so it can vary in length depending on the firm. With regard to allowing the reduction of employees' pension payment under the Act, the amount of past service cost can have high uncertainty and volatility.

Under Japanese accounting standards, these factors might allow firms to recognize past service cost over the average remaining service lives of the firm's employees. Therefore, the Act might represent a difference in accounting method between Japanese accounting standards and IAS19.

5.2.4 Actuarial Gains and Losses

Actuarial gains and losses are caused by the following (ASBJ Statement 26, par.11):

(a) a difference between the actual return on plan assets during a period and the expected return on plan assets for that period;

---

[71] Pension Fund Association, *Pension Systems in Other Countries*, Tokyo: Toyo Keizai, Inc., 1999, pp.237, 252-253.
[72] Yamaguchi, Osamu, "Transition of Japanese Corporate Pension Plans and Accounting," *Kigyo Kaikei*, Vol.62 No.7, July 2010, p.955.
[73] There is another private defined benefit pension fund, i.e., the employees' pension fund. It has a pension benefit guarantee system.

(b) a difference between the actual rate in calculating defined benefit obligations during a period and the estimated rate for that period; and

(c) a modification of estimated rates.

Therefore, a measurement of actuarial gains and losses permits firms to segregate the actual return into expected and unexpected elements. This feature of accounting standards for retirement benefits differs from those of other standards.[74] Actuarial gains and losses are treated as a part of defined benefit cost, and they are included in profit or loss for the period. Further, there is an approach for determining whether actuarial gains and losses are recognized, depending on whether a significant change in assumptions has occurred. ASBJ Guidance 25 states a significant change in a discount rate is considered to have occurred when the defined benefit obligations as measured using a discount rate at the end of the year are compared to it at the end of the previous year, and this amount exceeds 10% of the previous year's obligations (ASBJ Guidance 25, par.30). As for other assumptions, the effect on a profit or loss for the period or the change from the firm's past experience is considered to be the determinant of a significant change (ASBJ Guidance 25, pars.31, 32). Therefore, actuarial gains and losses are not recognized when there is no significant change in assumptions.

In contrast, when the actuarial gains and losses are recognized as a defined benefit cost, the cost can be spread over several years. Firms can choose the length of the period, and that choice tends to depend on the firm's financial condition. Kagaya (2009) indicates that over 70% of Japanese firms adopt amortization periods longer than six years for actuarial gains and losses. His paper shows that firms seem to be able to reduce the impact to their financial statements by spreading actuarial gains and losses over the longer period.

IAS19 eliminates the expected rate of return on plan assets from actuarial gains and losses, because IASB recognizes that firms might be able to have an opportunity to manipulate profit or loss when they determine the expected rate of return (IAS19ED, par.BC41). With regard to the determination of the recognition of actuarial gains and losses, Prior IAS19 also had a specific

---

[74] Barth, Mary E., William H. Beaver and Wayne R. Landsman, "The Market Valuation Implications of Net Periodic Pension Cost Components," *Journal of Accounting & Economics,* Vol.15 No.1, March 1992, p.33.

approach for recognition of defined benefit obligations and plan assets, which was called the *corridor approach*. Under this approach, as of the beginning of the year, if the net cumulative actuarial gains and losses exceed 10% of the greater of the present value of PBO or the fair value of any plan assets, the portion of unrecognized actuarial gains or losses are included as a component of net defined benefit cost of that year. When the portion of unrecognized actuarial gains or losses exceeds the 10% *corridor* at the end of the previous reporting period, the amount in excess of the 10% can be divided by the expected average remaining working lives of the employees participating in that plan (Prior IAS19, pars.92, 93). Under Prior IAS19, when a firm adopted a policy of recognizing actuarial gains and losses in the period in which they occurred, it might recognize them in other comprehensive income. They would not be recognized in profit or loss in a subsequent period (Prior IAS19, pars.93, 93A-D). The corridor approach differs somewhat from the Japanese approach. The approach in Japan entails determining whether or not the defined benefit obligations should be recalculated. Therefore, when the effect of the change in assumption rates on the defined benefit obligations is less than 10%, the actual amount of the obligations cannot be recognized. The method employed by Prior IAS19 is related to the amount of actuarial gains and losses, and firms adopting the corridor approach disclosed the actual amount of the defined benefit obligations by changing the assumption rates.[75]

IASB adopted the corridor approach due to the fact that actuarial gains and losses might offset one another in the long term (Prior IAS19, par.95). Under the current IAS19, the Board eliminates the corridor approach and uses immediate recognition for actuarial gains and losses for the following reasons (IAS19DP, pars. 2.10, 2.11):

(a) It is consistent with the framework and other accounting standards;

(b) It represents faithfully the firm's financial position;

(c) Amounts in the statements of financial position and comprehensive income under this recognition approach are transparent and easy to understand; and

(d) It improves comparability across firms.

Additionally, both the Japanese accounting standards and IAS19

---

[75] Imafuku, Aishi, *Accounting for Retirement Benefits,* Tokyo: Shinsei-Sha Co. Ltd., 2000, pp.105-106.

introduce accounting procedures to recognize defined benefit liability on the balance sheet. It is expected that these revisions will provide the most useful information to users of financial statements (IAS19ED, par.BC10).

5.2.5 Transitional Liability

In fiscal 2000, the Japanese accounting standards for retirement benefits were changed dramatically. Before the change, there was no certain standard for retirement benefits.[76] However, generally when firms funded pensions via trust funds, they recognized the amount of the contribution as a cost. Therefore, deficit funding could not be recognized on the balance sheet. Given this condition, retirement benefits could not be measured properly. In accordance with the accounting change, many firms had to recognize a lot of deficit funding at the end of the fiscal year in 2000. For these kinds of accounting changes, a transitional liability on accounting changes is recognized. Transitional liability is the difference between the PBO, and the total amount of the fair value of plan assets measured under the new standards and the accrued pension cost recognized under the prior standards.[77]

In Japan, the amount recognized by accounting changes can be amortized as income or expense on a straight-line basis over less than 15 years. When the accounting standards for retirement benefits were introduced in fiscal 2000, firms were given a one-time option: If the amortization period was less than 5 years, the cost could be recognized as an extraordinary loss. If it was more than 5 years, the cost had to be recognized as an ordinary loss. Therefore, this rule might encourage firms to amortize the cost over a shorter period. The length of the period firms chose depended on their financial condition.

Table 5.1 shows the amortization period for transitional liability that firms adopted in fiscal 2000 for this significant accounting change. Firms that are treated in Table 5.1 (excluding banks and insurance firms) are listed on the first section of the Tokyo Stock Exchange. Firms were selected that set and disclose both discount rates and expected rates of return on plan assets on their financial statements. Most firms adopted less than 5-year amortization periods,

---

[76] There was a standard only for the specific case when firms transferred their pension plan to another plan. The standard defined accounting methods only for the withdrawal of employee benefits, depreciation of past service cost, and disclosure on footnotes.

[77] Imafuku, Aishi, *op.cit.*, p.110.

Table 5.1 The Amortization Period for Transitional Liability Firms Adopted in Fiscal 2000

	No. of Firms	Average Amount of Transitional Liability in the Period (million yen)	Debt/Asset Ratio
1year	521	8,987	54.17%
2years	12	9,824	60.87%
3years	40	3,615	53.92%
4years	4	506	43.68%
5years	166	3,585	60.34%
6years	4	9,291	51.57%
7years	7	1,714	56.08%
8years	5	2,420	62.64%
9years	1	334	41.24%
10years	48	7,160	65.82%
11years	1	305	67.99%
12years	5	1,361	78.33%
13years	2	3,545	59.97%
14years	1	914	88.93%
15years	160	2,908	71.75%

Source: Nikkei Economic Electronic Databank System (2011)

because the cost could be recognized in an extraordinary loss. The shorter the amortization period is, the more transitional liability firms recognize. Firms adopting the longer amortization periods tend to have higher debt to asset ratios. Therefore, firms' financial condition affects the length of the period firms choose.

Prior IAS19 allowed firms to adopt one of following methods. Transitional liability is recognized (Prior IAS19, par.155):

(a) immediately, according to International Accounting Standard No.8: *Accounting Policies, Changes in Accounting Estimates and Errors* (IAS8); or

(b) as an expense on a straight-line basis over a period of up to five years from the date of adoption of IAS19.

A firm applying IAS19 for the first time would have been required to compute the effect of the corridor approach. However, some commentators felt the method would be impractical and would not generate useful information. Therefore, the corridor approach had not been adopted for this expense (Prior IAS19, par.BC96). Under current IAS19, this accounting procedure is deleted, and only the immediate recognition is allowed to recognize transitional liability.

The different length of the amortization period between the Japanese accounting standards and IAS8 might be due to the nature of transitional liability. The liability is not continuous and operational, so it is preferable to recognize it earlier, as prescribed by IAS19. Japanese accounting standards adopt the 15-year period to reduce the impact of accounting changes on financial statements. However they offered a one-time option to encourage firms to recognize the cost earlier.

5.2.6 The Expected Return on Plan Assets

The expected return on plan assets is an expected return resulting from the management of plan assets, and is subtracted from defined benefit cost (Statement on Establishing Accounting Standard for Retirement Benefits, par.4.2.(4)). Plan asset portfolio, management performance in the past, management policy, and market situation are considered in market expectations (ASBJ Guidance 25, par.25). The return is calculated based on the expected rate multiplied by plan assets at the beginning of the period to reduce the volatility in the actual rate, and equalize the defined benefit cost every year.[78] The difference between the actual rate and the expected rate is recognized as actuarial gains and losses.

5.2.7 Curtailments and Settlements

Prior IAS19 required disclosing gains or losses on the curtailment of a defined benefit plan as a component of defined benefit cost when the curtailment occurred (Prior IAS19, par.109).

A curtailment occurs when a firm either:
(a) is demonstrably committed to make a material reduction in the number of employees covered by a plan; or
(b) amends the terms of a defined benefit plan such that the material element of future service by current employees will no longer qualify for benefits, or will qualify only for reduced benefits.

Curtailments can accrue when a firm closes a plant, discontinues an operation, or terminates or suspends a plan (Prior IAS19, par.111). These were

---

[78] *Ibid.*, p.101.

recognized when they occurred. In accordance with the immediate recognition for unvested past service cost under current IAS19, the same accounting procedure is applied to recognize curtailments as past service cost. Therefore, curtailments are included in past service cost (IAS19, par.BC160). IASB retains only (a) definition for curtailments in Prior IAS19 under revised IAS19 (IAS19, par.BC162).

IAS19 states that "a settlement occurs when a firm enters into a transaction that eliminates all further legal or constructive obligation for part or all of the benefits provided under a defined benefit plan." For example, plan participants receive a lump-sum cash payment in exchange for their rights to have specified post-employment benefits (IAS19, par.111). The gain or loss on a settlement is recognized when it occurs. It results from the difference between (IAS19, par.109):

(a) the present value of the defined benefit obligation being settled, as determined on the date of settlement; and

(b) the settlement price, including any plan assets transferred and any payments made directly by the entity in connection with the settlement.

The Japanese accounting standards for retirement benefits do not state the accounting procedure for curtailments and settlements. However, Application Guideline for Accounting Standards No.1: *Accounting Procedure for Transition Between Retirement Benefit Plans* (Application Guideline 1) regulates an accounting procedure for the termination of defined benefit plans which is a similar accounting treatment to that of Prior IAS19.[79] The termination of defined benefit plans indicates the removal or amendment of defined benefit plans, and the transition between retirement benefit plans that results reducing the amount of defined benefit obligations (Application Guideline 1, par.4). The guideline also states the accounting procedure for mass retirement which includes the case of closing a plant or discontinuing an operation (Application Guideline 1, par.8). It basically requires firms to recognize gains or losses on the termination of defined benefit plans (Application Guideline 1, par.10). However, there is no definition for curtailments or settlements.

---

[79] Accounting Standards Board of Japan, *op.cit.*, p.34.

5.3 Transition of Defined Benefit Cost Presentation in IAS19

Under Japanese accounting standards, current service cost, interest cost, past service cost, actuarial gains and losses, transitional liability, and the expected return on plan assets are included in defined benefit cost. However, IAS19 regulates disclosing these components due to their characteristics. Firms distinguish these components among three categories; service cost, net interest on the net defined benefit liability, and remeasurements of the net defined benefit liability.

Before IASB revised IAS19 for defined benefit plans in 2011, the presentation of defined benefit cost was discussed in IAS19DP issued in 2008 and IAS19ED issued in 2010. Under IAS19DP, IASB suggested three approaches to present defined benefit cost. Table 5.2 shows the details of the accounting methods and presentation for defined benefit cost in IAS19DP.

In the prior accounting standard, the disclosure for defined benefit cost was designed to minimize volatility in recognition. This was achieved by employing deferred recognition in computing defined benefit cost. However,

Table 5.2 Accounting Methods and Presentation for Defined Benefit Cost Components in IAS19DP

Components of Defined Benefit Cost	① Japanese Accounting Standard · IAS19	② IAS19 (93D)	③ DP1 Approach	④ DP2 Approach	⑤ DP3 Approach
Current Service Cost	P/L	P/L	P/L	P/L	P/L
Interest Cost	P/L	P/L	P/L	OCI	P/L
The Expected Return on Plan Assets	P/L	P/L	—	—	P/L
Actuarial Gains and Losses					
Derives from:					
The Movement of Fair Value on Plan Assets	Deferred	OCI	P/L	OCI	OCI
Changes in Discount Rates	Deferred	OCI	P/L	OCI	OCI
Others	Deferred	OCI	P/L	P/L	P/L
Past Service Cost	Deferred	Deferred	P/L	P/L	P/L
Gains or Losses on Curtailments	P/L	P/L	P/L	P/L	P/L
Gains or Losses on Settlements	P/L	P/L	P/L	OCI	OCI
Transitional Liability	Deferred	Deferred	Deferred	Deferred	Deferred

Source: Accounting Standards Board of Japan, *Issues on Accounting Standards for Employee Benefits*, Tokyo: ASBJ, January 2009, p.24.

deferred recognition is eliminated from actuarial gains and losses and unvested past service cost, and applied only for transitional liability in IAS19DP. As explained above, IASB believes that immediate recognition will provide more useful information to financial statement users.

In DP1 approach, firms present all changes in the defined benefit obligations and in the value of plan assets in profit or loss (IAS19DP, par.3.11). This approach is consistent with other standards including the conceptual framework, IAS8, and IAS37 (IAS19DP, par.3.17). It is the simplest approach which eliminates arbitrariness and complexity in allocating defined benefit cost to profit or loss (IAS19DP, par.3.27). With regard to DP2 approach, firms present only the costs of service and gains or losses on curtailments in profit or loss; all other costs flow to other comprehensive income (IAS19DP, par.3.12). This approach distinguishes between the operating and financing components of post-employment benefit promises by recognizing only the service costs and the gains or losses on curtailments in profit or loss, while other components related to financing are recognized in other comprehensive income (IAS19DP, par.3.25).

For DP3 approach, firms present remeasurements that arise from changes in financial assumptions in other comprehensive income, and other changes in the amount of post-employment benefit cost in profit or loss (IAS19DP, par.3.15). Only this approach requires recognizing the expected return on plan assets. DP2 and DP3 approaches that recognize some components in other comprehensive income are inconsistent with the approach in some other standards (IAS19DP, par.3.17). Therefore, theoretically DP1 approach can be the most desirable method. However, it brings a lot of volatility to profit or loss in financial statements.

Kagaya (2009) examines the relationship between net income (characterized in various ways) under these three approaches and six attributes of earnings referred to in the paper of Francis et al. (2004). For the purposes of this study, the category *net income* includes net income before taxes, net income being calculated based on DP1, DP2, and DP3 approaches. The six attributes of earnings are persistence, predictability, smoothness, value relevance, timeliness, and conservatism. This paper proves which type of net income has the strongest relationship with each category of earnings attribute. It concludes that net income before taxes has the strongest relationships with persistence, predictability, smoothness, and value relevance. DP1 approach indicates the most desirable timeliness. DP2 approach has the highest degree of conservatism. This result shows net income before taxes reflects economic volatility on financial statements the most stably, and DP1 approach does it the most timely. The paper mentions that the change in presentation for defined benefit cost components might affect corporate systems, such as dividend policies or pension systems.

Table 5.3 represents a presentation approach for defined benefit cost stated in IAS19ED, and it is mostly based on DP3 approach in IAS19DP. IASB decided to adopt this presentation approach for the following reasons (IAS19ED, par.BC37):

(a) Some items that have different predictive value will be combined in DP1 approach;
(b) The DP1 approach gives high volatility in profit or loss that is not related to the firm's operations; and
(c) This approach helps clear presentation of the risk that results from measuring plan assets and defined benefit liabilities at present value.

The Board rejected recognition of the expected return on plan assets, because there is no objective way to determine the amount, and the recognition of the return might include a return that is not simply due to the passage of time (IAS19ED, par.BC26.(a)).

IAS19 adds some changes to IAS19ED. The new presentation approach for defined benefit cost under IAS19 is shown in Table 5.4. There are two changes made from IAS19ED: (1) gains or losses on curtailments are included in past service cost, and (2) gains or losses on settlement are disclosed as a component of service cost. With regard to gains or losses on curtailments, it was necessary to recognize and disclose past service cost and curtailments separately before IAS19 was revised, because curtailments were recognized immediately, whereas unvested past service cost was recognized over the vesting period. However, after the amendments in IAS19 were made in 2011, the standard requires recognizing all defined benefit cost components immediately, and there is no reason to make a distinction between recognizing gains or losses on curtailments and those on unvested past service cost (IAS19, par.BC161).

As for gains or losses on settlement, these were categorized into

Table 5.3 Accounting Methods and Presentation for Defined Benefit Cost Components in IAS19ED

Components of Defined Benefit Cost		Accounting Method
Service Cost	Current Service Cost	P/L
	Past Service Cost	P/L
	Gains or Losses on Curtailments	P/L
Finance Cost	Interest Cost	P/L
Remeasurements	Actuarial Gains and Losses	
	Derives from:	
	Experience Adjustments	OCI
	Changes in Actuarial Assumptions	OCI
	Return on Plan Assets	OCI
	Gains or Losses on Settlements	OCI
Accounting Change	Transitional Liability	P/L

Table 5.4 Accounting Methods and Presentation for Defined Benefit Cost Components in IAS19

Components of Defined Benefit Cost		Accounting Method
Service Cost	Current Service Cost	P/L
	Past Service Cost	P/L
	Gains or Losses on Settlement	P/L
Net Interest	Interest Cost	P/L
Remeasurements	Actuarial Gains and Losses	
	Derives from:	
	Experience Adjustments	OCI
	Changes in Actuarial Assumptions	OCI
	Return on Plan Assets	OCI
Accounting Change	Transitional Liability	P/L

remeasurements, and recognized in other comprehensive income in IAS19ED. However, they are treated in service cost, and recognized in profit or loss in IAS19, because (IAS19, par.BC166):

(a) there is overlap between the definitions of settlements, curtailments, and plan amendments and the transactions usually happen at the same time, so it can be difficult to allocate the gains and losses between them; and

(b) it is inconsistent with other IFRSs to recognize gains or losses on settlement in other comprehensive income.

Moreover, IASB concluded that past service cost and gains and losses on settlements should not be disclosed in remeasurements, because they are the result of a new transaction, as opposed to the remeasuement of a prior period transaction (IAS19, par.BC173).

5.4 Categories of Defined Benefit Cost

As explained above, IAS19 separates defined benefit cost into three categories as follows (IAS19, par.BC65):

(a) Service cost, relating to the cost of the services received;

(b) Net interest on the net defined benefit liability, representing the financing effect of paying for the benefits in advance or in arrears; and

(c) Remeasurements of the net defined benefit liability, representing the period-to-period fluctuations in the amounts of defined benefit obligations and plan assets.

Service cost and net interest components are useful for users of financial statements for estimating the amount and timing of future cash flows, and the remeasurement component indicates the uncertainty of future cash flows (IAS19, par.BC88).

5.4.1 Service Cost

The service cost component comprises current service cost, past service cost, and gains or losses arising from settlements (IAS19, par.8). It is presented in profit or loss. As mentioned in Section 5.2.3, IASB states unvested past service cost should be recognized immediately, because "the attribution of unvested benefits to past service results in a liability as defined in IAS19" (IAS19ED, par.BC13). IASB implements immediate recognition for all components of defined benefit cost.

5.4.2 Net Interest on the Net Defined Benefit Liability

The net interest component includes interest income on plan assets, interest cost on the defined benefit obligations, and interest on the effect of the asset ceiling mentioned in IAS19, paragraph 64 (IAS19, par.124).[80] It is presented in profit or loss. Net interest on the net defined benefit liability is the net defined benefit liability throughout the period multiplied by the discount rate specified in IAS19 as determined at the beginning of the period (IAS19, par.123). Interest income on plan assets is a part of the return on plan assets. The return on plan assets is classified into an amount that arises from the passage of time and other changes. The interest income on plan assets arising from the passage of time is calculated by multiplying the plan assets throughout the period by the discount rate used to discount the defined benefit obligations at the beginning of the period (IAS19, pars.BC77, 79).[81] IAS19 adopts the same rate as the rate used to discount the obligations, because a firm can avoid subjective judgment of how to divide the return on plan assets into net interest and remeasurement components (IAS19, par.BC82). The amount is included in the net interest component. The return on plan assets arising from other changes is disclosed in the remeasurement component.

5.4.3 Remeasurements on the Net Defined Benefit Liability

The remeasurement component comprises actuarial gains and losses on the defined benefit obligations, the return on plan assets, and any changes in the effect of the asset ceiling described in paragraph 64 (IAS19, par.8). These are presented in other comprehensive income, and it will not be reclassified to profit or loss in a subsequent period (IAS19, par.122). This component will help to assess the uncertainty and risk of future cash flows (IAS19, par.BC88).

---

[80] Paragraph 64 in IAS19 states when a firm has a surplus in a defined benefit plan, it measures at the lower of (IAS19, pars.64, 83):
    (a) the surplus in the defined benefit plan; and
    (b) the asset ceiling, determined using the discount rate determined by reference to market yields at the end of the reporting period on high quality corporate bonds.

[81] IASB acknowledged it was difficult to find a practical method to recognize the change in the fair value of plan assets arising from the passage of time. It rejected two approximations to the calculation of the change including (1) the expected return on plan assets, and (2) dividends received on equity plan assets and interest earned on debt plan assets (IAS19, par.BC78).

5.5 Effects of Income Measurement Approaches and Concepts of Incomes

There are two major differences between Japanese accounting standards and IAS19, namely, (1) deferred recognition and immediate recognition for actuarial gains and losses, past service cost, and transitional liability, and (2) the presentation of remeasurement component, especially actuarial gains and losses. These differences in accounting methods and presentation may be affected by different income measurement approaches and concepts of incomes.

5.5.1 Income Measurement Approaches and Concepts of Incomes

Under Japanese accounting standards, all defined benefit cost components are included in a single item, i.e., defined benefit cost, and are disclosed in profit or loss. With regard to the recognition of actuarial gains and losses, past service cost, and transitional liability, deferred recognition is adopted. On the other hand, IAS19 states how to recognize the remeasurement component, including actuarial gains and losses, return on plan assets, and any change in the effect of the asset ceiling in other comprehensive income. Immediate recognition is adopted for all defined benefit cost components.

There are two income measurement approaches: revenue-expense approach and asset-liability approach. Figure 5.2 shows that under the revenue-expense approach, income is recognized as the difference between revenues and expenses that occurred for the period, and based on the profit and loss statement. With regard to the asset-liability approach, income is recognized as the movement of net assets, the difference between total assets and total liabilities, in the end of the period from those in the beginning of the period, and based on the balance sheet.

Income under the asset-liability approach is recognized as total comprehensive income. It consists of profit or loss and other comprehensive

Revenue-Expense Approach		Asset-Liability Approach	
P/L		B/S	
Expenses	Revenues	Net Assets in the End of the Period	Net Assets in the Beginning of the Period
Profit or Loss			Total Comprehensive Income

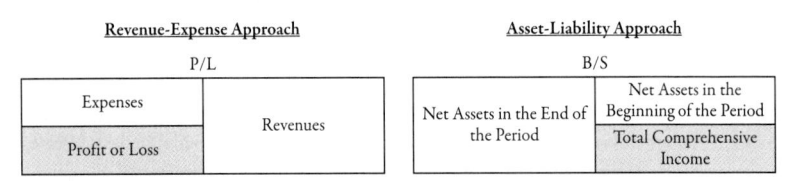

Figure 5.2   Revenue-Expense and Asset-Liability Approaches

income, which has a wider definition than the income, i.e., profit or loss, under the revenue-expense approach. Under International Accounting Standard No.1: *Presentation of Financial Statements* (IAS1), total comprehensive income is defined as "the change in equity during a period resulting from transactions and other events, other than those changes resulting from transactions with owners in their capacity as owners" (IAS1, par.7). With regard to profit or loss, IAS1 defines it as "the total of income less expenses, excluding the components of other comprehensive income" (IAS1, par.7). *Framework for the Preparation and Presentation of Financial Statements* (Framework) asserts profit is "a measure of performance or as the basis for other measures, such as return on investment or earnings per share" (Framework, par.69). *Presentation of Items of Other Comprehensive Income Amendments to IAS 1* (Amended IAS1) mentions IASB has no plan to eliminate profit or loss as a measure of performance (Amended IAS1, par.BC54C). IAS1 indicates that other comprehensive income comprises items of income and expense that are not recognized in profit or loss. It includes five components as follows (IAS1, par.7):

(a) changes in revaluation surplus;
(b) actuarial gains and losses on defined benefit plans;
(c) gains and losses arising from translating the financial statements of a foreign operation;
(d) gains and losses from investments in equity instruments measured at fair value through other comprehensive income; and
(e) the effective portion of gains and losses on hedging instruments in a cash flow hedge.

Firms had the option to present all items of income and expense either in a single statement of comprehensive income or two separate statements of profit or loss and other comprehensive income (IAS1, par.81). Amended IAS1 requires firms to present profit or loss and other comprehensive income separately in a statement of profit or loss and other comprehensive income statement (Amended IAS1, par.81A). Therefore, IASB recognizes that the nature of profit or loss is different from that of other comprehensive income, and both are important measures of performance. Representing these items separately would help financial statement users understand all non-owner changes in equity more clearly. However, IAS1 and *The Conceptual Framework for Financial Reporting* (IFRS Conceptual Framework) do not describe a principle for classifying the items to be recognized into other comprehensive income or into profit or loss (IAS19ED, par.BC42).

IFRS Conceptual Framework also defines income as including revenue and gains. It states that "revenue arises in the course of the ordinary activities of an entity," and "gains represent other items that meet the definition of income" (IFRS Conceptual Framework, pars.4.29, 4.30). It also mentions that "the definition of income includes unrealized gains; for example, those arising on the revaluation of marketable securities and those resulting from increases in the carrying amount of long-term assets" (IFRS Conceptual Framework, par.4.31). With regard to recognition of income, "income is recognized in the profit and loss statement when an increase in future economic benefits related to an increase in an asset or a decrease of a liability has arisen that can be measured reliably. This means, in effect, that recognition of income occurs simultaneously with the recognition of increases in assets or decreases in liabilities" (IFRS Conceptual Framework, par.4.47). IASB recognizes income as the difference between net assets at the beginning of the period and those at the end of the period, and categorize the income into profit or loss or other comprehensive income depending on the realization. Therefore, it adopts the asset-liability approach for income measurement.

Under the Japanese Conceptual Framework, comprehensive income is defined as "the change in net assets during a period resulting from transactions, other than those changes resulting from direct transactions with owners of a reporting entity including shareholders, minority shareholders of the consolidated subsidiaries, and future owners with options" (Conceptual Framework, par.3.8). In terms of this definition, comprehensive income is recognized as an increase or a decrease of the difference between net assets at the beginning of the period and those at the end of the period. Therefore, the asset-liability approach is adopted. On the other hand, profit or loss is defined as "an investment result discharged from a risk for the year, and a part of comprehensive income resulting from transactions with owners. It increases or decreases only shareholders' equity" (Conceptual Framework, par.3.9). The Conceptual Framework also states "the profit or loss is calculated by revenues less expenses with consideration of minority interests" (Conceptual Framework, par.3.11). As mentioned above, under IAS1, profit or loss is calculated as the difference between revenues and expenses, excluding the components of other comprehensive income. The amount of other comprehensive income has to be recognized to calculate profit or loss. However, Japanese Conceptual Framework defines the calculation for profit or loss. It recognizes profit or loss as an independent component for financial statements from other comprehensive income, and adopts the revenue-expense approach. Japanese accounting standards had adopted the revenue-expense approach in the past; however, corresponding to the convergence project with IASB, ASBJ has set out to adopt the asset-liability approach for some accounting standards. Both the asset-liability and revenue-expense approaches exist in Japanese accounting standards.

Under the revenue-expense approach, profit or loss is a firm's bottom line. Therefore, other comprehensive income components are recycled and recognized in the profit and loss statement when they are realized. On the other hand, with regard to the asset-liability approach, total comprehensive income is the main concept of income, and it does not attach importance on separating profit or loss from other comprehensive income. Therefore, some other comprehensive income components are not recycled under IFRS. With consideration of recognition of components for defined benefit cost, Japanese accounting standards adopt the revenue-expense approach. The approach allows firms to recognize past service cost, actuarial gains and losses, and transitional liability as other comprehensive income, and to recycle when they are realized. The asset-liability approach IASB adopts allows firms to recognize a remeasurement component in other comprehensive income without recycling. However, at one time previously IASB had agreed to recognize all components in profit or loss immediately, because the accounting procedure eliminates arbitrariness and complexity in allocating defined benefit cost and is consistent with other standards (IAS19DP, pars.3.17, 3.27). One possible reason it was rejected is that many responses to the IAS19DP might have reflected the view that the remeasurement component should be in other comprehensive income due to the volatility in profit or loss.[82] Therefore, there might be a different effect between profit or loss and other comprehensive

---

[82] IASB believes that "a measure should be volatile if it faithfully represents transactions and other events that are themselves volatile, and financial statements should not omit such information" (IAS19, par.BC72.(c)).

income on firms' valuation. To consider the effect, prior research studies and a field test Financial Accounting Standards Board (FASB) and IASB performed are referred.

5.5.2 Related Prior Research Studies

There are several prior research studies that have examined the usefulness of comprehensive income consisting of profit or loss and other comprehensive income. Cheng et al. (1993) and Dhaliwal et al. (1999) examine the relationship between estimated comprehensive income and stock returns. These studies find no evidence that comprehensive income is more useful for investors to predict better future cash flows or income than net income. Cahan et al. (2000), Dehning and Ratliff (2004), Biddle and Choi (2006), Kubota et al. (2006), Chambers et al. (2007), Dastgir and Velashani (2008), and Kanagaretnam et al. (2009) study the relationship between reported comprehensive income and stock prices or returns. Cahan et al. (2000) and Dehning and Ratliff (2004) find investors value the information in comprehensive income. However, there is no benefit in disclosing the components of comprehensive income separately. Dastgir and Velashani (2008) do not support the proposition that comprehensive income is superior to net income for evaluating firm performance on the basis of stock return and price. Biddle and Choi (2006) find that comprehensive income dominates in explaining equity returns, and net income dominates in explaining chief executive compensation. They conclude each definition of income provides different usefulness for decision-making in different applications, and the disclosure of comprehensive income components is useful.

Kubota et al. (2006) investigate net income as the most important income measure for investors. However, foreign currency translation adjustments and unrealized gains and losses from securities available for sale in other comprehensive income provide useful information to explain cumulative raw returns or risk adjusted returns. Chambers et al. (2007) find some other comprehensive income components, namely, unrealized gains and losses on marketable securities and foreign currency translation adjustments are valued by investors. Their evidence suggests that investors pay attention to other comprehensive income information. Kanagaretnam et al. (2009) recognize aggregate comprehensive income is more strongly associated with both stock prices and returns compared to net income and that it is a better predictor of future cash flows. They also observe that net income is a better predictor of future net income relative to comprehensive income.

Hirst and Hopkins (1998) report that different forms of accounting display can have some impact on analysts' valuation judgments. Comprehensive income is useful when it is reported separately from net income, not as part of the statement of changes in shareholders' equity. Maines and McDaniel (2000) also arrive at the same conclusion as Hirst and Hopkins (1998), i.e., that the volatility of comprehensive income is reflected in investors' judgments of corporate and management performance only when it is presented in a statement of comprehensive income.[83] Therefore, there is no consistent result for the usefulness of comprehensive income from these empirical research studies. Most research studies suggest profit or loss and other comprehensive income provide different useful information to investors, and are recognized separately for their decision-making.

FASB and IASB (2009) performed a field test with analyst participation and summarized the results to test the proposals of the October 2008 discussion paper *Preliminary Views on Financial Statement Presentation*. One of the purposes of the field test was "to determine whether the proposed presentation model improves the usefulness of a firm's financial statements for users in making decisions in their capacity as capital providers." In the field test, these accounting standards boards asked analysts some questions, such as:

(a) How much do they rely upon certain sources of information?;

(b) What metric do they create from the balance sheet?; and

(c) How useful are the aspects of the proposed presentation model?

The results of the test show about 70 percent of respondents rely more than 50 percent on information from the annual report to make judgments in their work as analysts. The test also indicates which primary performance metric they use or create from a firm's profit and loss statement. The results are shown in Figure 5.3.

---

[83] In the U.S. from 1997 to 2011, comprehensive income was required to be reported in either a statement of comprehensive income or a statement of changes in shareholders' equity. Currently, FASB does not permit firms to present other comprehensive income in the statement of changes in shareholders' equity.

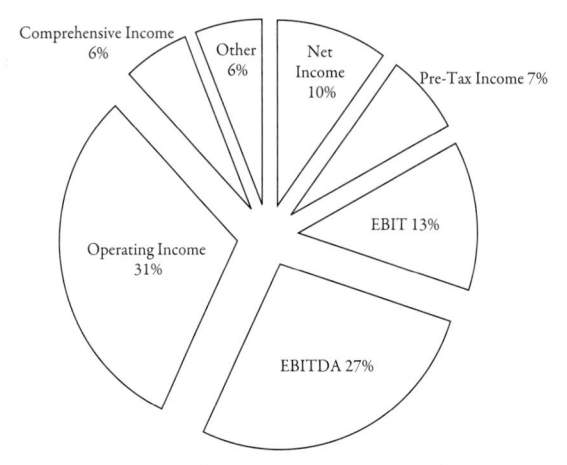

Figure 5.3 Primary Performance Metrics in Profit and Loss Statement

Source: Financial Accounting Standards Board and International Accounting Standards Board, "Financial Statement Presentation, Analyst Field Test Results," IASB Meeting September 2009 (IASB Agenda Reference 9B), and FASB - Information Board Meeting September 21, 2009 (FASB Memo Reference 66B), September 2009, p.9.

Operating income has the highest proportion, with 31 percent of respondents identifying it as a primary performance metric. Pre-tax income and income calculated based on pre-tax income, including earnings before interest and tax (EBIT) and earnings before interest, taxes, depreciation and amortization (EBITDA) represent 47 percent. Some 10 percent of respondents recognize net income as a primary performance metric to evaluate firms. Comprehensive income has the lowest percentage, with only 6 percent of respondents. Therefore, 88% of respondents choose incomes reported above net income as their primary performance metric.

As explained above, the asset-liability approach allows firms to recognize a remeasurement component in other comprehensive income. However, at one time previously IASB had agreed to recognize all components in profit or loss to remain consistent with other accounting standards. This situation might be created, because IASB has not set a principle for classifying the items to be recognized into other comprehensive income or into profit or loss (IAS19ED, par.BC42). Actuarial gains and losses included in a remeasurement component, especially, are somewhat affected by stock and bond prices, and the amount of the gains and losses are estimated to be quite significant. If the remeasurement component is included in profit or loss, it provides volatility to the firms' financial statements and affects all primary performance metrics for analysts shown in Figure 5.3. Profit or loss is an important factor for investors and financial analysts to estimate future stock prices and dividends. Therefore, the remeasurement component is included in other comprehensive income, which does not affect return on investment or earnings per share.

5.6 Summary and Conclusion

IFRS is basically set on an asset-liability approach. However, two approaches existed, the asset-liability approach and revenue-expense approach in Prior IAS19, owing to the adoption of deferred recognition. Currently, IAS19 adopts immediate recognition for actuarial gains and losses and past service cost. This is based on the asset-liability approach that reflects the change of fair value in profit or loss or other comprehensive income for the period. The IASB considered whether to disclose all defined benefit cost components in profit or loss and decided not to, because it would create too much volatility in financial statements.

There are two differences in accounting methods and presentation for defined benefit cost between Japanese accounting standards and IAS19: deferred recognition and immediate recognition for actuarial gains and losses, past service cost, and transitional liability, and presentation for remeasurement component. Japanese accounting standards adopt deferred recognition for actuarial gains and losses, past service cost, and transitional liability, and recognizes all defined benefit cost components in profit or loss to measure firms' core business activities more precisely, and reduce the volatility from other activities in profit or loss. On the other hand, IAS19 adopts immediate recognition for actuarial gains and losses and past service cost, and recognizes service cost and finance cost in profit or loss and remeasurement component in other comprehensive income. The FASB and IASB (2009) test shows that 88% of respondents indicate incomes reported above net income are the most important primary performance metrics for analysts, with comprehensive income representing only 6 percent of respondents' answers. From this result, IASB might reduce the volatility of remeasurement component by recognizing it in other comprehensive income, which does not have a significant effect on investors' judgments. Therefore, even though IFRS is adopted for Japanese firms, it can be predicted that the presentation of defined benefit cost will not have a significant negative impact on Japanese firms' financial statements.

Chapter 6
Fair Value of Plan Assets

6.1 Introduction

In pension accounting, the focus is always on how to calculate the amount of defined benefit obligations. This is true because it should be declared how much a firm has to make in payments of employee benefits for their employees in the future. In addition, plan assets are measured at fair value and deducted from the obligations to calculate a defined benefit liability (asset), which represents firm's underfunded (overfunded) status of employee benefits.

Plan assets have different characteristics from other assets in the balance sheet, because they are funded solely for the purpose of employee benefits, not for the gain that results from management of the assets. There are some requirements for them to be recognized as plan assets, and these requirements give distinctive characteristics to plan assets. With regard to recognition of plan assets, some accounting treatments are allowed that differ from those in other accounting standards, such as those for the recognition of a gain or loss from valuation of securities, and presentation of plan assets and defined benefit obligations. Therefore, there are some inconsistencies with other standards in the recognition of plan assets. This chapter mainly discusses requirements of plan assets, accounting treatment for plan assets in retirement benefit trusts, and presentation of a defined benefit liability (asset), and explains why different accounting procedures are allowed for recognition of plan assets.

6.2 Requirements of Plan Assets

Plan assets consist of domestic and foreign stocks and bonds, and other properties. In Japan, they are defined as assets funded for the payment of employees' retirement benefits based on corporate pension plans. Plan assets have to meet all requirements as follows (ASBJ Statement 26, par.7):

(a) They are available to be used only for retirement benefits;

(b) They are completely separated from the accounts of the employer and the creditors;

(c) It is prohibited to do prejudicial acts to the employer's pensioners. For example, plan assets may not be returned to the employer, terminated, or used for purposes other than retirement benefits, unless the plan assets are overfunded; and

(d) They cannot be traded with the employer's assets.

Plan assets are evaluated based on fair value and subtracted from defined benefit obligations at the end of the reporting period (ASBJ Statement 26, par.22). The pension system serves the important social function of supporting employees after retirement. Therefore, it is required to build a system whereby employees can receive their pensions with certainty. These requirements of plan assets help to protect employees' vesting.

IAS19 states that plan assets comprise assets held by a long-term employee benefit fund and qualifying insurance policies. The qualifying insurance policies are defined as "an insurance policy issued by an insurer that is not a related party of the reporting entity." These assets are required to be used to pay or fund only for employee benefits, and are not available to the reporting firm's creditors (IAS19, par.8). Therefore, the requirements for these assets are similar to those under Japanese accounting standards.

As explained in Section 4.2.5 in Chapter 4, Japanese firms tend to invest their plan assets in domestic stocks and bonds. Until 1997, the Japanese government restricted the investment of plan assets according to the 5:3:3:2 formula. It required firms to invest more than 50% of plan assets in bonds, less than 30% in stocks or foreign properties, and less than 20% in other properties. Because of the low proportion of stocks in pension fund portfolios, fund earnings were modest, even though a boom in Japanese stocks occurred during the 1980s. This restriction on plan assets was abolished in 1997, but the stock prices of Japanese firms have been low because of continuing depressed business conditions, causing more than 30% of plan assets to remain invested in bonds. As a result, Japanese firms cannot manage their plan assets efficiently. Moreover, the sub-prime mortgage loan crisis of the past few years has had a significant negative effect on domestic and foreign stock prices. Therefore, the proportion of domestic and foreign stocks in total assets was lower for the most recent 5 years than in previous years. Firms tend to reduce the negative impact of stock price movement on their financial statements and invest in bonds for stable pension management. Because of the earlier restrictions of the 5:3:3:2 formula and the lackluster Japanese economy over the last 20 years, it can be predicted that Japanese firms have substantial unfunded liabilities related to defined benefit plans.

In the U.S., the breakdown of plan assets of firms which adopt defined benefit plans for the latest 5-year period is about 50% for stocks, 30% for bonds, and the remaining 20% for other properties.[84] These relative proportions are similar to those for Japanese formula aggregate pension funds. In the U.K., however, the percentages are different. There, the percentages until 2007 were about 60-70% for stocks, 20% for bonds, and the rest for other properties. The relatively higher proportion invested in stocks might be appropriate as a hedge against inflation. In 2008 and 2009, due to the worldwide recession, the percentage of stocks fell to 50%, and of bonds rose as high as 30%.[85] By 2012, the percentage of stocks had decreased to 35%, while bonds had increased to around 40%.[86] Most firms in the U.K. determine employee benefits by using the employee's final-year salary or average salary for the last 3 to 5 years before retirement to estimate the employee's pension, so firms in the U.K. must consider the effect of inflation hedging when managing their plan assets.[87] Therefore, since 2008, the number of firms closing their defined benefit plans either to new employees or to future accrual has continued to rise, owing to the pressure on corporate sponsors and the higher costs and burdens of defined benefit plans.[88]

6.3 Measurement of Plan Assets

Plan assets are measured at fair value. Japanese accounting standard, ASBJ

---

[84] Employee Benefit Research Institute, "EBRI Databook on Employee Benefits Chapter11: Retirement Plan Finances," http://www.ebri.org/pdf/publications/books/databook/DB.Chapter%20 11.pdf, p.2.

[85] Hewitt Associates, *Pensions Pocket Book 2010*, UK: Economic and Financial Publishing Ltd., 2010, p16.

[86] The National Association of Pension Funds, *Trends in Defined Benefit Asset Allocation: the Changing Shape of UK Pension Investment*, July 2013, http://www.napf.co.uk/PolicyandResearch/ DocumentLibrary/~/media/Policy/Documents/0314_Trends_in_db_asset_allocation_changing_ shape_UK_pension_investment_NAPF_research_paper_July_2013_DOCUMENT.ashx, p.5.

[87] Pension Fund Association, *Management of Pension Funding without Legal Controls*, Tokyo: Toyo Keizai, Inc., 1999, p145.

[88] The National Association of Pension Funds, *op.cit.*, pp.2, 5.

Guidance 25, states that fair value is determined by the amount that parties with sufficient knowledge and information make in a negotiated transaction on the asset voluntarily (ASBJ Guidance 25, par.20). Generally, the fair value for securities is assessed based on the information from stock exchanges, securities industry associations, theoretical prices, or brokers.[89] IAS19 defines fair value as "the amount for which an asset could be exchanged or a liability settled between knowledgeable, willing parties in an arm's length transaction" (IAS19, par.8). In effect, there is no difference between Japanese accounting standards and IAS19 for these definitions. IAS19 mentions further that if there is no market price available, fair value of plan assets is estimated in the manner of discounting expected future cash flows using a discount rate that reflects both the risk related to the plan assets and the maturity or expected disposal date of those assets (IAS19, par.113). There is volatility in evaluating plan assets at fair value. However, fair value also offers the possibility of eliminating the risk of managers' subjectivity in assessing plan assets, and the enhancement of comparability among firms and reliability of financial statements.

6.4 Retirement Benefit Trusts

A retirement benefit trust is a contract that promises to distinguish plan assets from a firm's other assets, and to provide the assets only for retirement benefits. When the prior accounting standards were introduced in fiscal 2000, most firms had to recognize significant amounts of pension deficits due to their inefficient pension fund management, primarily owing to the effect of a long recession in Japan and the depressed prices of domestic and foreign securities. To reduce the effect of pension fund deficits on financial statements, firms have adopted the strategy of retirement benefit trusts because of its following advantages:[90]

(a) A firm can keep the voting rights on the stocks;
(b) The difference between book value and fair value of securities can be recognized as gain when they are contributed to the retirement benefit trust; and

---

[89] Yamaguchi, Osamu, "Discounted Cash Flow in Accounting for Retirement Benefits," *Kigyo Kaikei*, Vol.54 No.4, April 2002, pp.493-494.
[90] Imafuku, Aishi, *Accounting for Labor Obligations,* Tokyo: Hakuto-Shobo Publishing Company, 2001, p.107.

(c) A firm can keep cross-shareholding relationships with other firms after it contributes stocks under the relationships to the retirement benefit trust.

Therefore, firms have adopted the method as a solution to problems in their pension management and their ownership stakes.

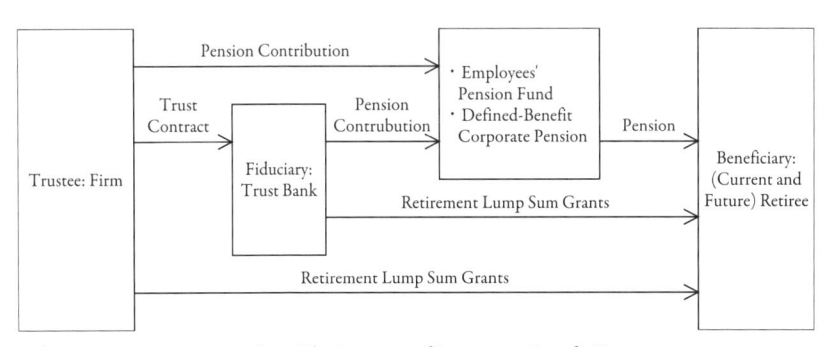

6.4.1 The Structure of Retirement Benefit Trusts

Figure 6.1 shows the structure of a retirement benefit trust. The first step in its establishment is that a firm makes a trust contract with the trust bank, and contributes listed securities it holds to the bank. The listed securities are managed by the trust bank, and the profits including dividends and interest from the securities management increase the firm's plan assets. The profits occurring from securities management are not returned to the firm. The trust bank makes a payment for current retirees' pension or retirement lump sum grants with the profits stemming from plan asset management and the proceeds of a sale of securities.[91]

It is required that assets contributed to retirement benefit trusts should be negotiable, and can be evaluated at fair value objectively (ASBJ Guidance 25, par.91). The registration name of the securities contributed to the trust bank transfers to the bank from the firm. However, the firm can keep the assignment rights for proxy on their securities (ASBJ Guidance 25, par.88).

Figure 6.1 The Structure of Retirement Benefit Trust

Source: Imafuku, Aishi, *Accounting for Retirement Benefits*, Tokyo: Shinsei-Sha Co. Ltd., 2000, p.160.

---
[91] Yamaguchi, Osamu, *Practice of Defined Benefit Obligations*, Tokyo: Chuokeizai-Sha, Inc., 2000, pp.104-105.

6.4.2 Requirements of Retirement Benefit Trusts Recognized as Plan Assets

Assets contributed to retirement benefit trusts have to meet all the following requirements to be recognized as plan assets (ASBJ Guidance 25, par.18):

(a) It is possible to ensure that the assets shall be available only for retirement benefits;

(b) It is a third-party benefit trust for retirement benefits;

(c) The retirement benefit trust is legally separated from the employer. It is prohibited to return the entrusted assets to the employer or do prejudicial acts to the employer's pensioners; and

(d) The fiduciary has rights to manage, operate, and dispose the trusted assets in accordance with the trust contract.

These requirements protect the fund for retirement benefits and ensure that it not be spent for other purposes. Basically they are similar to requirements for plan assets; item (d) clarifies who has the right for management of plan assets.

6.4.3 Recognition of Gain or Loss on Plan Assets in Retirement Benefit Trusts

Within six months from the start date of fiscal 2000 when the prior accounting standards were introduced, the amount of securities at fair value a firm contributed to the trust bank could be regarded as pension deficit-covering. In that case, the difference between book value and fair value on securities was recognized as gain on contribution of securities to retirement benefit trusts.[92] The contribution of securities to the retirement benefit trust could be offset with transitional liabilities. It was preferable for firms to reduce their defined benefit pension deficits due to their competitive positions in international markets or their grading. Therefore, this method was a valid approach for firms, especially for the first six months after the accounting change. However, there has been an inconsistency vis-à-vis other accounting standards with respect to gain or loss from valuations of securities.

Under the ASBJ Statement 26, a gain or loss from valuation of securities, including stocks for cross-shareholdings, is compared with the expected return

---

[92] Imafuku, Aishi, *Accounting for Retirement Benefits*, Tokyo: Shinsei-Sha Co. Ltd., 2000, p.163.

on the securities, and the difference between the gain or loss and the expected return on the securities can be recognized as actuarial gains and losses over the employees' average remaining service period (ASBJ Statement 26, par.24).

On the other hand, when the securities are not for the purpose of retirement benefits, they are treated under ASBJ Statement No.10: *Accounting Standard for Financial Instruments* (ASBJ Statement 10). The accounting standard classifies securities into four categories: trading securities, bonds held-to-maturity, stocks of subsidiaries and related firms, and other securities (ASBJ Statement 10, pars.15-18). Securities including stocks for cross-shareholdings are included in other securities, and evaluated at fair value. When the fair value of securities exceeds the book value, the gain is recognized in other comprehensive income. When the book value exceeds the fair value, the loss is recognized in either (1) other comprehensive income or (2) net income or loss on the basis of the principle of conservatism (ASBJ Statement 10, pars.18, 79, 80). In general, firms recognize their losses in other comprehensive income.

Under the ASBJ Statement 26, a gain or loss occurring from valuation of securities, including stocks for cross-shareholdings, is recognized as actuarial gains and losses which have an effect on net income over several years. The gain or loss which is not recognized for the period is disclosed in other comprehensive income. Under the accounting standard for financial instruments, ASBJ Statement 10, a gain or loss from the same securities is recognized in other comprehensive income. Thus there is an inconsistency in the recognition of gain or loss from securities, arising from whether they have a retirement benefits purpose.

IAS19 recognizes only the return on plan assets (securities) in other comprehensive income immediately (IAS19, par.8). It eliminated a recognition of the difference between actual and expected return on securities in actuarial gains and losses, because there is a possibility for firms to manipulate profit or loss when they determine the expected rate of return (IAS19ED, par.BC41). When these securities are not for employee benefits, they are treated under International Financial Reporting Standard No.9: *Financial Instruments* (IFRS9[93]). Securities including stocks for cross-shareholdings are evaluated at fair value, and the gain or loss is recognized in profit or loss, or other

---

[93] IFRS9 requires recognizing all financial assets at amortized cost or fair value (IFRS9, par.4.1.1). The amortized cost is applied if the following conditions are met (IFRS9, par.4.1.2): ↗

comprehensive income immediately.[94] Therefore, the treatment for securities including stocks for cross-holdings in IAS19 is consistent with IFRS9 if the gain or loss is recognized in other comprehensive income.

Basically, assets contributed to a trust bank cannot be returned to the firm, or exchanged with the firm's other assets. Therefore, securities contributed to a trust bank for retirement benefits have a different nature than that of securities treated under the accounting standard for financial instruments. The accounting method under IAS19 for recognition of securities including stocks for cross-shareholdings is more transparent and consistent with other accounting standards. However, it is acceptable to adopt the rules under the Japanese accounting standards for retirement benefits, because actuarial gains and losses are recognized in profit or loss, and the effect of the gains and losses is significant on financial statements.

Under the prior accounting standards, unrecognized actuarial gains or losses were off balance sheet, however, the new accounting standard, ASBJ Statement 26, states firms recognize them in other comprehensive income (ASBJ Statement 26, par.24). Therefore, the difference between the accounting standard for retirement benefits and that for financial instruments could be narrowed. The most important thing is whether these securities are solely for the purpose of retirement benefits, and if so, all rights belonging to the securities should be withdrawn from employers in order to manage plan assets efficiently without any other concerns. Leaving the voting rights on stocks in the hands of employers might encourage them to control plan assets. Therefore, voting rights also should be assigned to the firm's retirement benefit trust.

6.5 Offset with Defined Benefit Obligations

Plan assets are offset with defined benefit obligations. Until fiscal 2012, the difference between (a) defined benefit obligations and (b) plan assets and

---

    (a) the asset is held within a business model whose objective is to hold assets in order to collect contractual cash flows; and

    (b) the contractual terms of the financial asset give rise on specified dates to cash flows that are solely payments of principal and interest on the principal amount outstanding.

    The effective date of IFRS9 is 1 January 2015. Earlier application is permitted.

[94] IFRS9 states that "at initial recognition, a firm may make an irrevocable election to present in other comprehensive income subsequent changes in the fair value of an investment in a firm instrument" (IFRS9, par.5.7.5).

some other unrecognized items was recognized as a defined benefit liability at the end of the period. The accounting procedure is changed under the new accounting standard.

6.5.1 Measurement for Defined Benefit Liability

Defined benefit liability was calculated by the following formula until fiscal 2012 (Accounting Standard for Retirement Benefits, par.2.1).

> Defined benefit liability = Defined benefit obligations at present value at the balance sheet date
> ± Unrecognized actuarial gains or losses
> ± Unrecognized past service cost
> − Unrecognized transitional liability
> − Plan assets at fair value at the balance sheet date

From fiscal 2013, defined benefit liability will be calculated as the difference between defined benefit obligations and plan assets. It will be recognized as a liability on the balance sheet. When the amount determined by the difference between defined benefit obligations and plan assets is negative, it will be recognized as a defined benefit asset.

6.5.2 Recognition of Defined Benefit Asset

Under prior Japanese accounting standards, there were three cases in which a defined benefit asset resulted from the calculation in Section 6.5.1 (Statement on Establishing Accounting Standard for Retirement Benefits, par.4.4).

(a) Actual return on plan assets exceeds the expected return;
(b) The retirement benefit level was lowered by the employer; and
(c) The amount of contribution payable a firm contributed based on the pension financing calculation exceeds the defined benefit cost.

The defined benefit asset could be recognized as an asset on the balance sheet only for case (c). With regard to cases (a) and (b), the overfunded amount could not be recognized as a defined benefit asset, because these cases could

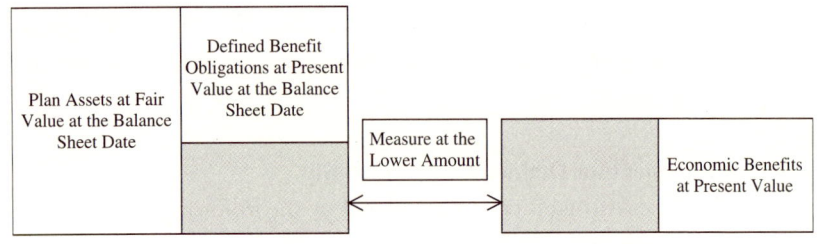

Figure 6.2 Recognition of Defined Benefit Asset under IAS19

be controlled by firms. However, it was possible to return the overfunded amount to the firm as a contribution payable or surplus fund. When all or a part of these amounts were returned to a firm under certain conditions,[95] it was recognized as an employer's asset (JICPA Report 13, par.31). Under the new accounting standard, this limitation is deleted, and the difference between defined benefit obligations and plan assets is recognized as a defined benefit asset (ED39, par.69).

IAS19 states that when a defined benefit asset occurs, the resulting asset shall be measured at the lower of (IAS19, pars.64, 83):

(a) the surplus in the defined benefit plan; and
(b) the asset ceiling, determined using the discount rate determined by reference to market yields at the end of the reporting period on high quality corporate bonds.

The asset ceiling is defined as "the present value of any economic benefits available in the form of refunds from the plan or reductions in future contributions to the plan" (IAS19, par.8). IFRIC Interpretation No.14: *IAS 19 -The Limit on a Defined Benefit Asset, Minimum Funding Requirements and their Interaction* (IFRIC14) clarifies the calculation for economic benefits. When the economic benefit is available as a refund, it is measured by the amount of the surplus (being the fair value of the plan assets less the present value of the defined benefit obligations) at the end of the reporting period, less any associated costs (IFRIC14, par.13). When the economic benefit is available as a contribution reduction, it is calculated by the future service cost to the firm for each period over the shorter of the expected life of the plan and the expected

---

[95] It was required that the asset amount in excess had to meet all requirements for the recognition of plan assets in Section 6.2 to return it to a firm (JICPA Report 13, par.31).

life of the firm. The future service cost to the firm excludes amounts that will be covered by employees (IFRIC14, par.16). The asset can be recognized, because the firm controls a resource which has the ability to generate future benefits, the control is a result of past events, and the firm can have future economic benefits in the form of a reduction in future contributions or a cash refund (IAS19, par.65). However, IAS19 has a limitation on the recognition of a defined benefit asset, and the IASB is reluctant to allow its declaration on the balance sheet, due to the characteristic of plan assets being used only for employee benefits. Japanese accounting standards have eliminated the limitation on the recognition of a defined benefit asset. The ASBJ, in light of the convergence project with the IASB, discussed adopting the asset ceiling IAS19 states. However, the Board decided not to adopt it, owing to the different circumstances in Japan, namely, that more firms tend to have pension deficits in their defined benefit plans than those in other countries adopting IFRS (ED39, par.70).

6.5.3 Net Approach and Gross Approach

There are two approaches for presentation of defined benefit liability (asset) which represents firm's pension funding status, a net approach and a gross approach. Under the net approach, a firm's entire obligation is recognized as a liability after deducting the assets at the fair value held by the fund. Under the gross approach, a firm's entire obligation is recognized as a liability and the rights to a refund from the fund are recognized as a separate asset (IAS19, par.BC179). In principle, Japanese Corporate Accounting Principles require firms to disclose assets, liabilities, and net assets on their financial statements based on a gross approach. Any assets should not be offset with liabilities or netted, or receive off balance sheet treatment (Corporate Accounting Principles, par.3.1.B). However, as explained above, the accounting standards for retirement benefits state plan assets should be offset with defined benefit obligations, and be recognized as a defined benefit liability (asset). IAS19 also adopts the same treatment for the presentation of defined benefit obligations and plan assets.

The Japanese accounting standards discuss the reason why the net approach is adopted in the standards for retirement benefits. Plan assets are funded systematically and used only for retirement benefits, so they should not

Table 6.1 Average Ratios of Defined Benefit Obligations and Plan Assets to Total Liabilities and Total Assets

(%)

	Defined Benefit Obligations / Total Liabilities	Plan Assets / Total Assets	Defined Benefit Liability / Total Liabilities
2001	27.99	8.05	9.95
2002	31.27	7.79	10.36
2003	29.74	5.98	9.74
2004	27.35	6.33	9.00
2005	25.85	6.36	8.31
2006	24.77	7.30	7.60
2007	24.07	7.40	6.68
2008	24.45	6.72	6.11
2009	26.74	5.96	6.25
2010	30.31	8.39	6.12
2011	26.24	6.52	6.24

Source: Nikkei Economic Electronic Databank System (2011)

be recognized on the balance sheet with other assets held to generate profits (Statement on Establishing Accounting Standard for Retirement Benefits, par.4.4). Other reasons generally discussed are as follows:

(a) Under defined benefit plans, employers make a certain amount of payment for employees' pension to their trust banks or insurance firms, and these institutions grant an annuity to their beneficiaries. Therefore, plan assets cannot be controlled by firms; and

(b) Plan assets account for a significant proportion of firm's total assets, and it might mislead financial statement users.

Table 6.1 shows the average ratios of defined benefit obligations and plan assets to total liabilities and total assets of Japanese firms (excluding banks and insurance firms) listed on the first section of the Tokyo Stock Exchange. The results indicate that the average ratios of defined benefit obligations to total liabilities range around 25 to 30%. With regard to average ratios of plan assets to total assets, the range is around 5 to 8%.

Both defined benefit obligations and plan assets have high proportions on the balance sheet. These average ratios are not stable, because the amount of defined benefit obligations and plan assets are affected by economic conditions, especially stock and bond prices. As for the average ratio of defined benefit liability to total liabilities, it gets lower every year. When the prior accounting standards were introduced in fiscal 2000, firms had to recognize significant amounts of defined benefit liabilities which represent firms' pension deficits. Therefore, this result shows that firms have decreased their pension deficits after the accounting change.

IAS19 states some reasons a net approach is adopted, as follows:

(a) International Accounting Standard No.32: *Financial Instruments: Presentation* states that a financial asset and a financial liability should be offset and the net amount reported in the balance sheet when a firm has a legally enforceable right to set off the recognized amounts, and intends to either to settle on a net basis, or to realize the asset and settle the liability simultaneously (IAS19, par.BC174);

(b) A gross presentation would be misleading, because plan assets held by the fund are not controlled by the firm (IAS19, par. BC180.(a)); and

(c) A gross presentation would be an unnecessary change from current practice, which generally permits a net presentation (IAS19, par.180.(b)).

IAS19 also mentions some advantages a gross approach has, as follows:

(a) A firm has a right to receive reimbursement from the fund which is a source of economic benefits (IAS19, par.BC181. (b)); and

(b) IAS37 adopts a gross presentation for reimbursements related to provisions, which was not previously general practice (IAS19, par.BC181.(c)).

As a result, the IASB concluded that it is justified to adopt a net presentation for IAS19 due to the restriction on the use of plan assets (IAS19, par.BC184).

6.6 Treatment for Multi-Employer Plans

A multi-employer plan is a private corporate pension plan established by several employers. There are two types of multi-employer plans for employees' pension fund: (1) a multi-employer plan established by a leading firm and associated firms, and (2) by firms in the same industry or the same area. Firms adopting multi-employer plans need to recognize the amount of defined benefit obligations and plan assets belonging to them. Each firm calculates their defined benefit obligations based on the information firms have, such as number of employees, employees' salaries, or rate of employee turnover. Plan assets are managed by the employees' pension fund with assets from other employers collectively. Therefore, the assets under multi-employer plans are calculated and allocated by one of four methods, as follows (ASBJ Guidance 25, pars.63, 119).

(1) Ratio based on defined benefit obligations

Plan assets are calculated based on a ratio of a firm's defined benefit obligations to the total amount under the multi-employer plan.

(2) Ratio based on obligations under pension financing method

Plan assets are calculated based on a ratio of a firm's obligations measured by a pension financing method[96] to total amount of obligations under the same method in the multi-employer plan.[97]

(3) Ratio based on the amount of accumulated total contribution payable

Plan assets are calculated based on a ratio of the accumulated amount of the firm's contribution payable to the total amount of contribution payable of all firms under the multi-employer plan.

(4) Ratio based on plan assets under pension financing method

This method can be adopted only when plan assets are controlled by each firm. The return realized from plan asset management with other firms is divided based on the contribution amount.

ASBJ Statement No.14: *Amendments to Accounting Standard for Retirement Benefits (Part 2)* (ASBJ Statement 14) states when plan assets are not reasonably assessed, the firm's contribution payable to a fund is recognized as defined benefit cost (ASBJ Statement 14, par.2). The case where plan assets are not reasonably assessed is when each firm contributes an across-the-board amount of contribution payable. Firms adopting a multi-employer plan established by firms in the same industry or area often fit into this category,

---

[96] Under a pension funding method, the obligation is calculated by the present value of the total amount of premiums for employees in the future, subtracted from the present value of the amount of benefits paid in the future. To estimate these present values, both are discounted.

[97] There is another case to use the ratio of a firm's obligations excluding unrecognized past service cost measured by a pension financing method to total amount of obligations under the same method in the multi-employer plan.

because the contribution payable is not linked to employees' service periods or ages, and the amount is equal in each firm.[98] When the proportion of retirement benefits belonging to a specific employer to the total amount is quite high, plan assets are regarded as being reasonably assessed (ASBJ Guidance 25, par.121). There was a requirement to disclose the amount of plan assets in footnotes, even when plan assets were not reasonably assessed under a prior practical guidance issued by the Japanese Institute of Certified Public Accountants (JICPA), because there was a risk that a parent firm would simply add one or more of its subsidiaries to meet the requirements of a multi-employer plan (which was to be preferred, since it required simpler disclosure than a regular defined benefit plan). The amount of plan assets was calculated by one of the following ratios: a ratio based on the amount of contribution payable, the number of pension plan participants, or total amount of employees' salaries.[99] However, the requirement is eliminated in a current guidance, because it is not rational to calculate plan assets that are not reasonably assessed (ASBJ Guidance 25, par.121).

Under IAS19, when a multi-employer plan is a defined benefit plan, a firm recognizes its proportionate share of the defined benefit obligations, plan assets, and cost related to the plan in the same way as for any other defined benefit plan (IAS19, par.33). When sufficient information is not available to use defined benefit accounting for a multi-employer plan, a firm can account for the plan in the same way as it does for recognition in a defined contribution plan (IAS19, par.34). Under a defined contribution plan, a firm recognizes the contribution payable to the plan as a liability, after deducting any contribution already paid and, as an expense (IAS19, par.51). Therefore, there is no difference between the Japanese accounting standards and IAS19.

6.7 Summary and Conclusion

Because of their particular characteristics, there are some distinctive accounting procedures allowed in recognition and presentation of plan assets. Plan assets are solely for the purpose of retirement benefits, and separated from the accounts of the firm's employer or creditors. There are many requirements

---

[98] Tagaya, Mitsuru, *Accounting Standards for Retirement Benefits*, Tokyo: Zeimu Kenkyukai, 2000, p.126.
[99] *Ibid.*, pp.123-124.

and a restriction on recognition of plan assets. Pension is defined as a future salary payment for a firm's employees after their retirement. Therefore, part of the reason there are some requirements for recognition of plan assets is that they belong to employees, and their pensions should be protected for their retirement.

There are two different accounting procedures for recognition of plan assets from other standards: recognition of a gain or loss from valuation of securities in a retirement benefit trust, and adoption of a net approach. With regard to the recognition of a gain or loss from valuation of securities in a retirement benefit trust, under prior accounting standards for retirement benefits, the gain or loss from the valuation of securities compared with the expected return on the securities was deferred, and a part of it was recognized as actuarial gains and losses in defined benefit cost for the period. The rest was off balance sheet and noted in a footnote as unrecognized actuarial gains or losses. However, in ASBJ Statement 26, it is stated that unrecognized actuarial gains or losses are included in other comprehensive income (ASBJ Statement 26, par.24). Therefore, the difference between the accounting standards for retirement benefits and that for financial instruments is narrowed. However, leaving voting rights on stocks to employers might give them an opportunity to control plan assets. As for adopting a net approach, this accounting procedure is allowed, because plan assets are funded for retirement benefits and are not controlled by firms' employers to generate their earnings.

Retirement benefits including pensions perform an important social function in stabilizing employees' livelihoods after they retire. There are some cases in which firms have reduced their employees' pension owing to their financial condition and management results in Japan. However, these situations might be considered harmful to the social system. Therefore, under accounting standards for retirement benefits, plan assets should be separated from other assets and secured in order to guarantee payments to employees' pensions.

Chapter 7
Disclosure of Defined Benefit Liability

7.1 Introduction

The ASBJ issued ASBJ Statement 26 in 2012. This accounting change will have some significant effects on financial statements and financial ratios. The accounting standards for retirement benefits have several distinctive features in the recognition and measurement of some components of defined benefit obligations. One of these features is deferred recognition for past service cost, actuarial gains and losses, and transitional liabilities. When recognizing these components, firms can amortize them over several years. Amounts that are not recognized in that period are shown as unrecognized obligations. This approach to recognition is allowed because these obligations are not related to the firm's operating business. Under the prior accounting standards introduced in fiscal 2000, these unrecognized obligations were disclosed only in footnotes. The amount of defined benefit liability was calculated with consideration given to these unrecognized obligations. This accounting procedure was relatively complex and demonstrated inconsistency with other standards, and made financial statements difficult to understand. The new accounting standard, ASBJ Statement 26, states that these unrecognized obligations be shown on the balance sheet, and this treatment will be applied from fiscal years beginning on or after April 1, 2013. This accounting change affects levels of total assets, total liabilities, and net assets, and for most firms it will have a significant negative effect on their financial statements.

This chapter, as a first step, will consider whether the defined benefit liability meets the definition of a liability, with a view to determining if it is appropriate to recognize these obligations on the balance sheet, given the many estimations required in the calculation. Second, to investigate the impact of this accounting standard change, the chapter will explain the difference between prior and new accounting standards, and how the change affects financial statements and some financial ratios, including the amount of total assets, total liabilities, and net assets in those calculations.

7.2 Definition and Recognition of a Liability

Japanese accounting standards have not stated a definition of a liability. One of these standards, Corporate Accounting Principles, states only the definition of a *provision*, which is defined as a future cost or loss. When the provision results from past events and is probable to occur, and the amount can be estimated reliably, the amount accrued in the period is recognized as a provision on the profit and loss statement. The amount not accrued in that period is disclosed on the balance sheet (Corporate Accounting Principles, par. footnote18).

Currently, ASBJ is considering whether to establish a conceptual framework that systematizes premises and concepts underlying financial accounting in the Conceptual Framework (Conceptual Framework, Introduction). In the Conceptual Framework, a liability is defined as "an obligation or the equivalent of a reporting entity to transfer or disclaim the economic resources as a result of past transactions or events. The equivalent includes a legal obligation" (Conceptual Framework, par.3.5). A liability is recognized in the balance sheet when at least one of two sides has executed the contract, and it is probable that the event will occur in the future (Conceptual Framework, pars.4.3, 4.6). There are four measurement methods for a liability that ASBJ states in the Conceptual Framework, as follows (Conceptual Framework, pars.4.30-43):

(a) expected amount of payment (settlement value or future payment amount);
(b) cash receivable amount;
(c) discounted value; and
(d) market value.

Expected amount of payment is the sum of future cash flows required to repay a liability. In general, it indicates the liability principal of the contract (Conceptual Framework, par.4.30). Cash receivable amount is cash or cash equivalents received in exchange of an obligation to provide goods or services (Conceptual Framework, par.4.32). Discounted value is calculated as the estimated amount of future cash flows discounted by any discount rate on the measurement date. The discount rate can be determined by a firm with consideration of such factors as increase or decrease of future cash outflow, the movement of risk-free rate, passage of time, or credit risk of the firm (Conceptual Framework, pars.4.36, 4.38). The timing of future cash flows has to be able to be predicted reasonably to adopt this measurement method (Conceptual Framework, par.4.19). Market value is a value that is accrued on the secondary market for a given asset (Conceptual Framework, par.4.11). To measure a defined benefit obligation, the future amount of a defined benefit obligation at an employee's retirement is estimated, and discounted to its present value on the balance sheet date. Therefore, the measurement of the defined benefit obligation is categorized into (c).

In IFRS Conceptual Framework, the IASB defines a liability as "a present obligation of the entity arising from past events, the settlement of which is expected to result in an outflow from the entity of resources embodying economic benefits" (IFRS Conceptual Framework, par.4.4.(b)). An obligation is "a duty or responsibility to act or perform in a certain way." Obligations might be enforceable by law as a result of a binding contract or statutory requirement. Obligations also result from normal business practice, custom, and a desire to maintain good business relations or act in an equitable manner (IFRS Conceptual Framework, par.4.15). IASB states that a provision which can be measured only by using a substantial degree of estimation, such as a provision for payments to cover defined benefit obligations should be included in liabilities when it involves a present obligation and satisfies the rest of the definition of liabilities (IFRS Conceptual Framework, par.4.19). A liability is recognized in the balance sheet when it is probable that an outflow of resources incorporating economic benefits will arise due to the settlement of a present obligation and the amount at the settlement date can be measured reliably (IFRS Conceptual Framework, par.4.46).

The IFRS Conceptual Framework includes the following three components in its definitions of a liability: an obligation arising from past events, a probable future outflow of entity's resources, and a present obligation. The component of "an obligation arising from past events" acknowledges that financial statements are historically based.[100] With regard to a probable future

---

[100] Murray, Dennis, "What Are the Essential Features of a Liability?" *Accounting Horizons*, Vol.24 No.4, December 2010, p.624.

outflow of an entity's resources, the IFRS Conceptual Framework includes the phrase "expected to result in an outflow from the entity of resources embodying economic benefits" in its liability definition. IASB clarifies that "the phrase *expected to* is not intended to imply that there must be a particular degree of certainty that an outflow of benefits will occur before an item meets the Framework's definition of a liability." The Board also notes that the word *expected* is consistent with the meaning of the word *probable* in the definition of a liability that FASB provides.[101] Statement of Financial Accounting Concepts No.6: *Elements of Financial Statements* (SFAS Conceptual Framework 6) states that "*probable* refers to that which can reasonably be expected or believed on the basis of available evidence or logic but is neither certain nor proved" (SFAS Conceptual Framework 6, par.footnote18). On the other hand, the Japanese Conceptual Framework includes the phrases "to transfer or disclaim the economic resources" in the definition, and "a liability is recognized when it is probable that the event will occur in the future" in the recognition. These phrases indicate that a liability involves a future event which transfers or disclaims economic resources.

The IFRS Conceptual Framework states clearly that a liability is a present obligation of an entity (IFRS Conceptual Framework, par.4.4.(b)). Firms can recognize expenses as a liability only when they cannot avoid paying them in the future. The definition of a liability in the Japanese Conceptual Framework does not include the phrase *a present obligation.* Under the Japanese Conceptual Framework, the recognition of some liability items is based on the revenue-expense approach, and these items are not required to be legal or constructive obligations. It is one of the issues Japanese accounting standards have, namely, that there are mixed approaches to asset-liability and revenue-expense in one standard. Specifically, it can be seen in an accounting procedure for provision of repairs, which is a provision to prepare for costs of repairs in the future. However, firms can avoid the payment in the future if they suspend operations or dispose of their equipment. There are no legal or constructive obligations for this provision. Under IAS37, it is required that there be a

---

[101] International Accounting Standards Board, Liabilities-Amendments to IAS 37 *Provisions, Contingent Liabilities and Contingent Assets* and IAS 19 *Employee Benefits,* June 2009, http://www.iasb.org/NR/rdonlyres/B2EE99F3-C48E-40A1-8827-5137C92C0EF4/0/LiabIAS37projectJune08.pdf, par.64.

present obligation (legal or constructive) when these items are recognized as a liability, therefore the provision of repairs is not recognized as a liability.[102] On the other hand, under Japanese accounting standards, it is possible to recognize the provision as a liability. The lack of the component of a present obligation in the definition of a liability does not affect the recognition of a defined benefit liability. However, it is important to understand there is a difference between Japanese and IFRS Conceptual Frameworks, and it has an effect on some other standards.

The IASB and FASB are working together on several joint projects, including the conceptual framework project, business combination project, financial statement presentation, and revenue recognition project. The definition of a liability is discussed in the conceptual framework project. The Boards have proposed to adopt the following definition: "A liability of an entity is a present economic obligation for which the entity is the obligor." Two conditions should be satisfied for recognition as a present economic obligation: (1) the economic obligation exists, and (2) the entity is the obligor on the date of the financial statements. Regarding the first condition, an economic obligation is an unconditional promise or other requirement to provide economic resources.[103] An unconditional obligation requires performance to occur now or over a period of time, whereas a conditional obligation requires performance to occur only if an uncertain future event occurs.[104] As for the second condition, an entity is the obligor if the economic obligation the entity

---

[102] Under IAS37, legal and constructive obligations are defined as follows (IAS37, par.10):
A legal obligation is an obligation that derives from:
  (a) a contract (through its explicit or implicit terms);
  (b) legislation; or
  (c) other operation of law.
A constructive obligation is an obligation that derives from an entity's actions where:
  (a) by an established pattern of past practice, published policies or a sufficiently specific current statement, the entity has indicated to other parties that it will accept certain responsibilities; and
  (b) as a result, the entity has created a valid expectation on the part of those other parties that it will discharge those responsibilities.
[103] Financial Accounting Standards Board, "Minutes of the October 20, 2008 Conceptual Framework (Phase B) Board Meeting," October 22, 2008, http://www.fasb.org/board_meeting _minutes/10-20-08_cf.pdf, p.2.
[104] Financial Accounting Standards Board, "Board Meeting Handout Conceptual Framework," June 25, 2008, http://www.fasb.org/jsp/FASB/Document_C/DocumentPage&cid=1218220092264, par.8.

is required to bear is enforceable by legal or equivalent means.[105] This proposed definition is different from the one under the current IFRS Conceptual Framework, because it does not include the following components: an obligation arising from past events and a probable future outflow of an entity's resources. Obligations including bank loans and purchases on account are present obligations. However, there are some obligations that do not meet the first condition, which encompasses unvested benefit obligations and product warranties. Under the definition, these items are not recognized as a liability, because a present obligation does not exist for them.[106]

Therefore, there is one difference in the definition and recognition of a liability between Japanese and IFRS Conceptual Frameworks. Under the Japanese Conceptual Framework, a liability is not defined as a present obligation in terms of a revenue-expense approach, which leads to different accounting treatments in some accounting standards from those in IFRS, although the recognition of defined benefit liability adopts the same treatment in the Japanese accounting standards and IAS19. There are two issues concerning the recognition of a defined benefit liability that have been generally discussed, and also mentioned in the IASB and FASB project, namely, the recognition of unvested benefit obligations as a liability and the consideration of future salary increases in the projected unit credit method. These accounting treatments are inconsistent with the recognition of liabilities in other accounting standards (IAS19DP, par.1.11). With regard to unvested benefit obligations, the IASB has decided to recognize them immediately, because the obligations arise from employees' past service (IAS19DP, par.2.17). However, unvested benefit obligations are not a present obligation, because the employer can terminate the employees' contract and avoid the payment for their pensions (IAS19DP, par.6.2). Therefore, IASB states in its conceptual framework that a defined benefit liability does not meet the definition of a liability. On the other hand, the Japanese accounting standards do not include a present obligation as a component of the recognition of a liability. Unvested benefit obligations can be recognized as a liability if they are likely to occur in their future. As explained in Chapter 3, employees in Japan tend to work longer than those in other countries. The possibility that unvested benefit obligations

---

[105] Financial Accounting Standards Board, *Ibid*, October 22, 2008, p.2.
[106] Murray, Dennis, *Ibid.*, p.632.

will be realized must be high. Thus it is appropriate to recognize unvested benefit obligations considering the probability these obligations will be realized based on the past experience of the firm under the Japanese accounting standards. As for future salary increases, they do not meet any component in the definitions that Japanese and IFRS Conceptual Frameworks state, because they are related to future events and are not probable to occur in the future due to the current economic situation. Therefore, they should not be included as a liability.

7.3 Recognition and Measurement of Defined Benefit Liability under Prior Accounting Standards

As explained in Chapter 6, until fiscal 2012 a defined benefit liability was calculated with consideration of unrecognized past service cost, unrecognized actuarial gains or losses, and unrecognized transitional liability. In the calculation of a defined benefit liability, first, plan assets at fair value at the balance sheet date were deducted from defined benefit obligations at present value. Second, unrecognized obligations were added to or subtracted from the difference between plan assets and defined benefit obligations. The amount calculated from these formulas was recognized as a defined benefit liability. Figure 7.1 shows the structure of defined benefit liability.

It would be simple and easy for financial statement users to understand the defined benefit liability if it had been calculated by plan assets deducted from defined benefit obligations. However, there were three other components

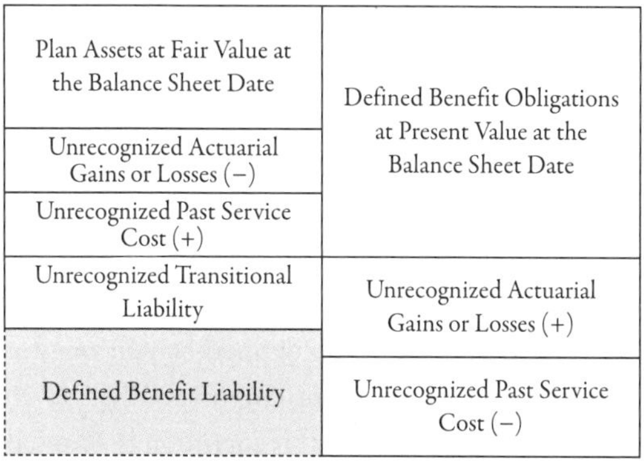

Plan Assets at Fair Value at the Balance Sheet Date	Defined Benefit Obligations at Present Value at the Balance Sheet Date
Unrecognized Actuarial Gains or Losses (−)	
Unrecognized Past Service Cost (+)	
Unrecognized Transitional Liability	Unrecognized Actuarial Gains or Losses (+)
Defined Benefit Liability	Unrecognized Past Service Cost (−)

Figure 7.1 Structure of Defined Benefit Liability

to be considered: unrecognized past service cost, unrecognized actuarial gains or losses, and unrecognized transitional liability under the prior accounting standards. The prior accounting standards for retirement benefits required firms to disclose defined benefit obligations, plan assets, prepaid defined benefit cost, defined benefit cost, unrecognized past service cost, unrecognized actuarial gains or losses, and *others* in the footnotes. Unrecognized transitional liability was included in *others* as a component of defined benefit obligations, because it occurred only when firms changed their accounting standards for retirement benefits (Accounting Standard for Retirement Benefits, par.6.2.(1)).

7.4 Unrecognized Obligations

Japanese accounting standards adopt deferred recognition for past service cost, actuarial gains and losses, and transitional liability. These amounts are amortized over several years, and amounts which are not recognized as a part of defined benefit cost in the period were disclosed as unrecognized obligations only in a footnote under the prior accounting standards. These unrecognized obligations including unrecognized past service cost, unrecognized actuarial gains or losses, and unrecognized transitional liability will be on the balance sheet from the end of annual periods beginning on or after April 1, 2013.

7.4.1 Unrecognized Past Service Cost

Past service cost is recognized when a firm changes the benefits payable under an existing defined benefit plan (ASBJ Statement 26, par.12).

In Japan, past service cost is recognized over the average remaining service lives of the firms' employees. The average remaining service lives is the average period of the firms' current employees from the balance sheet date to their retirement date (ASBJ Guidance 25, par.103). JICPA Report 13 states that in principle, it is calculated based on a decrement table of pension mathematics including mortality rates and rates of employee turnover. Firms are also allowed to use the average age of current employees on the balance sheet date deducted from a standard age. The standard age refers to a retirement age, average age of retirees, or the final age stated in the defined benefit pension plan (JICPA Report 13, par.24). Past service cost for employees that have already retired can be recognized immediately. Deferred recognition is adopted, because firms expect to increase employees' incentives to work for them in the future when they introduce or change their defined benefit plans (ASBJ Statement 26, pars.67, 68). Therefore, firms might incur the effect of changes in their plans on employees' incentives in the future, and they are allowed to adopt deferred recognition for past service cost.

The IASB formerly held that firms should recognize past service cost as an expense on a straight-line basis over the average period until the benefit became vested (Prior IAS19, par.96). It indicated the following reasons to support deferred recognition (Prior IAS19, par.BC50):
(a) a firm introduces or improves employee benefits for current employees in order to generate future economic benefits; and
(b) immediate recognition is too revolutionary.

However, under the current IAS19, IASB recognizes unvested past service cost immediately, because IAS19DP states that "past service cost can be assumed as increasing the present obligation that arises from employees' past service" (IAS19DP, par.2.17).

7.4.2 Unrecognized Actuarial Gains or Losses

Actuarial gains and losses are caused by a difference between the actual rates and the estimated rates to assess plan assets or to calculate defined benefit obligations, and a modification of estimated rates (ASBJ Statement 26, par.11).

In Japan, actuarial gains and losses are recognized when there is a significant change in assumptions, which indicates when defined benefit obligations as measured using assumptions at the end of the year are compared to those at the end of the previous year, and this amount exceeds 10% of the previous year's obligations (ASBJ Guidance 25, par.30). When the gains and losses are recognized as defined benefit cost, the cost can be spread over the average remaining service lives of the firms' employees. The amortized period can be different from the one set for past service cost (ASBJ Guidance 25, pars.34, 43). Deferred recognition is adopted for actuarial gains and losses, because actuarial gains and losses comprise not only a difference between the actual rates and the estimated rates but also a modification of estimated rates. Therefore, recognizing the gains and losses as a cost in the period does not express the condition of defined benefit obligations faithfully (ASBJ Statement 26, pars.67, 68).

IASB adopted a corridor approach to recognize actuarial gains and losses, because gains and losses might offset one another in the long run (Prior IAS19, par.95). Under the corridor approach, the portion of actuarial gains and losses that exceeded 10% of the greater of the present value of PBO or the fair value of any plan assets was divided by the expected average remaining working lives of the employees participating in that plan (Prior IAS19, pars.92, 93). IASB recognized that deferred recognition and the corridor approach were complex, artificial, and difficult to understand, and recognition attempted to reduce volatility in actuarial gains and losses (Prior IAS19, par.BC40). The IASB also mentioned that the immediate recognition approach was attractive, and when the Board resolved substantial issues about performance reporting,[107] it would be possible to adopt immediate recognition (Prior IAS19, par. BC41). In the current IAS19, the corridor approach has been eliminated and immediate recognition is adopted for actuarial gains and losses, due to the objectives of consistency with the framework and other accounting standards, faithful representation of the firm's financial position, and improvements in comparability across firms (IAS19DP, pars.2.10, 2.11).

7.4.3 Unrecognized Transitional Liability

In fiscal 2000, the Japanese accounting standards on retirement benefits were changed dramatically. Before the change, generally firms recognized the amount contributed to their trust funds to fund their employees' pensions as a cost. After the accounting standards were introduced, firms recognized their PBO, plan assets, defined benefit liability, and defined benefit cost on their financial statements. Unrecognized transitional liability is the difference between the PBO, and the total amount of the fair value of plan assets measured under the new accounting standards and the accrued pension cost recognized under the prior accounting standards.[108]

---

[107] The substantial issues includes (Prior IAS19, par.BC41):
  (a) whether financial performance includes those items that are recognized directly in equity;
  (b) the conceptual basis for determining whether items are recognized in the profit and loss statement or directly in equity;
  (c) whether net cumulative losses should be recognized in the profit and loss statement, rather than directly in equity; and
  (d) whether certain items reported initially in equity should subsequently be reported in the profit and loss statement ('recycling').
[108] Imahuku, Aishi, *Accounting for Retirement Benefits*, Tokyo: Shinsei-Sha Co. Ltd., 2000, p.110.

In Japanese accounting standards, the amount recognized by this accounting change can be recognized as expense or revenue on a straight-line basis over less than 15 years. On the other hand, IASB recognizes a transitional liability immediately, according to IAS8. In prior IAS19, IASB allowed firms to recognize it as an expense on a straight-line basis over five years or less from the date of adoption of IAS19 (Prior IAS19, par.155). However, deferred recognition was eliminated, and only immediate recognition is adopted in the current IAS19.

In the prior Japanese accounting standards for retirement benefits, unrecognized obligations were disclosed only in footnotes. Deferred recognition has been allowed, because it can reduce volatility in light of the fact that these obligations are not related to firms' operations. However, since the amount of these obligations is significant and the amortization period is determined by each firm, there was a possibility that it would be difficult for investors to understand financial statements if these obligations were disclosed in footnotes.

Additionally, with respect to the definition of a liability under Japanese Conceptual Framework, it contains two components; an obligation arising from past events, and a probable future outflow of entity resources. Defined benefit liability is recognized as future salary payment for employees' services in the past. The amount is calculated by discounting the estimated amount at employees' retirement date to the balance sheet date. Japanese accounting standards mention that deferred recognition is adopted for unrecognized past service cost and unrecognized actuarial gains or losses, because the effect of changes in the benefit level on employees' incentives will remain in the future, and a modification of estimated rates is included in actuarial gains and losses. However, changes in benefit level and the modification of *estimated* rates should be reflected in a defined benefit liability immediately, because it has been already changed in consideration of a probable future outflow of entity resources. Regarding unrecognized transitional liabilities, they should be treated in the same way as the other liabilities occurring from any accounting changes. Therefore, there is no appropriate reason to adopt deferred recognition and recognize these obligations off balance sheet, except for reducing volatility in financial statements.

7.5 Presentation of Defined Benefit Liability under the New Accounting Standard

In 2012, ASBJ issued ASBJ Statement 26, which states that unrecognized past service cost, unrecognized actuarial gains or losses, and unrecognized transitional liability are to be disclosed in accumulated other comprehensive income as a net asset (ASBJ Guidance 25, pars.33, 130). These unrecognized obligations are recycled to profit or loss in later periods. Under prior accounting standards, deferred recognition made it difficult for financial statement users to understand the financial position of defined benefit plans, because the information did not indicate the funding status of these plans correctly owing to the recognition of unrecognized obligations off balance sheet. Referring to other international accounting standards including IAS19 and SFAS158, ASBJ has decided to disclose unrecognized obligations on the balance sheet (ED39, par.52). This accounting standard will be adopted from fiscal 2013 (ASBJ Statement 26, par.85).

IASB requires recognizing all changes in the value of plan assets and the defined benefit obligations in the period in which they occur (IAS19DP, par. IN5). The main criticisms of deferred recognition are as follows (IAS19DP, par.2.7):

(a) a firm may recognize an asset when a plan is in deficit or a liability may be recognized when a plan is in surplus; and
(b) prior IAS19 had a level of complexity, and it made financial statements difficult for users to understand.

The Board also mentions that immediate recognition would be consistent with the IFRS Conceptual Framework and other IFRSs, and it represents faithfully the firm's financial position (IAS19DP, pars.2.10, 2.11). IAS19 states that immediate recognition is adopted to recognize past service cost and actuarial gains and losses. IASB does not permit the recycling method that firms could use to reclassify or recycle amounts recognized in other comprehensive income to profit or loss in later periods, because (IAS19ED, par.BC45):

(a) there is not a consistent policy on recycling in IFRSs;
(b) the question of recycling remains open in IFRSs;
(c) a general decision on the matter should not be made in the context of amendments to IAS19; and

(d) there is no pragmatic ability to identify a suitable basis for recycling.

The defined benefit liability (asset) includes the effect of an asset ceiling, which is explained in Chapter 6 (IAS19ED, par.BC64.(b)).

The FASB has issued SFAS158 which requires disclosure of unrecognized obligations on the balance sheet as of the end of the fiscal year ending after December 15, 2006. Under SFAS87, FASB had already noted that "it would be conceptually appropriate to recognize a net pension liability or asset measured as the difference between defined benefit obligations and plan assets, either with no deferred recognition, or with gains and losses recognized in comprehensive income. However, this approach might be too great a change from past practice to be adopted at the present time" (SFAS87, par.107). The amendment on unrecognized obligations in SFAS158 states that unrecognized past service cost, unrecognized actuarial gains or losses, and unrecognized transitional liability[109] would be recognized as accumulated other comprehensive income (SFAS158, par.16a). This amendment on unrecognized obligations does not change past practice of deferred recognition as a component of net periodic benefit cost. The treatment is also consistent with the practice of including in other comprehensive income certain changes in value that have not been recognized in earnings (SFAS158, par.B36). FASB states that this treatment of unrecognized obligations is simple, transparent, and symmetrical, and is consistent with the definitions of an asset and a liability in the SFAS Conceptual Framework (SFAS158, par.B41). FASB believes the statement will improve existing reporting for defined benefit postretirement plans and provide information that is useful for stakeholders.

There are several papers that examine the effect of SFAS158 on firms' financial statements. Bryan et al. (2007) estimate the effect of SFAS158 on financial statements for Dow 30 firms. Their calculation shows that aggregate

---

[109] FASB proposed recognition of a transitional liability as adjusted retained earnings in an Exposure Draft of a proposed statement which was issued in March 2006. FASB believed that "any remaining transition asset or obligation was similar to the cumulative effect resulting from a change in accounting principle, and should not affect current or future reported earnings" (SFAS158, pars.B44, B45). However, FASB has elected to recognize unrecognized transitional liability as accumulated other comprehensive income, which is the same procedure as other unrecognized obligations. The FASB believes "the benefit of recognizing unrecognized net obligation on accounting changes does not exceed the cost and was inconsistent with the intent of FASB not to change amounts reported as net periodic benefit cost as part of the first phase of the project" (SFAS158, par.B47).

shareholders' equity would decrease by over 12%, aggregate total liabilities increase by around 4%, and aggregate total retained earnings are reduced by almost 16% if SFAS158 were introduced. They also indicate the change in three common financial ratios with and without applying SFAS158: market to book, return on equity (ROE), and debt to equity. The decrease in equity leads to an increase in the market to book ratio of 35%, of ROE by more than 60%, and of total debt to equity by 19%. They conclude that the impact of SFAS158 on financial statements would be significant. Soroosh and Espahbodi (2007) also examine how SFAS158 affects a firm's financial statements. They choose Merck's 2004 financial statements and examine how they would be affected by the accounting standard change. They also select some financial ratios, and show how the ROE, ROA, debt to equity, and debt to asset ratios are increased due to the introduction of SFAS158. In addition, VanDerhei (2007) shows that in the two years before the enactment of the Pension Protection Act of 2006 and SFAS158, a third of their respondents had closed the plan to new hires or frozen their defined benefit plans, and another third planned to close or freeze their pensions in the next few years.

Houmes and Boylan (2010) examine the impact of SFAS158 on discount rates used to estimate defined benefit liabilities. Under the prior accounting standard, SFAS87 required firms to disclose PBO only in the footnotes. It also adopted an additional minimum liability requirement, which recognized the difference between ABO and the fair value of plan assets under a certain condition (explained in Chapter 3). ABO was calculated based on employees' current salaries, whereas PBO was based on employees' future salaries. Therefore, this accounting change might increase firms' defined benefit liabilities. They investigate whether firms have changed their discount rates to help reduce the PBO and defined benefit liabilities. They conclude that, after SFAS158 was enacted, firms used higher discount rates to reduce estimated PBO and defined benefit liabilities. Houmes et al. (2011) test how firms' stock prices will be affected by the defined benefit liability calculated based on PBO. They form high and low financial risk portfolios, and use standard event study methodology to estimate abnormal returns around relevant SFAS158 event dates for each portfolio. Their results show that firms with high financial risk have a negative impact from SFAS158, whereas firms with low financial risk have a positive impact from the accounting standard change. Therefore, these results show that recognizing a defined benefit liability on the balance sheet has a negative effect on the firm's financial statements.

7.6 The Significance of Unrecognized Obligations

Under the new accounting standard, unrecognized obligations including unrecognized past service cost, unrecognized actuarial gains or losses, and unrecognized transitional liability are recognized on the balance sheet. The difference between PBO and plan assets is recognized as a defined benefit liability in total liabilities. Deferred tax assets in total assets are increased by the amount of unrecognized obligations multiplied by the firm's tax rate. The balance of unrecognized obligations is recognized as accumulated other comprehensive income in net assets. Therefore, all of these unrecognized obligations affect the levels of total assets, total liabilities, and net assets, and have no effect on profit or loss.

To estimate the impact of the accounting standard change, some financial ratios under both the prior and new accounting standards have been calculated. The firms (excluding banks and insurance firms) that have been selected are Japanese firms that are listed on the first section of the Tokyo Stock Exchange and disclose both discount rates and the expected rates of return on plan assets.

Table 7.1 shows the average ratios of defined benefit liability to total liabilities under the prior and new accounting standards. It reveals that the

Table 7.1 Ratios of Defined Benefit Liability to Total Liabilities

	Defined Benefit Liability / Total Liabilities (%) (Under Prior Standards)	Defined Benefit Liability / Total Liabilities (%) (Under New Standard)	No. of Firms	Firms with Underfunded Status	Firms with Overfunded Status
2001	7.71	11.45	1,027	1,022	5
2002	8.58	13.43	1,233	1,224	9
2003	8.70	14.51	1,201	1,194	7
2004	8.47	12.00	1,160	1,132	28
2005	8.10	10.41	1,157	1,118	39
2006	7.57	7.76	1,152	1,009	143
2007	7.08	7.11	1,171	1,054	117
2008	6.71	6.96	1,177	1,086	91
2009	7.36	10.58	1,166	1,142	24
2010	7.47	9.19	1,142	1,097	45
2011	7.44	9.12	1,106	1,064	42

Source: Nikkei Economic Databank System (2011)

Table 7.2 Ratios of Unrecognized Obligations and Their Components to Total Liabilities

(%)

	Unrecognized Obligations / Total Liabilities	Unrecognized Past Service Cost / Total Liabilities	Unrecognized Actuarial Gains or Losses / Total Liabilities	Unrecognized Transitional Liability / Total Liabilities
2001	4.26	-0.20	2.32	2.12
2002	5.76	-0.40	4.41	1.76
2003	7.14	-0.40	6.15	1.39
2004	4.65	-0.61	4.20	1.06
2005	3.37	-0.93	3.45	0.85
2006	0.85	-0.85	0.97	0.73
2007	0.63	-0.65	0.66	0.62
2008	1.82	-0.86	2.25	0.43
2009	5.15	-0.60	5.34	0.41
2010	3.56	-0.71	3.94	0.33
2011	3.43	-0.61	3.79	0.26

Source: Nikkei Economic Databank System (2011)

proportion of defined benefit liability in total liabilities increases when unrecognized obligations are on the balance sheet. It also indicates the number of firms that would have underfunded and overfunded status under the new accounting standard. Most firms have always had underfunded pension plans. However, in 2006 and 2007, over 100 firms had overfunded status, owing to the high Japanese stock prices. As shown in Table 7.2, unrecognized actuarial gains or losses are a high proportion of total unrecognized obligations. They are affected by stock and bond prices, because they result from a difference between the actual rates and the estimated rates on plan assets and defined benefit obligations. Therefore, firms can have overfunded status when they manage their pension assets efficiently.

With regard to unrecognized past service cost, firms tend to decrease the benefits payable of their defined benefit plans, because most have underfunded status. Therefore, ratios of unrecognized past service cost to total liabilities indicate negative signs. With respect to unrecognized actuarial gains or losses, the proportion of unrecognized actuarial gains or losses in total unrecognized obligations is the highest. The ratio of unrecognized actuarial gains or losses to total liabilities has rapid swings, because the amount is affected by stock and bond prices which represent current economic conditions. Ratios of unrecognized transitional liabilities to total liabilities decrease every year. The

Table 7.3 Ratios of Unrecognized Obligations to Net Assets and Total Assets
(%)

	Unrecognized Obligations*60% / Net Assets	Unrecognized Obligations*40% / Total Assets
2001	9.98	1.06
2002	9.17	1.41
2003	10.07	1.66
2004	8.42	1.04
2005	4.99	0.76
2006	1.94	0.24
2007	1.40	0.19
2008	1.72	0.41
2009	3.59	0.96
2010	2.94	0.66
2011	3.04	0.65

Source: Nikkei Economic Databank System (2011)

Accounting Standard for Retirement Benefits was introduced in fiscal 2000. The amount recognized by the accounting change can be amortized as income or expense on a straight-line basis over less than 15 years. As explained in 5.2.5, most Japanese firms amortize their transitional liabilities in five years due to the one-time option in fiscal 2000 that gave firms the ability to recognize them as extraordinary loss if they are recognized within five years or less. Therefore, the ratio in 2001 is the highest, and it decreases every year.

Table 7.3 shows the effect of unrecognized obligations on net assets and total assets. As mentioned above, the amount of unrecognized obligations multiplied by the firm's tax rate (assumed to be 40%) is recognized as deferred tax assets in total assets, and the rest of the amount is recognized as accumulated other comprehensive income in net assets. Therefore, unrecognized obligations increase the amount of total assets, and reduce the amount of net assets.

Ratios of unrecognized obligations to net assets from 2001 to 2004 are relatively high, due to the accounting change in fiscal 2000 and the decline in Japanese stock prices. From 2004 to 2007, these ratios decrease because most firms had finished amortizing all of their transitional liabilities, and Japanese stock prices increased. The average ratios of unrecognized obligations to net assets range from 1 to 10%, whereas ratios of those obligations to total assets range within a span of only a few percentage points or less. This indicates that

Table 7.4 ROE

(%)

	ROE (Off-Balance-Sheet)	ROE (On-Balance-Sheet)
2001	1.14	1.45
2002	0.36	0.65
2003	2.83	3.56
2004	6.12	6.93
2005	6.47	9.22
2006	7.57	9.82
2007	5.61	5.70
2008	5.82	6.45
2009	1.99	2.01
2010	3.04	3.64
2011	5.21	5.33

Source: Nikkei Economic Databank System (2011)

Table 7.5 ROA

(%)

	ROA (Off-Balance-Sheet)	ROA (On-Balance-Sheet)
2001	5.58	5.54
2002	4.46	4.42
2003	5.08	5.01
2004	5.68	5.64
2005	6.35	6.33
2006	6.41	6.41
2007	6.63	6.63
2008	6.68	6.67
2009	4.23	4.21
2010	3.58	3.58
2011	5.60	5.59

Source: Nikkei Economic Databank System (2011)

Japanese firms tend to have low net assets compared with total assets, and the effect of unrecognized obligations to net assets is significant.

As Tables 7.2 and 7.3 reveal, unrecognized obligations have some effects on total liabilities, total assets, and net assets. It is expected that unrecognized obligations will have some substantial effects on financial ratios that are related to total assets, total liabilities, and net assets after these obligations are disclosed on the balance sheet under the new accounting standard. Tables 7.4, 7.5, 7.6, and 7.7 indicate the effect of unrecognized obligations on some financial ratios before and after unrecognized obligations are recognized on the balance sheet, including ROE, ROA, debt to asset, and debt to equity ratios. Table 7.4 shows the effect of unrecognized obligations on the balance sheet on ROE.

The ROE shows the firms' profitability. In this calculation of before and after recognition of unrecognized obligations on the balance sheet, since the amount of net income (the numerator) is the same and the amount of equity (the denominator) is decreased by unrecognized obligations, ratios after recognition should be higher than ratios before recognition. Therefore, Table 7.4 shows that all ratios after recognition are higher than ratios before recognition.

Table 7.5 shows the effect of unrecognized obligations on the balance sheet on ROA. ROA represents how efficiently a firm manages its assets to generate earnings. As explained above, the new accounting standard for retirement benefits makes no change to the profit and loss statement. Therefore, the numerator is the same, and only the denominator, total assets, is increased by unrecognized obligations. ROA after recognition of unrecognized obligations on the balance sheet should be lower than those before recognition. Table 7.5 indicates that most yearly ROA ratios after recognition are lower than those before recognition. However, there are some cases in which ROA before and after recognition are the same. That might be because the ratio of unrecognized obligations to total assets is quite low, as shown in Table 7.3.

Table 7.6 represents the effect of unrecognized obligations before and after the accounting change on the debt to asset ratio. The debt to asset ratio is used to describe a firm's capital structure. If the proportion of debt in assets is higher, the long-term solvency risk is greater.[110] It is preferable if the ratio is lower. When unrecognized obligations are recognized on the balance sheet, those obligations are added to the amount of both debt (liability) and assets. In this chapter, firms' tax rate is assumed to be 40%, and 40% of unrecognized obligations is added to the amount of assets and the total amount of those affects the amount of debt (liability). The effect of unrecognized obligations on

---

[110] Stickney, Clyde P., Paul R. Brown and James M. Wahlen, *Financial Reporting, Financial Statement Analysis, and Valuation: A Strategic Perspective*, Sixth Edition, Mason, OH: Thomson South-Western, 2006, p.297.

Table 7.6 Debt to Asset Ratio

(%)

	Debt to Asset Ratio (Off-Balance-Sheet)	Debt to Asset Ratio (On-Balance-Sheet)
2001	58.48	60.39
2002	56.03	58.49
2003	55.67	58.60
2004	54.33	56.12
2005	53.42	54.66
2006	51.83	52.13
2007	51.89	52.09
2008	50.60	51.08
2009	50.17	51.67
2010	49.23	50.18
2011	50.02	50.95

Source: Nikkei Economic Databank System (2011)

Table 7.7 Debt to Equity Ratio

(%)

	Debt to Equity Ratio (Off-Balance-Sheet)	Debt to Equity Ratio (On-Balance-Sheet)
2001	332.34	421.91
2002	253.34	292.65
2003	265.51	273.46
2004	211.30	269.50
2005	193.94	281.89
2006	170.00	182.63
2007	169.17	176.51
2008	156.63	162.68
2009	164.43	173.34
2010	154.16	160.86
2011	148.07	169.18

Source: Nikkei Economic Databank System (2011)

debt (liability) is greater than on assets. Therefore, all ratios after recognition are higher than those before recognition. Unrecognized obligations have an effect of one to three percentage points on these ratios.

With regard to the debt to equity ratio where unrecognized obligations are on or off balance sheet, as Tables 7.2 and 7.3 show, ratios of unrecognized obligations to total liabilities and net assets are high. Thus it can be predicted that the ratios when they are on balance sheet are much higher than when off balance sheet. This ratio sustained the most significant effect from this accounting standard change, because the numerator is increased, and the denominator is decreased by unrecognized obligations. The lower the debt to equity ratio, the better the management of capital, because it indicates the firm manages its own capital without any risk. This ratio is one of the most important financial ratios. Table 7.7 shows the effect of unrecognized obligations on and off balance sheet on the debt to equity ratio.

As mentioned above, the effect of unrecognized obligations on both debt and equity is significant. Especially notable is the fact that the difference in the ratio before and after recognition is greater in 2001 when the accounting standards were dramatically changed than in later years. When firms have defined benefit pension plans, they have to recognize the unfunded pension amount on the balance sheet. However, firms that have defined contribution pension plans have to recognize only the pension costs occurring in the year and do not have any unrecognized obligation. Therefore, if the effect of unrecognized obligations is too significant, firms might shift to defined contribution pension plans to eliminate the negative impact of unrecognized obligations on financial statements.

7.7 Summary and Conclusion

The new accounting standard, ASBJ Statement 26 will be applied from the end of annual periods beginning on or after April 1, 2013, and it requires firms to disclose unrecognized obligations that had been off balance sheet on the balance sheet. It is expected that this accounting change will provide more useful information for financial statement users, and make it easier to understand the accounting procedures for retirement benefits. Unrecognized obligations include unrecognized past service cost, unrecognized actuarial gains or losses, and unrecognized transitional liability. The impact of these obligations on total assets, total liabilities, and net assets will be significant.

The calculation of defined benefit liability needs many assumptions because pensions are provided to employees after their retirement. There is more complexity in the calculation than for liabilities affected by other standards. A defined benefit liability does not meet the definition and recognition of a liability, because it includes unvested benefit obligations and future salary increases.

With regard to unvested benefit obligations, employees have the right to receive their pension after their vesting is granted. Firms have no obligations until they provide vesting to their employees. Therefore, the obligations should not be recognized as a liability under the IFRS Conceptual Framework, because they are not present obligations. On the other hand, under the Japanese Conceptual Framework, unvested benefit obligations meet the definition of a liability, because the Framework does not require a liability to be a present obligation. However, the definition of a liability has much uncertainty, and the recognition might provide firms an opportunity to control incomes.

Nonetheless, unvested benefit obligations are recognized as a liability under both Japanese and IFRS Conceptual Frameworks, because they result from employees' service in the past. Under the definition of the IASB & FASB project, unvested benefit obligations are not recognized as a liability. However, as mentioned, it might be appropriate to recognize unvested benefit obligations given the probability that these obligations will be realized (because Japanese employees tend to work longer for their firms and there is a high possibility that unvested benefit obligations will be realized) in order to provide useful information on the amount, timing, and uncertainty of future cash flows.

As for future salary increases, they are related to future events, and are not probable to occur in the future due to the current economic situation. Recognizing these obligations as a liability would also require that employees perform additional work. Future salary increases do not meet any component stated under both Japanese and IFRS Conceptual Frameworks. It might be appropriate not to recognize them as a liability.

With regard to the effect of the accounting standard change in Japan, unrecognized obligations have significant effects on financial statements and financial ratios after they are placed on the balance sheet. The proportion of unrecognized actuarial gains or losses in the total amount of unrecognized obligations is quite high. Therefore, the amount of unrecognized obligations is affected by stock and bond prices, and fluctuates according to economic conditions. These obligations have some effects on total assets, total liabilities, and net assets under the new accounting standard. Specifically, the impact of these obligations on net assets is significant, because historically Japanese firms tend to have a lower proportion of net assets than those in other countries.

As for financial ratios including total assets, total liabilities, and net assets in their calculations, ROA, debt to asset ratio, and debt to equity ratio incurred a negative effect from the accounting standard change, and only ROE has incurred a positive effect. Most notably, the debt to equity ratio becomes much higher by the accounting standard change, which leads to increased liabilities and decreased net assets. From these results, it appears the new accounting standard which requires the recognition of unrecognized obligations on the balance sheet will have a significant negative effect on financial statements and financial ratios, because it adversely affects firms' capital structures.

Chapter 8
The Effect of Defined Benefit Liability on Firms' Valuations

8.1 Introduction

A new accounting standard for retirement benefits, ASBJ Statement 26, will be adopted from the end of annual periods beginning on or after April 1, 2013. The significant effect of this accounting standard change is to recognize unrecognized obligations on the face of the balance sheet, which previously had been disclosed only in footnotes. As explained in Chapter 7, unrecognized obligations will increase the amount of a defined benefit liability in total liabilities. The amount of these obligations multiplied by the firm's tax rate will be recognized as deferred tax assets in total assets, and the balance of these obligations will be subtracted from accumulated other comprehensive income in net assets. Unrecognized obligations consist of unrecognized past service cost, unrecognized actuarial gains or losses, and unrecognized transitional liability. The unrecognized actuarial gains or losses account for a large proportion of these obligations, and are affected by bond or stock prices. Therefore, it can be assumed that the unrecognized obligations will give more volatility in the amounts of total assets, total liabilities, and net assets under the new accounting standard.

As mentioned in Chapter 1, SAAJ states that investors and financial analysts generally consider the effect of unrecognized obligations in footnotes when they evaluate firms. If that is true, the recognition of these obligations on the balance sheet would not have a significant effect on stock prices. On the other hand, ASBJ has decided not to disclose these obligations on the balance sheet for non-consolidated financial statements, due to the negative impact on firms' financial statements and their valuations. In addition, Chapter 7 explained there are several prior research studies which examine the effect of the introduction of a new accounting standard, SFAS158, on firms' financial statements. Their results show that the recognition of a defined benefit liability on the balance sheet has a negative effect on firms' financial statements.

On and off balance sheet pension components consist of PBO, plan assets, a defined benefit liability, and unrecognized obligations. Only a defined benefit liability was on the balance sheet under the prior accounting standards. If all these components are recognized by investors and financial analysts, the introduction of the new accounting standard will not have a significant effect on stock prices. To examine the effect of these off balance sheet pension components under the prior accounting standards, multiple regression models and Vuong (1989) test are employed in this chapter.

8.2 Prior Research

There are several prior research studies that examine the effect of pension accounting components and stock prices in their analyses. Oldfield (1977) studies the impact on stock valuation of unfunded obligations. He employs the cross-section econometric model to investigate whether common stock values reflect the existence of defined benefit obligations. His results show that the unfunded vested obligation variable has been consistently negative, because firms can have a net tax advantage through defined benefit pension funding. Therefore, these unrecognized obligations influence the value of a firm's common stock.

Feldstein and Seligman (1981) study the effect of unfunded defined benefit obligations on stock prices. To examine the effect, they use data from about 200 manufacturing firms for 1976 and 1977. The data includes the replacement cost of plant, equipment, inventories, market value of corporate equity and debt, accounting earnings with depreciation, inventory gains adjusted for inflation, and the reported values of defined benefit liabilities and plan assets. They use a multiple regression model with this information and conclude that defined benefit liabilities reflect stock prices.

Feldstein and Morck (1983) use the same basic specifications as those used in Feldstein and Seligman (1981). Their analysis is based on data of large manufacturing firms for 1979. The sample of 132 manufacturing firms used a wide range of discount rates from 5.0 to 10.5%. Therefore, they examine whether the financial markets see the manipulation of defined benefit obligations and evaluate them. Their results show that market values of firms are related much more closely to defined benefit obligations evaluated at the average rate used by all of the firms. The financial markets appear to see through the manipulation of defined benefit obligations.

Barth et al. (1992) examine whether market participants implicitly assign different coefficients to defined benefit cost components when stock prices are determined. Their study suggests two findings. One is that the coefficients on the defined benefit cost components are generally different from each other. The coefficient on the unrecognized net obligations on accounting changes is lower than the other defined benefit pension coefficients, because information on obligations does not provide any incremental valuation-relevant information. The other finding is that the pension-related components generally have a larger impact on stock prices than non-pension components of income. Also, Barth et al. (1993) analyze the pension components. They mention that defined benefit cost components, except an unrecognized net obligation on accounting changes, are assigned earnings multiples. They also examine the relationship between balance sheet and profit and loss statement information and which data is needed to explain the market value of equity. Their results show that defined benefit pension balance sheet and profit and loss statement data are so correlated, and balance sheet information in addition to earnings data is important for understanding the structure of stock prices.

Coronado and Sharpe (2003) employ the residual income model advanced by Feltham and Ohlson (1995) to study whether corporate stock prices reflect the fair market value of plan assets and defined benefit liabilities from 1993 to 2001. In this model for analytical purposes, they divide corporate financial statements into two parts: core operations and financial operations related to outstanding defined benefit liabilities. Their results support their hypothesis that when investors make a decision, they recognize the importance of a corporate defined benefit pension plan to the firm value, in accordance with the associated stream of accounting earnings. Moreover, the authors consider whether the results they have obtained necessarily imply mispricing. They conclude that although there are some elements that might mislead investors in understanding financial statements, such as accounting earnings and costs associated with the pension plan, the market seems to have largely focused on these accruals. They also suggest that serious consideration should be given to defined benefit pension accounting.

Okumura (2005) studies the value relevance of net assets, defined benefit obligations, plan assets, defined benefit cost, unrecognized obligations, and others including after-tax ordinary income, growth rate of sales, research and development cost, and debt ratio. This study shows that, with the exception of the debt ratio, there is a relationship between these accounting items and a firm's total market value, and these coefficients have predictable signs. As for the debt ratio, it is generally thought that a firm's total market value is low when the debt ratio is high. However, during the research period, from 2001 to 2004, Japan had an unusually low interest rate for liabilities, and the leverage effect was significant. Therefore, the coefficient indicates an opposite sign.

The research studies cited above conclude that there is a relationship between pension accounting components, especially a defined benefit liability, and a firm's stock price. From a different standpoint, the following studies investigate the importance of the information for pension accounting in footnotes. Barth (1991) studies which measures of defined benefit obligations and plan assets most closely reflect investors' valuation for firms. The study employs cross-sectional regressions, and the model includes the market values of equity, the book values of total assets and liabilities other than pensions, and the alternative measures of defined benefit obligations (VBO, ABO, and PBO) and plan assets. It concludes that several measures of defined benefit obligations and plan assets are found to be significant for investors to evaluate firms; however, the ABO and the fair value of plan assets have less measurement errors than other measurements. Therefore, it suggests that investors consider pension information that is required in the footnotes to be more important than that on the face of the balance sheet. Choi et al. (1997) use an extension of the model employed by Barth (1991) and conclude the same result as she does.

On the other hand, there are several studies that lead to an opposite conclusion. Landsmand and Ohlson (1990) study whether the difference between defined benefit obligations and plan assets, i.e., a defined benefit liability including unrecognized obligations, are fully reflected in firms' stock prices during the period from 1979 to 1982. They conclude the defined benefit liability is relevant in a firm's stock price. However, investors and analysts appear to under-react to the accounting information contained in a defined benefit liability, due to the fact that excess returns are realized over several years.

Yano (2005) examines whether investors evaluate the actual conditions of plan assets and defined benefit obligations properly, because deferred recognition and the setting of the discount rate in accounting standards for retirement benefits make it difficult for investors to understand financial information. He develops a cross-section model employed by Feldstein and Morck (1983) and a residual income model used by Coronado and Sharpe (2003). He concludes that it seems investors cannot evaluate actual plan assets and defined benefit obligations, including unrecognized obligations, because defined benefit pension revenue that is not actual revenue is significant in this statistical analysis. Therefore, there is a possibility that investors overvalue firm stocks.

Picconi (2006) examines whether investors and analysts recognize all available pension information on financial statements to evaluate firms and make earnings forecast. The model includes the following components: the PBO, the firm's funded status (both the on balance sheet and off balance sheet liabilities), the expected return on plan assets, the discount rate, and the rate of future salary increases. These assumption rates are included because they are made at the discretion of a firm, and the return difference will be recognized as unrecognized actuarial gains or losses, which increase the amount of off balance sheet liabilities. The result shows that the PBO and the off balance sheet liabilities are predictive of future returns; however, on balance sheet liabilities are not significant. This means that investors do not take into account the full amount of information from defined benefit liabilities in prices and forecasts.

Under SFAS158, the FASB has already mandated disclosure of the difference between PBO and plan assets as a defined benefit liability. The accounting standard requires recognition of unrecognized obligations that had been shown in footnotes under the prior accounting standard, and reduces the off balance sheet amount of defined benefit plans. There are several studies on whether the accounting change affects firms' stock prices or their behavior. Mitra and Hossain (2009) employ several cross-sectional regression analyses to examine the relationship between the level and change in stock returns and the magnitude of pension transition adjustments in the first year of adoption of SFAS158, which requires the disclosure of unrecognized obligations on the balance sheet. Their results show that the coefficient of pension transition adjustments is negative and statistically significant. Their work suggests that capital markets evaluate firms with pension transition adjustments following SFAS158 negatively.

Houmes and Boylan (2010) find that firms tend to use higher discount rates to reduce the impact of the accounting change on the amount of their defined benefit liabilities after the enactment of SFAS158. Houmes et al. (2011) study how firms' stock prices will be affected by the accounting change. The period of the empirical research is in 2005, when the Securities and Exchange Commission called for the accounting change, and in 2006, when SFAS158 was mandated. The results show that firms with high financial risk have negative price returns, whereas firms with low financial risk have positive returns in both years. Therefore, the accounting change has an effect on firms' stock prices.

As these studies suggest, there is no consistent result when examining the relationship between a defined benefit liability and firms' stock prices. However, as shown in Chapter 7, it can be assumed that the impact of the new accounting standard, which requires recognition of unrecognized obligations on the balance sheet, on financial statements will be significant. If investors and analysts have not recognized unrecognized obligations under the accounting standards introduced in fiscal 2000, it can be predicted that the accounting change will have a significant effect on firms' stock prices. If they have already recognized these obligations in evaluating firms, the accounting change will not have a significant impact on firms' stock prices. Therefore, the following sections will investigate whether unrecognized obligations are reflected in firms' stock prices.

8.3 Hypothesis Development

Unrecognized obligations are expensed as a part of defined benefit cost when they are depreciated. Under the accounting standards introduced in fiscal 2000, these items, unrecognized past service cost, unrecognized actuarial gains or losses, and unrecognized transitional liability were treated as off balance sheet items. Therefore, they only could be recognized in footnotes before the depreciation. As mentioned in Chapter 1, investors and financial analysts might consider the effect of unrecognized obligations disclosed in footnotes when they evaluate firms. In that case, accounting information for retirement benefits including unrecognized obligations would have a stronger relationship with stock prices than information not including these obligations would have. Therefore, the following hypothesis is employed:

Hypothesis: Accounting information for retirement benefits including on and off balance sheet data reflects stock prices more precisely than only the on balance sheet information.

To develop this hypothesis, two models considering with and without the introduction of the new accounting standard should be employed. Comparing the results of these models, the impact of the new accounting standard would be explained. Under the prior accounting standards for retirement benefits, a defined benefit liability is recognized in total liabilities and defined benefit cost is disclosed as operating expense. In explaining the structure of stock prices, a model of Barth et al. (1993) is referenced:

$$MV_t = \alpha_0 + \alpha_1 ASTS_t + \alpha_2 LIAB_t + \alpha_3 PA_t + \alpha_4 PBO_t + \alpha_5 NIBP_t + \alpha_6 SVC_t + \alpha_7 INT_t + \alpha_8 RPA_t + \alpha_9 DEFRET_t + \alpha_{10} ATRANS_t + \varepsilon_t$$

They include non-pension and pension data on financial statements in the model to examine "what is the degree of redundancy between non-pension balance sheet data and non-pension earnings data." They explain that there is a relation between the balance sheet and the profit and loss statement data. With regard to pension components, plan assets are related to actual return on plan assets (RPA) and the deferred portion of the return on plan assets (DEFRET), and PBO are related to service cost (SVC) and interest cost (INT). Their study focuses on examining whether investors and financial analysts need both sets of data to set firm's stock prices. Therefore, defined benefit cost components are separated in their model.[111] On the other hand, this analysis examines the effect of the new accounting standard, ASBJ Statement 26, which does not affect the amount of defined benefit cost. It is not important to recognize each component related to the defined benefit cost. Therefore, the total amount of defined benefit cost is included in following cross-section models:

$$MVE_t = \alpha_0 + \alpha_1 ASTS_t + \alpha_2 (LIAB - DBL)_t + \alpha_3 (OPI + DBC)_t + \alpha_4 DBL_t + \alpha_5 DBC_t + \text{Year Dummies} + \varepsilon_t \qquad (1)$$

---

[111] However, their study concludes that defined benefit cost components are less important, once defined benefit pension balance sheet variables are included in the same model.

$$MVE_t = \alpha_0 + \alpha_1(NA + DBL)_t + \alpha_2(OPI + DBC)_t + \alpha_3 DBL_t + \alpha_4 DBC_t$$
$$+ \text{Year Dummies} + \varepsilon_t \qquad (2)$$

MVE: Market Value of Equity
ASTS: Total Assets
LIAB: Total Liabilities
NA: Net Assets
OPI: Operating Income
DBL: Defined Benefit Liability
DBC: Defined Benefit Cost

This model consists of non-pension and pension components on both the profit and loss statement and the balance sheet. MVE indicates market value of equity. Stock prices are average prices for the day firms disclosed their financial statements, because the research of Morse (1981) has shown that financial markets react most significantly on the day firms disclose their consolidated financial statements. Net assets are included in Model (2) instead of total assets and total liabilities, because there might be a strong correlation between total assets and total liabilities. As explained above, all defined benefit cost components are disclosed in operating expense under Japanese accounting standards. Therefore, operating income is included in these models, which represents firms' core businesses. The amounts of total liabilities, net assets, and operating income include the amount of a defined benefit liability or a defined benefit cost in their calculations. They are adjusted to separate the impact of these components to see whether they have a different effect on stock prices from other non-pension components. Each component is scaled by total sales. Kothari and Zimmerman (1995) explain that a price model, which examines a relationship between stock prices and earning per share, has a problem related to heteroscedasticity. They suggest using a suitable deflator to reduce the problem. Therefore, deflating variables by total sales would lead to less unbiased results.

Currently only a defined benefit liability is recognized on the balance sheet. PBO, plan assets, and unrecognized obligations, which are disclosed only in footnotes, are necessary to calculate the defined benefit liability. The defined benefit liability is a part of the PBO, and the amount of PBO is calculated with the following model:

PBO = PA + DBL + TUO

To avoid the effect of multicollinearity, PBO is not included in a model. If all other items including plan assets, a defined benefit liability, and total unrecognized obligations are recognized by investors and financial analysts, the amount of PBO is also recognized by them. Therefore, the following cross-section models are employed to explain how non-pension and pension components on and off balance sheet affect firm's stock prices:

$$MVE_t = \beta_0 + \beta_1 ASTS_t + \beta_2(LIAB - DBL)_t + \beta_3(OPI + DBC)_t \\ + \beta_4 DBL_t + \beta_5 DBC_t + \beta_6 PA_t + \beta_7 TUO_t + \text{Year Dummies} \\ + \varepsilon_t \qquad (3)$$

$$MVE_t = \beta_0 + \beta_1(NA + DBL)_t + \beta_2(OPI + DBC)_t + \beta_3 DBL_t + \beta_4 DBC_t \\ + \beta_5 PA_t + \beta_6 TUO_t + \text{Year Dummies} + \varepsilon_t \qquad (4)$$

PA: Plan Assets
TUO: Total Unrecognized Obligations

If the result shows that Model (3) or (4) explains stock prices more precisely than Model (1) or (2), off balance sheet pension components provide useful information to investors and financial analysts when they evaluate firms.

This research also adopts the Vuong (1989) test to reveal whether the adoption of the new accounting standard for retirement benefits would provide additional information to investors. Vuong (1989) states that "this approach is based on testing if the competing models are as close to the true distribution against the hypothesis that one model is closer than the other." The accounting information can be proved useful if it has information content, which consists of relative information content and incremental information content. Relative information content examines what accounting information has more information than others. With regard to incremental information content, it evaluates whether given information content X or Z provides any additional information to the other.[112]

Vuong (1989) mentions that a pair of competing models are categorized into non-nested, overlapping, or nested model. The non-nested model examines two competing models which include no common explanatory variable. The overlapping model examines two competing models which have some common and inherent explanatory variables. These models are useful to test the relative content information. As for the nested model, a model consists of all explanatory variables in the other. The nested model determines if there is any additional information in a model to the other. Therefore, it is adopted to examine the relative information content.[113] In this research, plan assets and total unrecognized obligations in Model (3) and (4) are added to Model (1) and (2). These pairs of competing models are deemed to the nested model. The Vuong (1989) test for the nested model is also employed to examine whether there is any difference in determination coefficients between the Model (1) and (3), and the Model (2) and (4).

8.4 Research Design

This empirical analysis is based on 10 years of annual report. The time period of this study is from 2002 through the latest year, 2011, for which data are available. Year 2001, the year Accounting Standard for Retirement Benefits was required, is excluded, owing to the impact from changes in accounting standards for employee benefits and financial instruments on firms' stock prices in the year.

Firms which are treated in this research design (excluding banks and insurance firms) are listed on the first section of the Tokyo Stock Exchange within the 12-month fiscal years ending in March from 2002 to 2011 after accounting standards for retirement benefits had been changed. Firms were selected which set both discount rates and expected rates of return for accounting standards for retirement benefits, and disclose plan assets on financial statements. The total sample number selected for this empirical research is 9,128 firms. Financial data used in this study were collected from Nikkei Economic Electronic Databank System (2011) which is provided by the

---

[112] Ota, Koji and Akihiko Matsuo, "The Vuong (1989) Test and Its Application," *The Journal of Musashi University*, Vol.52 No.1, July 2004, pp.50, 51.
[113] *Ibid.*, pp.46-48, 57, 58.

Table 8.1 Number of Sample Firms Selected

	2002	2003	2004	2005	2006	2007	2008	2009	2010	2011	Total
Firms Listed on the First Section of the Tokyo Stock Exchange	1,418	1,447	1,461	1,479	1,494	1,502	1,511	1,522	1,527	1,535	14,896
Excluding Firms:											
with Fiscal Years Ending in Months Other Than March	315	320	322	325	328	329	333	336	336	337	3,281
with Less-Than-12-Month Accounting Periods	9	5	7	9	2	0	0	1	2	2	37
without Plan Assets	97	112	119	132	143	152	155	162	170	189	1,431
not Disclosing Discount Rates	43	45	41	36	40	38	37	33	33	32	378
not Disclosing Expected Rates of Return	24	48	79	81	70	57	58	65	82	77	641
Total	930	917	893	896	911	926	928	925	904	898	9,128

Table 8.2 Descriptive Statistics from 2002 to 2011

	MVE	ASTS	LIAB	NA	OPI	DBL	DBC	PA	TUO
Mean	0.646	1.151	0.558	0.594	0.065	0.038	0.012	0.075	0.023
Median	0.455	1.058	0.456	0.508	0.057	0.027	0.010	0.057	0.012
Min	0.009	0.150	0.079	-1.116	-0.619	-0.191	-0.072	0.000	-0.127
Max	9.397	11.576	10.206	6.005	0.617	0.621	0.210	0.633	0.340
Std. Dev.	0.689	0.578	0.418	0.425	0.058	0.045	0.012	0.068	0.037

MVE = market value of equity, ASTS = total assets, LIAB = total liabilities, NA = net assets, OPI = operating income, DBL = defined benefit liability, DBC = defined benefit cost, PA = plan assets, TUO = total unrecognized obligations; all variables are deflated by total sales

Nikkei Digital Media, Inc., and stock prices were obtained from Stock Chart CD-ROM (2011) which is provided by the Toyo Keizai Inc.

Table 8.2 shows the descriptive statistics from 2002 to 2011 for all models. The correlation coefficients for the variables for Model (1) and (3) are shown in Table 8.3. The table and Figure 8.1 indicate that there is a strong relationship between total assets and total liabilities. To examine the effect of multicollinearity, Model (2) and (4) are employed. Pension components are related each other. The more defined benefit liabilities or total unrecognized obligations firms disclose, the more defined benefit cost they recognize.

The result of the regression analysis on the effect of non-pension and pension components including total assets and total liabilities on stock prices is

Table 8.3 Correlation including ASTS and LIAB

	MVE	ASTS	LIAB	OPI	DBL	DBC	PA	TUO
MVE	1.000							
ASTS	0.499	1.000						
LIAB	0.017	0.679	1.000					
OPI	0.592	0.326	0.049	1.000				
DBL	0.007	0.217	0.134	0.035	1.000			
DBC	0.039	0.199	0.128	0.112	0.397	1.000		
PA	0.177	0.227	0.048	0.129	0.195	0.410	1.000	
TUO	-0.111	0.057	0.130	-0.036	0.242	0.517	0.380	1.000

MVE = market value of equity, ASTS = total assets, LIAB = total liabilities, OPI = operating income, DBL = defined benefit liabillity, DBC = defined benefit cost, PA = plan assets, TUO =total unrecognized obligations; all variables are deflated by total sales

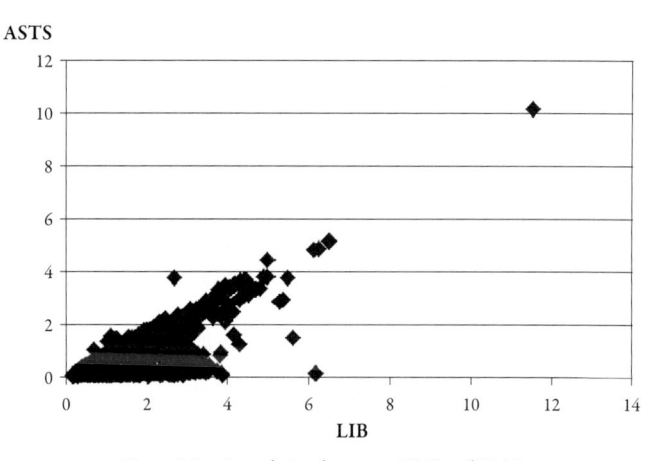

Figure 8.1 Correlation between ASTS and LIAB

in Table 8.4.

It reveals that there is a positive relationship between stock prices and total assets, operating income, and plan assets, and a negative relationship between stock prices and total liabilities, a defined benefit liability, a defined benefit cost, and total unrecognized obligations as expected. These effects of non-pension and pension components on the profit and loss statement or the balance sheet are significant at the 0.1% level, and those for the off balance sheet pension components are significant at the 5% level. All year dummies are significant at 0.1% level in Model (1) and (3). These results for Model (1)

Table 8.4 The Effect of ASTS, LIAB, OPI and Pension Components on Stock Prices

Variables	Expected Signs	Model (1) On-Balance-Sheet	Model (3) On and Off-Balance-Sheet
Intercept		-0.28	-0.28
ASTS	+	0.87	0.86
		(71.83)***	(68.36)***
LIAB	−	-0.79	-0.78
		(-51.00)***	(-48.91)***
OPI	+	4.45	4.44
		(50.40)***	(50.32)***
DBL	−	-1.29	-1.28
		(-11.51)***	(-11.42)***
DBC	−	-2.70	-2.63
		(-6.15)***	(-5.22)***
PA	+		0.19
			(2.42)*
TUO	−		-0.36
			(-2.17)*
Adjusted R^2		0.600	0.600
Vuong Test			8.101*
N			9,128

MVE = market value of equity, ASTS = total assets, LIAB = total liabilities, OPI = operating income, DBL = defined benefit liability, DBC = defined benefit cost, PA = plan assets, TUO = total unrecognized obligations; all variables are deflated by total sales; ***, **, *, †indicate statistical significance at 0.1, 1, 5, 10% levels respectively.

and (3) indicate that investors and financial analysts recognize and consider pension components on financial statements to evaluate and set firm's stock prices. Recognizing both total unrecognized obligations and a defined benefit cost implies that they also take account of a firm's depreciation method for past service cost, actuarial gains and losses, and a transitional liability. As for plan assets, a firm's funding status was a big issue when Accounting Standard for Retirement Benefits was introduced in fiscal 2000. Furthermore, as mentioned in Chapter 3, Japan has a problem on requirements of vesting. There have been some cases where firms reduce or do not pay their employees' retirement benefits when they go bankrupt or their financial condition grows worse. Therefore, plan assets can be an important factor in knowing a firm's financial and management conditions.

Comparing Model (1) with Model (3), their adjusted R-squares are not different. This is because the off balance sheet independent variables, i.e., plan assets and total unrecognized obligations, have less effect on stock prices than other independent variables. The following models explain the effect of each non-pension and pension component on stock prices:

$$MVE_t = \alpha_0 + \alpha_1 ASTS_t + \alpha_2 (LIAB - DBL)_t + \alpha_3 (OPI + DBC)_t + \alpha_4 DBL_t$$
$$\quad\quad (1.002) \quad\quad (-0.440) \quad\quad\quad (0.291) \quad\quad (-0.049)$$
$$+ \alpha_5 DBC_t + \text{Year Dummies} + \varepsilon_t$$
$$(-0.032) \quad\quad\quad\quad\quad\quad\quad\quad\quad\quad\quad\quad\quad\quad (1)$$

$$MVE_t = \beta_0 + \beta_1 ASTS_t + \beta_2 (LIAB - DBL)_t + \beta_3 (OPI + DBC)_t + \beta_4 DBL_t$$
$$\quad\quad (0.990) \quad\quad (-0.435) \quad\quad\quad (0.290) \quad\quad (-0.049)$$
$$+ \beta_5 DBC_t + \beta_6 PA_t + \beta_7 TUO_t + \text{Year Dummies} + \varepsilon_t$$
$$(-0.031) \quad (0.014) \quad (-0.008) \quad\quad\quad\quad\quad\quad\quad\quad (3)$$

With regard to the Vuong (1989) test, the result shows that LR statistic is significant at 5% level. Therefore, it indicates Model (3) provides more additional information to investors and financial analysts than Model (1). These results from the multiple regression analysis and the Vuong (1989) test indicate that off balance sheet pension components, i.e., plan assets and unrecognized obligations, are recognized by investors and financial analysts. However, the effect of these components on stock prices is less than other non-pension and pension components on the profit and loss statement or the balance sheet. After the new accounting standard is introduced in fiscal 2013, unrecognized obligations will increase the amount of defined benefit liability, and a part of them will reduce the amount of accumulated other comprehensive income. Therefore, the effect of unrecognized obligations on stock prices will be stronger than under the prior accounting standards.

The correlation coefficients for the variables for Model (2) and (4) are shown in Table 8.5. As mentioned above, pension components are related, because calculations for these components are linked. However, the relationship is not strong enough to lead to a problem of multicollinearity. Firms with high net assets tend to have higher operating income.

Table 8.6 shows that net assets have a positive effect on stock prices as expected. These effects of non-pension and pension components on the profit and loss statement and the balance sheet are significant at 0.1% level, and of the

Table 8.5 Correlation including NA

	MVE	NA	OPI	DBL	DBC	PA	TUO
MVE	1.000						
NA	0.662	1.000					
OPI	0.592	0.395	1.000				
DBL	0.007	0.164	0.035	1.000			
DBC	0.039	0.144	0.112	0.397	1.000		
PA	0.177	0.261	0.129	0.195	0.410	1.000	
TUO	-0.111	-0.050	-0.036	0.242	0.517	0.380	1.000

MVE = market value of equity, NA = net assets, OPI = operating income, DBL = defined benefit liability, DBC = defined benefit cost, PA = plan assets, TUO = total unrecognized obligations; all variables are deflated by total sales

Table 8.6 The Effect of NA, OPI and Pension Components on Stock Prices

Variables	Expected Signs	Model (2) On-Balance-Sheet	Model (4) On and Off-Balance-Sheet
Intercept		-0.24	-0.24
NA	+	0.86	0.85
		(71.32)***	(67.82)***
OPI	+	4.50	4.49
		(51.02)***	(50.97)***
DBL	−	-1.21	-1.20
		(-10.82)***	(-10.74)***
DBC	−	-2.49	-2.50
		(-5.67)***	(-4.94)***
PA	+		0.19
			(2.39)*
TUO	−		-0.30
			(-1.80)†
Adjusted R^2		0.598	0.598
Vuong Test			6.942*
N			9,128

MVE = market value of equity, NA = net assets, OPI = operating income, DBL = defined benefit liability, DBC = defined benefit cost, PA = plan assets, TUO = total unrecognized obligations; all variables are deflated by total sales; ***, **, *, †indicate statistical significance at 0.1, 1, 5, 10% levels respectively.

off balance sheet pension components are significant at 5 or 10% level. All year dummies are significant at 0.1% level in Model (2) and (4). The result in Table 8.6 does not show any significant difference from that in Table 8.4. Therefore, there is no effect of multicollinearity in Model (1) and (3).

These models also indicate the same adjusted R-squares, 0.598. The following models explain the effect of each non-pension and pension component on stock prices:

$$MVE_t = \alpha_0 + \alpha_1(NA+DBL)_t + \alpha_2(OPI+DBC)_t + \alpha_3 DBL_t + \alpha_4 DBC_t$$
$$(0.511)(0.293)(-0.046)(-0.030)$$
$$+\text{ Year Dummies} + \varepsilon_t \tag{2}$$

$$MVE_t = \beta_0 + \beta_1(NA+DBL)_t + \beta_2(OPI+DBC)_t + \beta_3 DBL_t + \beta_4 DBC_t$$
$$(0.505)(0.292)(-0.046)(-0.030)$$
$$+ \beta_5 PA_t + \beta_6 TUO_t + \text{Year Dummies} + \varepsilon_t \tag{4}$$
$$(0.014)(-0.007)$$

The result also suggests that the effect of off balance sheet pension components on stock prices are less than that of other non-pension and pension components on the profit and loss statement or the balance sheet. As explained above, unrecognized obligations will increase a defined benefit liability, and a part of them will decrease other accumulated comprehensive income which is included in net assets under the new accounting standard. The coefficients on net assets and a defined benefit liability are greater than those on unrecognized obligations. It can be assumed that the effect of unrecognized obligations on stock prices will be stronger than calculated under the prior accounting standards introduced in fiscal 2000 once they are on the balance sheet.

8.5 Summary and Conclusion

The SAAJ states that unrecognized obligations are considered by investors and financial analysts to set firms' stock prices. There are also several research studies that indicate unrecognized obligations in footnotes on financial statements affect firms' stock prices when investors and financial analysts evaluate firms. The ASBJ has now decided to require firms to disclose these obligations on the balance sheet. The FASB has already required firms to disclose the difference between PBO and plan assets as a defined benefit liability. Some firms have closed or frozen their defined benefit plans due to the significant impact of the accounting change on their financial statements. Therefore, deferred recognition might have allowed firms to reduce the volatility on their financial statements.

The results of this empirical research show that all non-pension and pension components on financial statements have an effect on firms' stock prices. Unrecognized obligations in footnotes are also recognized by investors and financial analysts, and models including off balance sheet pension components improve the value relevance of stock prices more than without these components. However, the coefficients for off balance sheet pension components are less than non-pension and pension components on the profit and loss statement or the balance sheet. Under the new accounting standard, the amount of unrecognized obligations is added to a defined benefit liability in total liabilities. The amount of these obligations multiplied by the firm's tax rate is recognized as deferred tax assets in total assets, and the rest of the obligations is recognized as accumulated other comprehensive income in net assets. It is expected that the effect of these obligations on stock prices could be stronger than under the prior accounting standards after they are on the balance sheet.

The new accounting standard, ASBJ Statement 26, will have an effect on the relationship among total assets, total liabilities, and net assets. The effect on total liabilities and net assets are especially significant. The debt to equity ratio is one of the most important financial ratios for revealing firms' leverage and capital risk. Unrecognized obligations on the balance sheet might have some negative impacts on firms' capital structure after the new accounting standard is adopted. In addition, these obligations are affected by social conditions or the economic environment firms are in, and bring some volatility to firms' financial conditions. Unrecognized obligations in footnotes are recognized by investors and financial analysts; however, recognizing them on the balance sheet would have a stronger negative effect on firms' stock prices, due to the change in the balance among total assets, total liabilities, and net assets. After SFAS158 was introduced in the U.S. in 2006, many firms have frozen or closed their defined benefit plans because of the significant negative impact on their financial statements. Therefore, there is a possibility that firms with a huge amount of unrecognized obligations might do the same with consideration of the change in the balance of their capital structure.

Chapter 9
Discussion and Summary

This book examined the effect of unrecognized obligations (unrecognized past service cost, unrecognized actuarial gains or losses, and unrecognized transitional liability) arising from firms' retirement benefits on firms' financial statements and their valuations, and predicted the impact of the introduction of the new accounting standard, ASBJ Statement 26. Under the prior accounting standards, deferred recognition and off balance sheet pension items had made financial statements difficult for users to understand the measurement and recognition of defined benefit pension components. As noted in Chapter 1, the SAAJ states that financial analysts have taken into account unrecognized obligations in footnotes when they evaluate firms; however, they have been required to perform additional work to include these obligations as if they were on the balance sheet. On the other hand, the ASBJ has decided not to adopt recognition of these obligations on the balance sheet for non-consolidated financial statements due to the significant negative effect on firms' reported results. The Board suggests that if unrecognized obligations are recognized on the balance sheet for non-consolidated statements, procedures should be introduced to reduce the fluctuation in results caused by the accounting change. In addition, as prior research studies indicated, the recognition of unrecognized obligations on the balance sheet for consolidated financial statements had a significant negative impact on firms' financial statements and their valuations when SFAS158 was introduced in the U.S. in 2006. Several firms adopting SFAS158 have already frozen or terminated their defined benefit plans. It can be assumed that Japanese firms also will experience a negative effect on their financial statements and their valuations after the accounting change.

Therefore, there are two questions which should be considered: (1) whether the SAAJ is correct in its assessment that unrecognized obligations have been taken into account by investors and financial analysts under the prior accounting standards, and (2) whether disclosing such defined benefit pension components on the balance sheet as opposed to off balance sheet will have any significant effect on firms' valuations.

Defined benefit pension components consist of defined benefit obligations, plan assets, defined benefit liability, and defined benefit cost. Under the new accounting standard, the defined benefit liability is calculated by subtracting plan assets from defined benefit obligations. Japanese accounting standards continue to adopt deferred recognition. Unrecognized obligations incurred for the period are recognized as past service cost, actuarial gains and losses, and a transitional liability which are a part of defined benefit cost.

To answer the questions stated above, it is important to understand the measurement and recognition of each component, and clarify related problems in these components. Therefore, Chapter 2 provided background on the Japanese pension system as a basis for understanding the treatment of this area under Japanese accounting standards. Chapters 3, 4, 5, 6, and 7 described each defined benefit pension component, including defined benefit obligations, plan assets, defined benefit liability, and defined benefit cost. Chapter 8 examined the effect of unrecognized obligations on firms' valuations under the prior accounting standards. The summary and conclusion of each chapter from Chapters 2 to 8 is as follows.

Chapter 2 described the development of retirement lump sum grants and corporate pension plans in Japan, and these structures. Japanese retirement benefits began with lump sum grants with the purpose of harmonious labor relations, which have a feature of merit reward, specifically for longevity at the firm. This feature still exists in current retirement benefit systems, and affects accounting standards for retirement benefits. There were three corporate defined benefit pension plans, including employees' pension fund, defined-benefit corporate pension, and tax-qualified pension plan. However, the tax-qualified pension plan was abolished in March 2012. Under this plan, vesting was not defined clearly, and there were some cases where firms reduced or did not make payments for their employees' pensions when they had gone bankrupt or their financial condition became worse. Employees' pension fund and defined-benefit corporate pension still have some problems pertaining to requirements for vesting. Pension payments are not guaranteed to employees with certainty. This situation also affects the content and implementation of the accounting standards for retirement benefits in Japan.

Chapter 3 explained how to measure defined benefit obligations at a future date. The concept of PBO as currently adopted has two problems in the benefit formula: (1) the recognition of unvested benefits as a liability, and (2) the consideration of future salary increases in the projected unit credit method. Regarding unvested benefits, Japanese corporate defined benefit pension plans do not state requirements of vesting clearly, as noted above. Vesting is not defined as a nonforfeitable right, and the grant date of vesting is set depending on each firm. Under these conditions, it is difficult to assess the recognition of unvested benefits before incorporating the grant date of vesting in each firm. In reference to ERISA, if the vesting is granted five to seven years after employees' hire date, there is a high possibility that unvested benefit obligations would be realized in Japan. Therefore, the probability that these obligations will be realized in each firm can be considered to calculate defined benefit obligations, which would provide more useful information about the amounts, timing, and uncertainty of cash flows. As for future salary increases, they represent the difference between PBO and ABO. In most research, they are recognized as liabilities of the firm by investors. However, conceptually, they should not be included as a liability, because they do not arise from past events. These amounts of PBO and ABO can be equal at the employees' retirement date. Therefore, adopting PBO smoothes the periodic service cost to reduce volatility. On the other hand, ABO reduces the uncertainty in the calculation of defined benefit obligations. Greater consistency with other accounting standards would be achieved by recognizing only liabilities resulting from past events.

Chapter 4 explained how actuarial assumptions are determined under the Japanese accounting standards for retirement benefits, and discussed whether other financial factors affect the determination of actuarial assumptions. There are several assumptions made to calculate defined benefit obligations, because the obligations occur at some future date. Changing these assumptions has a significant effect on the amount of these obligations. Several prior studies prove that firms' managers change their discount rates or expected rates of return on plan assets for earnings management. This chapter revealed how Japanese firms changed their discount rates and expected rates of return from 2001 to 2011. Most Japanese firms tended to change these assumptions depending on the economic circumstances they were in. Especially after 2007, when a world economic slump started, the number of firms reducing their assumptions increased. Therefore, changing actuarial assumptions is just a way to avoid a problem for firms which have a significant amount of pension deficits; ultimately, it cannot be a solution.

Chapter 5 clarified the difference between Japanese accounting standards for retirement benefits and IAS19 on the disclosure for defined benefit cost components. The defined benefit cost components consist of current service cost, interest cost, past service cost, actuarial gains and losses, transitional liability, and the expected return on plan assets. Under Japanese accounting standards, these components are recognized as a single item, i.e., defined benefit cost, in profit or loss. Deferred recognition is adopted for past service cost, actuarial gains and losses, and transitional liability. On the other hand, IAS19 categorizes these components into service cost, net interest on the net defined benefit liability, and remeasurements of the net defined benefit liability due to their characteristics. Actuarial gains and losses and return on plan assets are included in remeasurements, and recognized in other comprehensive income. Other components are disclosed in profit or loss. All components are recognized immediately. These differences in accounting procedures between Japanese accounting standards and IAS19 would be affected by different income measurement approaches, and concepts of incomes. IFRS is basically founded on an asset-liability approach. The immediate recognition of all components is based on an approach which reflects the change of fair value in profit or loss, or other comprehensive income. On the other hand, under Japanese accounting standards, deferred recognition and the recognition of all pension components in profit or loss are based on the revenue-expense approach. Profit or loss is an important measurement for investors and financial analysts to estimate future stock prices and dividends. Therefore, both Japanese accounting standards and IAS19 might reduce the volatility in profit or loss from some defined benefit cost components, especially actuarial gains and losses, by adopting deferred recognition or recognizing them in other comprehensive income.

Chapter 6 explained requirements and measurement of plan assets, accounting procedures for retirement benefit trusts, and a net approach for the recognition of a defined benefit liability. To recognize assets as plan assets, the assets must be solely for the purpose of retirement benefits, and separated from the accounts of the firm's employer or creditors. These requirements are set because retirement benefits have an important social function in stabilizing employees' livelihoods after their retirement. As for the net approach for the recognition of a defined benefit liability, Corporate Accounting Principles require firms to disclose assets, liabilities, and net assets on their financial statements based on a gross approach. However, they allow firms to adopt a net approach for accounting standards for retirement benefits. As explained above, there are some requirements to recognize assets as plan assets, and plan assets have different characteristics from other assets. Therefore, it would be thought that recognizing plan assets in total assets might mislead financial statement users.

Chapter 7 discussed whether the defined benefit liability meets the definition of a liability to consider whether it is appropriate to recognize it on the balance sheet. The chapter also explained the difference between prior accounting standards and the new accounting standard, ASBJ Statement 26, and revealed the effect of the new accounting standard on financial statements and some financial ratios. Under the Japanese Conceptual Framework, a liability is defined as an obligation arising from past events, and a probable future outflow of economic resources. However, it is not required to be a present obligation in terms of a revenue-expense approach. As explained in Chapter 3, there are two issues concerning the recognition of a defined benefit liability, namely, the recognition of unvested benefits as a liability and the consideration of future salary increases in the projected unit credit method. With regard to unvested benefits, under the IFRS Conceptual Framework, a liability has to be a present obligation; therefore, the unvested benefit obligations which are related to a future event should not be recognized as a liability. However, under the Japanese Conceptual Framework, unvested benefit obligations can be recognized as a liability if they are likely to occur in the future. As for future salary increases, they do not meet any component in the definition of a liability stated under both Japanese and IFRS Conceptual Frameworks. It would be appropriate to recognize only liabilities resulting from past events due to the consistency with other accounting standards. Therefore, the defined benefit liability does not meet the definition of a liability. The new accounting standard, ASBJ Statement 26, requires firms to disclose unrecognized obligations on the balance sheet, which were in the footnotes under the prior accounting standards. This accounting change will have an effect on the amount of total assets, total liabilities, and net assets. This chapter clarified that the recognition of unrecognized obligations on the balance sheet would have a significant effect on financial statements, and financial ratios including ROE, debt to asset ratio, and debt to equity ratio.

Chapter 8 discussed the empirical research performed to examine the effect of the new accounting standard, ASBJ Statement 26, on firms' valuations. The research employed two cross-section models: (1) a model consisting of non-pension and pension components on the balance sheet, and (2) a model consisting of non-pension and pension components on and off balance sheet. The Vuong (1989) test was also adopted to predict whether the adoption of the new accounting standard would provide additional information to investors. The result of cross-section models indicated that non-pension and pension components both on and off balance sheet were recognized by investors and financial analysts. However, their adjusted R-squares were not different, because the off balance sheet independent variables (i.e., plan assets and total unrecognized obligations) had less effect on stock prices than other independent variables. As for the Vuong (1989) test, the result showed that a model including non-pension and pension components on and off balance sheet provided more additional information to investors and financial analysts than a model including only on balance sheet components. These results showed that all non-pension and pension components on financial statements had an effect on firms' stock prices. However, the off balance sheet pension components had less effect on stock prices. Unrecognized obligations would be recognized on the balance sheet after the new accounting standard is introduced. Therefore, it is expected that the effect of these obligations on stock prices could be stronger than under the prior accounting standards.

Through these chapters, we found answers for two questions cited above. First, unrecognized obligations have been taken into account by investors and financial analysts under the prior accounting standards as the SAAJ suggested. The empirical research in Chapter 8 revealed that the effects of unrecognized obligations on stock prices were negative and significant, and investors and financial analysts considered the off balance sheet defined benefit pension components to evaluate and set firms' stock prices. However, the effect of the off balance sheet defined benefit pension components including unrecognized obligations and plan assets on stock prices was less than that of those on the balance sheet. Therefore, it can be predicted that disclosing defined benefit pension components on the balance sheet as opposed to off balance sheet will have a significant effect on firms' valuations after the introduction of ASBJ Statement 26.

There are several topics which should be considered for further research. In Chapter 3, it was mentioned that IASB suggests using alternative measurement methods to calculate defined benefit obligations, including projected benefit, accumulated benefit, fair value, and settlement value, because the method currently adopted in IAS19 is fundamentally different from the measurement models in other accounting standards. Chapter 3 treated two problems on the recognition of defined benefit obligations related to future events under the current benefit formula. Therefore, it would be useful to examine other benefit formulas, and consider which represents more precisely the amount of present obligations firms have, and is consistent with other accounting standards. Chapter 4 explained that Japanese firms tended to change their discount rates or expected rates of return on plan assets due to the economic circumstances they were in. However, there were still several firms increasing these rates, even though yields of government bonds or average actual rate of return decreased. There is a possibility that some firms might increase these rates to manage their earnings. Therefore, it may be useful to perform empirical research to examine this issue further. In Chapter 8, the empirical research used only financial statement data prior to the new accounting standard being introduced. It would be more useful to examine the data after unrecognized obligations are on the balance sheet under the new accounting standard. In addition, the effect of unrecognized obligations on net assets is more than simply that on total assets and total liabilities. It may be useful to perform empirical research focusing on the effect of unrecognized obligations on the structure of net assets.

The introduction of the new accounting standard, ASBJ Statement 26, will have an effect on firms' financial statements and their stock prices, because it will change the proportion of total assets, total liabilities, and net assets. Further study is necessary to see the actual impact of the new accounting standard on firms' financial statements, their stock prices, and firms' behavior on their defined benefit pension plans.

References

(Literature)

Accounting Standards Board, Financial Reporting Standard No.17: *Retirement Benefits,* UK: ASB, November 2000.

Accounting Standards Board of Japan, Application Guideline for Accounting Standards No.1: *Accounting Procedure for Transition Between Retirement Benefit Plans,* Tokyo: ASBJ, January 2002.

Accounting Standards Board of Japan, Discussion Paper: *Conceptual Framework for Financial Accounting,* Tokyo: ASBJ, December 2006.

Accounting Standards Board of Japan, ASBJ Statement No.14: *Amendments to Accounting Standard for Retirement Benefits (Part 2),* Tokyo: ASBJ, May 2007.

Accounting Standards Board of Japan, ASBJ Statement No.10: *Accounting Standard for Financial Instruments,* Tokyo: ASBJ, March 2008.

Accounting Standards Board of Japan, ASBJ Statement No.3: *Amendments to Accounting Standard for Retirement Benefits,* Tokyo: ASBJ, July 2008.

Accounting Standards Board of Japan, ASBJ Statement No.19: *Amendments to Accounting Standard for Retirement Benefits (Part 3),* Tokyo: ASBJ, July 2008.

Accounting Standards Board of Japan, *Issues on Accounting Standards for Retirement Benefits,* Tokyo: ASBJ, January 2009.

Accounting Standards Board of Japan, Exposure Draft of Guidance No.35: *Exposure Draft of Implementation Guidance on Accounting Standard for Retirement Benefits,* Tokyo: ASBJ, March 2010.

Accounting Standards Board of Japan, Exposure Draft of Statement No.39: *Exposure Draft of Accounting Standard for Retirement Benefits,* Tokyo: ASBJ, March 2010.

Accounting Standards Board of Japan, ASBJ Guidance No.25: *Guidance on Accounting Standard for Retirement Benefits,* Tokyo: ASBJ, May 2012.

Accounting Standards Board of Japan, ASBJ Statement No.26: *Accounting Standard for Retirement Benefits,* Tokyo: ASBJ, May 2012.

Amir, Eli and Shlomo Benartzi, "The Expected Rate of Return on Pension Funds and Asset Allocation as Predictors of Portfolio Performance," *The Accounting Review*, Vol.73 No.3, July 1998, pp.335-352.

Apostolou, Barbara and Nicholas G. Apostolou, "Recent Developments in Pension Accounting," *The CPA Journal*, Vol.79 No.11, November 2009, pp.46-50.

Asthana, Sharad, "Determinants of Funding Strategies and Actuarial Choices for Defined-Benefit Pension Plans," *Contemporary Accounting Research*, Vol.16 No.1, Spring 1999, pp.39-74.

Bader, Lawrence N., "Treatment of Pension Plans in a Corporate Valuation," *Financial Analysts Journal*, Vol.59 No.3, May/June 2003, pp.19-24.

Barth, Mary E., "Relative Measurement Errors Among Alternative Pension Asset and Liability Measures," *The Accounting Review*, Vol.66 No.3, July 1991, pp.433-463.

Barth, Mary E., William H. Beaver and Wayne R. Landsman, "The Market Valuation Implications of Net Periodic Pension Cost Components," *Journal of Accounting & Economics*, Vol.15 No.1, March 1992, pp.27-62.

Barth, Mary E., William H. Beaver and Wayne R. Landsman, "A Structural Analysis of Pension Disclosures under SFAS87 and Their Relation to Share Prices," *Financial Analysts Journal*, Vol.49 No.1, January/February 1993, pp.18-26.

Beaver, William H., "Commentary on Problems and Paradoxes in the Financial Reporting of Future Events," *Accounting Horizons*, Vol.5 No.4, December 1991, pp.122-134.

Bergstresser, Daniel, Mihir Desai and Joshua Rauh, "Earnings Manipulations, Pension Assumptions, and Managerial Investment Decisions," *The Quarterly Journal of Economics*, Vol.121 No.1, February 2006, pp.157-195.

Biddle, Gary C., Gim S. Seow and Andrew F. Siegel, "Relative versus Incremental Information Content," *Contemporary Accounting Research*, Vol.12 No.1, Fall 1995, pp.1-23.

Biddle, Gary C. and Jong-Hag Choi, "Is Comprehensive Income Useful?" *Journal of Contemporary Accounting & Economics*, Vol.2 No.1, June 2006, pp.1-32.

Blankley, Alan I. and Edward P. Swanson, "A Longtidinal Study of SFAS 87 Pension Rate Assumptions," *Accounting Horizon*, Vol.9 No.4, December 1995, pp1-21.

Bodie, Zvi, Jay O. Light, Randall Morck and Robert A. Taggart, Jr., "Funding and Asset Allocation in Corporate Pension Plans: An Empirical Investigation," in *Issues in Pension Economics*, eds. Bodie, Zvi et al., University of Chicago Press, 1987, pp.15-47.

Brown, Stephen, "The Impact of Pension Assumptions on Firm Value," *Working paper*, Goizueta Business School at Emory University, September 2004.

Bryan, Stephen H., Steven Lilien and Jane Mooney, "How the New Pension Accounting Rules Affect the Dow 30's Financial Statements," *The CPA Journal,* Vol.77 No.3, March 2007, pp.16-25.

Business Accounting Council, *Accounting Standard for Retirement Benefits,* Tokyo: BAC, June 1998.

Business Accounting Council, *Statement on Establishing Accounting Standard for Retirement Benefits,* Tokyo: BAC, June 1998.

Cahan, Steven F., Stephen M. Courtenay, Paul L. Gronewoller and David R. Upton, "Value Relevance of Mandated Comprehensive Income Disclosures," *Journal of Business Finance & Accounting,* Vol.27 No.9&10, November/December 2000, pp.1273-1301.

Chambers, Dennis, Thomas J. Linsmeier, Catherine Shakespeare and Theodore Sougiannis, "An Evaluation of SFAS No.130 Comprehensive Income Disclosures," *Review of Accounting Studies,* Vol.12 No.4, December 2007, pp.557-593.

Cheng, C. S. Agnes, Joseph K. Cheung and V. Goparakrishnan, "On the Usefulness of Operating Income, Net Income and Comprehensive Income in Explaining Security Returns," *Accounting and Business Research,* Vol.23 No.91, Spring 1993, pp.195-203.

Choi, Byeonghee, Daniel W. Collins and W. Bruce Johnson, "Valuation Implications of Reliability Differences: The Case of Nonpension Postretirement Obligations," *The Accounting Review,* Vol.72 No.3, July 1997, pp.351-383.

Chuo Audit Corp. and NLI Research Institute, *Accounting and Tax Practice for Corporate Pensions,* Tokyo: Nikkei Inc., 1999.

Collinson, David, "Actuarial Methods and Assumptions used in the Valuation of Retirement Benefits in the EU and Other European Countries," *Groupe Consultatif Actuariel Europeen,* United Kingdom, December 2001.

Coronado, Julia Lynn and Steven A. Sharpe, "Did Pension Plan Accounting Contribute to a Stock Market Bubble?," *Brookings Papers on Economic Activity1,* August 1, 2003, pp.323-371.

Daigo, Satoshi, *Coursework for Accounting,* Tokyo: University of Tokyo Press, 1998.

Dastgir, Mohsen and Ali Saeedi Velashani, "Comprehensive Income and Net Income as Measures of Firm Performance: Some Evidence for Scale Effect," *European Journal of Economics, Finance and Administrative Sciences,* Issue 12, October 2008, pp.123-133.

Dehning, Bruce and Paulette A. Ratliff, "Comprehensive Income: Evidence on the Effectiveness of FAS 130," *The Journal of American Academy of Business,* Cambridge, Vol.4 No.1/2, March 2004, pp.228-232.

Devine, Carl Thomas, *Essays in Accounting Theory,* Sarasota, Fla.: American Accounting Association, 1985.

Dhaliwal, Dan S., K. R. Subramanyam and Robert Trezevant, "Is Comprehensive Income Superior to Net Income as a Measure of Firm Performance?" *Journal of Accounting & Economics,* Vol.26

No.1-3, January 1999, pp.43-67.

Employees' Pension Fund Association, *Pension Systems in Other Countries*, Tokyo: Toyo Keizai, Inc., 1999.

Emura, Hiroshi and Masahiko Inoue, *The New Retirement Benefit Scheme and the Practical Accounting*, Tokyo: Nikkei Inc., 2002.

Ernst & Young ShinNihon LLC, *Comparison of IFRS and Japanese Accounting Standards*, Tokyo: Yushodo Press Co., Ltd., 2009.

Feldstein, Martin and Randall Morck, "Pension Funding Decisions, Interest Rate Assumptions, and Share Prices," in *Financial Aspects of the United States Pension System*, eds. Bodie, Zvi, and Shoven, John B., pp.177-207, Chicago: University of Chicago Press, 1983.

Feldstein, Martin and Stephanie Seligman, "Pension Funding, Share Prices, and National Savings," *The Journal of Finance*, Vol. 36 No. 4, September 1981, pp.801-824.

Feltham, Gerald A. and James A. Ohlson, "Valuation and Clean Surplus Accounting for Operating and Financial Activities," *Contemporary Accounting Research*, Vol.11 No.2, Spring 1995, pp.689-731.

Financial Accounting Standards Board, Statement of Financial Accounting Concepts No.6: *Elements of Financial Statements*, Norwalk, CT: FASB, December 1985.

Financial Accounting Standards Board, Statement of Financial Accounting Standards No.87: *Employers' Accounting for Pensions*, Stamford, CT: FASB, December 1985.

Financial Accounting Standards Board, Exposure Draft of a Proposed Statement of Financial Accounting Standards: *Employers' Accounting for Defined Benefit Pension and Other Postretirement Plans - an Amendment of FASB Statements No. 87, 88, 106, and 132(R)*, Norwalk, CT: FASB, March 2006.

Financial Accounting Standards Board, Statement of Financial Accounting Standards No.158: *Employers' Accounting for Defined Benefit Pension and Other Postretirement Plans*, Norwalk, CT: FASB, September 2006.

Financial Accounting Standards Board and International Accounting Standards Board, "Financial Statement Presentation, Analyst Field Test Results," IASB Meeting September 2009 (IASB Agenda Reference 9B), and FASB – Information Board Meeting September 21, 2009 (FASB Memo Reference 66B), September 2009.

Fitzpatrick, Brian D., Sudhakar S. Raju and Anthony L. Tocco, "Comprehensive Income Options: A Detriment To Transparency," *International Business & Economics Research Journal*, Vol.9 No.8, August 2010, pp.21-28.

Francis, Jennifer, Ryan LaFond, Per M. Olsson and Katherine Schipper, "Cost of Equity and Earnings Attributes," *The Accounting Review*, Vol.79 No.4, October 2004, pp.967-1010.

Ghicas, Dimitrios C., "Determinants of Actuarial Cost Method Changes for Pension Accounting and Funding," *The Accounting Review*, Vol.65 No.2, April 1990, pp.384-405.

Godwin, Joseph H., Stephen R. Goldberg and Jon E. Duchac, "An Empirical Analysis of Factors Associated with Changes in Pension-Plan Interest-Rate Assumptions," *Journal of Accounting, Auditing and Finance*, Vol.11 No.2, April 1996, pp.305-322.

Gopalakrishnan, V. and Timothy F. Sugrue, "An Empirical Investigation of Stock Market Valuation of Corporate Projected Pension Liabilities," *Journal of Business Finance & Accounting*, Vol.20 No.5, September 1993, pp.711-724.

Gopalakrishnan, V. and Timothy F. Sugrue, "The Determinants of Actuarial Assumptions under Pension Accounting Disclosures," *Journal of Financial and Strategic Decisions*, Vol.8 No.1, Spring 1995, pp.35-41.

Hamamura, Akira and Eriko Takino, "On the Valuation Gain and Loss of Entrusted Securities," *Journal of the University of Marketing and Distribution Sciences*, Vol.16 No.2, November 2003, pp.29-47.

Hann, Rebecca N., Frank Heflin and K. R. Subramanyam, "Fair-Value Pension Accounting," *Journal of Accounting & Economics*, Vol.44 No.3, December 2007 (2007a), pp.328-358.

Hann, Rebecca N., Yvonne Y. Lu and K. R. Subramanyam, "Uniformity versus Flexibility: Evidence from Pricing of the Pension Obligation," *The Accounting Review*, Vol.82 No.1, January 2007 (2007b), pp.107-137.

Hewitt Associates, *Pensions Pocket Book 2010*, UK: Economic and Financial Publishing Ltd., 2010.

Hirano, Yoshiaki, *Tax Practice For 401(k) and Corporate Pensions –In Preparation for the Introduction of Japanese 401(k)-*, Tokyo: Zeimu Kenkyukai, 1999.

Hirano, Yoshiaki, *New Corporate Pension System -Legal Work, Tax Practice, and Accounting-*, Tokyo: Okura Zaimu Kyokai, 2002.

Hirst, D. Eric and Patrick E. Hopkins, "Comprehensive Income Reporting and Analysts' Valuation Judgments," *Journal of Accounting Research*, Vol.36, Supplement, 1998, pp.47-75.

Houmes, Robert and Bob Boylan, "Has the Adoption of SFAS 158 Caused Firms to Underestimate Pension Liability? A Preliminary Study of the Financial Reporting Impact of SFAS158," *Academy of Accounting and Financial Studies Journal*, Vol.14 No.4, October 2010, pp.55-66.

Houmes, Robert, Bob Boylan and Inga Chira, "The Valuation Effect of Accounting Standard 158 on Firms with High and Low Financial Risk," *Atlantic Economic Journal*, Vol.39 No.1, March 2011, pp.47-57.

Imafuku, Aishi, *Accounting for Retirement Benefits*, Tokyo: Shinsei-Sha Co. Ltd., 2000.

Imafuku, Aishi, *Accounting for Labor Obligations*, Tokyo: Hakuto-Shobo Publishing Company, 2001.

Inoue, Masahiko, "Current Condition and Future Prospects of Accounting Standard for Employee Benefits -Summary of IASB Discussion Paper and the Effect-," *Weekly Keiei Zaimu*, No.2897, December 8, 2008.

International Accounting Standards Board, *Framework for the Preparation and Presentation of Financial Statements*, London: IASB, April 2001.

International Accounting Standards Board, International Accounting Standard No.8: *Accounting Policies, Changes in Accounting Estimates and Errors*, London: IASB, December 2003.

International Accounting Standards Board, International Accounting Standard No.32: *Financial Instruments: Presentation*, London: IASB, December 2003.

International Accounting Standards Board, International Accounting Standard No.39: *Financial Instruments: Recognition and Measurement*, London: IASB, December 2003.

International Accounting Standards Board, International Accounting Standard No.19: *Employee Benefits,* London: IASB, December 2004.

International Accounting Standards Board, IFRIC Interpretation No.14: *IAS 19 - The Limit on a Defined Benefit Asset, Minimum Funding Requirements and their Interaction,* London: IASB, July 2007.

International Accounting Standards Board, International Accounting Standard No.1: *Presentation of Financial Statements*, London: IASB, September 2007.

International Accounting Standards Board, Discussion Paper: *Preliminary Views on Amendments to IAS19 Employee Benefits*, London: IASB, March 2008.

International Accounting Standards Board, Discussion Paper: *Preliminary Views on Financial Statement Presentation*, London: IASB, October 2008.

International Accounting Standards Board, Exposure Draft: *Discount Rate for Employee Benefits -Proposed Amendments to IAS19*, London: IASB, August 2009.

International Accounting Standards Board, Exposure Draft: *Defined Benefit Plans -Proposed Amendments to IAS19*, London: IASB, April 2010.

International Accounting Standards Board, Exposure Draft: *Presentation of Items of Other Comprehensive Income -Proposed Amendments to IAS 1,* London: IASB, May 2010.

International Accounting Standards Board, *The Conceptual Framework for Financial Reporting,* London: IASB, September 2010.

International Accounting Standards Board, International Financial Reporting Standard No.9: *Financial Instruments,* London: IASB, October 2010.

International Accounting Standards Board, International Accounting Standard No.19: *Employee*

Benefits (revised), London: IASB, June 2011.

International Accounting Standards Board, *Presentation of Items of Other Comprehensive Income Amendments to IAS1*, London: IASB, June 2011.

International Accounting Standards Committee, International Accounting Standard No.7: *Statement of Cash Flows*, London: IASC, December 1992.

International Accounting Standards Committee, International Accounting Standard No.22: *Business Combinations*, London: IASC, September 1998.

International Accounting Standards Committee, International Accounting Standard No.37: *Provisions, Contingent Liabilities and Contingent Assets*, London: IASC, September 1998.

Ippolito, Rechard A., *Pension Plans and Employee Performance: Evidence, Analysis, and Policy*, Chicago: The University of Chicago Press, 1997.

Izumi, Nobutoshi, *Corporate Pension Plans*, Tokyo: Productivity Center for Socio-Economic Development, 2007.

Japanese Society of Certified Pension Actuaries, *Practical Standard for Defined-Benefit Corporate Pension*, Tokyo: JSCPA, April 2009.

Kagaya, Tetsuyuki, "Does the Convergence of the Pension Cost Presentation Affect Earnings Attributes?," *PIE/CIS Discussion Paper*, No. 438, Tokyo: Institute of Economic Research, Hitotsubashi University, August 2009.

Kanagaretnam, Kiridaran, Robert Mathieu and Mohamed Shehata, "Usefulness of Comprehensive Income Reporting in Canada," *Journal of Accounting and Public Policy*, Vol.28 No.4, July/August 2009, pp.349-365.

Kasaoka, Eriko, "The Market Valuation of a Revision to Accounting Standards for Employee Benefits in SFAS," *Indian Accounting Review*, Vol.11 No.2, December 2007, pp.43-55.

Kasaoka, Eriko, "Determinants of Changes and Levels in Discount Rates for Defined-Benefit Pension Plans," *International Review of Business*, No.11, March 2011, pp.65-94.

Kasaoka, Eriko, "Presentation of Defined Benefit Cost," *International Review of Business*, No.12, March 2012, pp.45-66.

Kasaoka, Eriko, "Fair Value of Defined Benefit Obligations in Japan," *International Review of Business*, No.13, March 2013, pp.59-85.

Kobayashi, Nobuyuki and Satoru Fujiwara, *Accounting Practice on Retirement Benefits*, Tokyo: Toyo Keizai, Inc., 1999.

Kothari, S. P. and Jerold L. Zimmerman, "Price and Return Models," *Journal of Accounting & Economics*, Vol.20 No.2, September 1995, pp.155-192.

KPMG Azusa LLC, *Q&A for Japanese Accounting Standards,* Tokyo: Seibunsha Co. Ltd., 2010.

Kubo, Tomoyuki, *Defined Contribution Pension Plan Act & Defined Benefit Corporate Pension Plan Act,* Tokyo: Nippon Keidanren Publishing Department, 2001.

Kubota, Keiichi, Kazuyuki Suda and Hitoshi Takehara, "Reporting of the Current Earnings plus Other Comprehensive Income: Information Content Test of Japanese Firms," *A Paper Presented at the 2006 Annual Meeting of American Accounting Association,* 2006.

Labor Standards Bureau, *Current Situation and Issues for Retirement Benefits,* Tokyo: The Institute of Labour Administration, 2000.

Landsman, Wayne R., "An Empirical Investigation of Pension Fund Property Rights," *The Accounting Review,* Vol.61 No.4, October 1986, pp.662-691.

Landsman, Wayne R. and James A. Ohlson, "Evaluation of Market Efficiency for Supplementary Accounting Disclosures: The Case of Pension Assets and Liabilities," *Contemporary Accounting Research,* Vol.7 No.1, Fall 1990, pp.185-198.

Li, Yong and Paul Klumpes, "Determinants of Expected Rate of Return on Pension Assets: Evidence from the UK," SSRN *Working Papers ID989559,* March 2007, pp.1-45.

Lorensen, Leonard and Paul Rosenfield, "Vested Benefits -A Company's Only Pension Liability," *Journal of Accountancy,* Vol.156 No.4, October 1983, pp.64-76.

Maines, Laureen A. and Linda S. McDaniel, "Effects of Comprehensive-Income Characteristics on Nonprofessional Investors' Judgments: The Role of Financial-Statement Presentation Format," *The Accounting Review,* Vol.75 No.2, April 2000, pp.179-207.

Ministry of Finance, *Order for Enforcement of the Corporation Tax Act,* Tokyo: MOF, November 2011.

Ministry of Health, Labour and Welfare, *Defined Benefit Corporate Pension Plan Act,* Tokyo: MHLW, June 2001.

Ministry of Health, Labour and Welfare, *Standards for Fiscal Management of Employees' Pension Fund,* Tokyo: MHLW, September 2007.

Ministry of Health, Labour and Welfare, *Amendments of Financial Administration Policy on Employees' Pension Fund,* Tokyo: MHLW, September 30, 2009.

Ministry of Health, Labour and Welfare, *Employees' Pension Insurance Act,* Tokyo: MHLW, August 2011.

Ministry of Health, Labour and Welfare, *Enforcement Regulation for Defined Benefit Corporate Pension Plan Act,* Tokyo: MHLW, August 2011.

Mitra, Santanu and Mahmud Hossain, "Value-Relevance of Pension Transition Adjustments and Other Comprehensive Income Components in the Adoption Year of SFAS No.158," *Review of*

Quantitative Finance and Accounting, Vol.33 No.3, October 2009, pp.279-301.

Morris, Michael H., William D. Nichols and Gregory R. Niehaus, "Considerations Driving Interest Rate Assumption Changes," *Financial Analysts Journal*, Vol.39 No.6, November/December 1983, pp.13-15.

Morse, Dale, "Price and Trading Volume Reaction Surrounding Earnings Announcements: A Closer Examination," *Journal of Accounting Research,* Vol.19 No.2, Autumn 1981, pp.374-383.

Murakami, Kiyoshi, *Corporate Pensions*, Tokyo: Nikkei Inc., 1999.

Murray, Dennis, "What Are the Essential Features of a Liability?" *Accounting Horizons,* Vol.24 No.4, December 2010, pp.623-633.

Nakakita, Toru, *The Future of Corporate Pension,* Tokyo: Chikumashobo Ltd., 2001.

Nakano, Makoto, "Measurement of Defined Benefit Obligations under Corporate Pension Accounting -ABO and PBO-," *The Japan Industrial Management & Accounting,* Vol.56 No.3, October 1996, p.90-101.

Nakano, Makoto, "Empirical Research on ABO v.s. PBO in Corporate Pension Accounting -Analysis of Incremental Information Content and Relative Information Content-," *Kigyo Kaikai*, Vol.52 No.5, May 2000, pp.101-110.

Nihon Economic Newspaper (Evening), March 18, 2010.

Nihon Economic Newspaper (Morning), February 26, 2012.

Nihon Economic Newspaper (Morning), March 23, 2012.

Nihon Economic Newspaper (Morning), May 16, 2012.

Nihon Economic Newspaper (Morning), November 3, 2012.

Obinata, Takashi, "Choice of Pension Discount Rate in Financial Accounting and Stock Prices," *Discussion Paper CIRIE-F-82*, University of Tokyo, July 2000.

Okumura, Masashi, "Discretion in the Choice of Pension Discount Rate, Projected Benefit Obligation and Stock Price," *The Waseda Commercial Review*, No.404, June 2005, pp.27-49.

Oldfield, George S., "Financial Aspects of the Private Pension System," *Journal of Money, Credit and Banking*, Vol.9 No.1, February 1977, pp.48-54.

Ota, Koji and Akihiko Matsuo, "The Vuong (1989) Test and Its Application," *The Journal of Musashi University*, Vol.52 No.1, July 2004, pp.39-75.

Pension Fund Association, *Management of Pension Funding without Legal Controls*, Tokyo: Toyo Keizai, Inc., 1999.

Pension Fund Association, *Pension Systems in Other Countries*, Tokyo: Toyo Keizai, Inc., 1999.

Picconi, Marc, "The Perils of Pensions: Does Pension Accounting Lead Investors and Analysts Astray?" *The Accounting Review*, Vol.81 No.4, July 2006, pp.925-955.

Reiter, Sara A., "Pension Obligation and the Determination of Bond Risk Premiums: Evidence from the Electric Industry," *Journal of Business Finance & Accounting*, Vol.18 No.6, November 1991, pp.833-859.

Rue, Joseph C. and David E. Tosh, "Continuing Unresolved Issues of Pension Accounting," *Accounting Horizons*, Vol.1 No.4, December 1987, pp.21-27.

Sawa, Etsuo, "Reporting (No.2) and Comment on IASC "Retirement Benefits and Other Costs for Employee Benefits" from Drafting Committee," *JICPA Journal*, Vol.8 No.8, August 1996, pp.21-26.

Schmidt, George L. and Dorothy A. Thompson, "The Effect on Firms Defined Pension Plans & Financial Statements Due to FAS158," *International Journal of Business, Accounting, and Finance*, Vol.4 No.1, Winter 2010, pp.63-69.

Schneider, Douglas K., Mark G. McCarthy and Lizabeth Austen-Jaggard, "Change in Reporting the Funded Status of Pensions: Impact on Debt-Asset and Debt-Equity Ratios," *The Coastal Business Journal*, Vol.10 No.1, Spring 2011, pp.31-40.

Sekine, Aiko, "Accounting Procedure for Pensions," *JICPA Journal*, Vol.10 No.3, March 1998, pp.39-43.

Soroosh, Jalal and Pouran Espahbodi, "New Accounting Rules for Postretirement Benefits," *The CPA Journal*, Vol.77 No.1, January 2007, pp.28-35.

Stickney, Clyde P., Paul R. Brown and James M. Wahlen, *Financial Reporting, Financial Statement Analysis, and Valuation: A Strategic Perspective*, Sixth Edition, Mason, OH: Thomson South-Western, 2006.

Suda, Kazuyuki, *Empirical Analysis of Accounting Reform*, Tokyo: Dobunkan Shuppan, Co. Ltd., 2004.

Tagaya, Mitsuru, *Accounting Standards for Retirement Benefits*, Tokyo: Zeimu Kenkyukai, 2000.

Takino, Eriko, "Gains and Losses on Employee Benefits in Japan," *Annual Report of Japanese Association for International Accounting Studies in 2004*, March 2005, pp.123-138.

Takino, Eriko, "Unrecognized Obligations and Deferred Recognition on Employee Benefits in Japan," *International Review of Business*, No.9, March 2007, pp.21-39.

The First Audit Committee, First Audit Committee Report No.33: *Accounting Procedures and Presentation, and Audit Treatment on Transition to a Tax-Qualified Pension Plan etc.*, Tokyo, April 10, 1979.

The Institute of Actuaries of Japan & The Japanese Society of Certified Pension Actuaries, *Practices on Accounting for Retirement Benefits*, Tokyo: IAJ&JSCPA, December 2008.

The Investigation Committee on Financial Accounting Systems, *Corporate Accounting Principles*, Tokyo, 1949.

The Japanese Institute of Certified Public Accountants, JICPA Accounting Practice Committee Report No.13: *Practical Guidance on Accounting for Retirement Benefits (Interim Report)*, Tokyo: JICPA, February 2009.

The Japanese Institute of Certified Public Accountants, *Questions and Answers on Accounting for Retirement Benefits*, Tokyo: JICPA, February 2009.

Utani, Ryoji, *History of Corporate Pensions -Trajectory of Failures,* Tokyo: Corporate Pension Research Institute Co., Ltd, 1993.

VanDerhei, Jack, "Retirement Income Adequacy after PPA and FAS158: Part One - Plan Sponsors' Reactions," EBRI Issue Brief, No.307, July 2007.

Vuong, Quang H., "Likelihood Ratio Tests for Model Selection and Non-Nested Hypotheses," *Econometrica*, Vol.57 No.2, March 1989, pp.307-333.

Watts, Ross L. and Jerold L. Zimmerman, *Positive Accounting Theory*, Englewood Cliffs, NJ: Prentice-Hall Inc., 1986.

Yamaguchi, Osamu, *Practice of Defined Benefit Obligations,* Tokyo: Chuokeizai-Sha, Inc., 2000.

Yamaguchi, Osamu, *Retirement Benefit Plans,* Tokyo: Kindai-Sales Co., Ltd., 2001.

Yamaguchi, Osamu, "Discounted Cash Flow in Accounting for Retirement Benefits," *Kigyo Kaikei*, Vol.54 No.4, April 2002, pp.490-495.

Yamaguchi, Osamu, "A Study on the Present Value of Defined Benefit Obligations in Japan," *Yokohama Business Review,* The Society for Business Administration of Yokohama National University, Vol.25 No.2/3, December 2004, pp.35-58.

Yamaguchi, Osamu, "Transition of Japanese Corporate Pension Plans and Accounting," *Kigyo Kaikei,* Vol.62 No.7, July 2010, pp.954-961.

Yano, Manabu, "Accounting Standards for Corporate Pension and Evaluation of Stock Prices," *Nenkin to Keizai,* Vol.23 No.4, February 2005, pp.38-45.

Yoshida, Kazuo, "Determinants of Expected Rate of Return on Plan assets in Japan," *KAIKEI,* Vol.175 No.5, May 2009, pp.676-690.

Zimmerman, Jerold L., "Taxes and Firm Size," *Journal of Accounting & Economics,* No.5, April 1983, pp.119-149.

(Homepages)

Accounting Standards Board of Japan, "A Report on the Progress of Retirement Benefits (Step1)," January 19, 2012, https://www.asb.or.jp/asb/asb_j/minutes/20120119/20120119_02.pdf, (accessed 9-20-2013).

Accounting Standards Board of Japan, "A Report on the Progress of Retirement Benefits (Step1) Discussion for Developing a Standard," June 2, 2011, https://www.asb.or.jp/asb/asb_j/minutes/20110602/20110602_06.pdf, (accessed 9-20-2013).

Employee Benefit Research Institute, "EBRI Databook on Employee Benefits Chapter11: Retirement Plan Finances," http://www.ebri.org/pdf/publications/books/databook/DB.Chapter%2011.pdf, (accessed 9-20-2013).

Ernst & Young, *IFRS -Observations on the Implementation of IFRS-*, September 2006, http://www2.eycom.ch/publications/items/ifrs/single/200609_observations_on_ifrs/200609_EY_Observations_on_IFRS.pdf, (accessed 9-20-2013).

Financial Accounting Standards Board, "Board Meeting Handout Conceptual Framework," June 25, 2008, http://www.fasb.org/jsp/FASB/Document_C/DocumentPage&cid=1218220092264, (accessed 9-20-2013).

Financial Accounting Standards Board, "Minutes of the October 20, 2008 Conceptual Framework (Phase B) Board Meeting," October 22, 2008, http://www.fasb.org/board_meeting_minutes/10-20-08_cf.pdf, (accessed 9-20-2013).

International Accounting Standards Board, Liabilities-Amendments to IAS 37 *Provisions, Contingent Liabilities and Contingent Assets* and IAS 19 *Employee Benefits*, June 2009, http://www.iasb.org/NR/rdonlyres/B2EE99F3-C48E-40A1-8827-5137C92C0EF4/0/LiabIAS37projectJune08.pdf, (accessed 5-19-2011).

JP Actuary Consulting Co., Ltd, "Glossary of Pension Terms," http://www.jpac.co.jp/english/glossary/, (accessed 9-20-2013).

Ministry of Finance, "Auction Announcement and Result," http://www.mof.go.jp/jgbs/auction/past_auction_schedule/index.html, (accessed 9-20-2013).

Ministry of Health, Labour and Welfare, "Average Lifetime," http://www.mhlw.go.jp/toukei/saikin/hw/life/life10/01.html, (accessed 9-20-2013).

Ministry of Health, Labour and Welfare, "Average Lifetime in Each Country," http://www.mhlw.go.jp/toukei/saikin/hw/life/life10/03.html, (accessed 9-20-2013)

Ministry of Health, Labour and Welfare, "Defined-Contribution Pension," http://www.mhlw.go.jp/topics/bukyoku/nenkin/nenkin/kyoshutsu/kiyakusu.html, (accessed 9-20-2013).

Ministry of Health, Labour and Welfare, "Enforcement Status of Defined-Contribution Pension," http://www.mhlw.go.jp/topics/bukyoku/nenkin/nenkin/kyoshutsu/sekou.html, (accessed 9-20-2013).

References 187

Ministry of Health, Labour and Welfare, "Outline of Defined-Benefit Corporate Pension Plan Act," http://www.mhlw.go.jp/topics/0102/tp0208-1a.html, (accessed 9-20-2013).

Ministry of Health, Labour and Welfare, "Overview of Pension System1," http://www.mhlw.go.jp/english/org/policy/dl/p36-37p1-2.pdf, (accessed 9-20-2013).

Nakata, Tadashi, "Review of Discussion Paper: Preliminary Views on Amendments to IAS19 Employee Benefits," *NFI Research Review,* July 2008, http://www.nikko-fi.co.jp/uploads/photos1/648.pdf, (accessed 9-20-2013).

National Personnel Authority, "Table 2 Current Status of Corporate Pension Plans and Retirement Lump Sum Grants in Private Firms," http://www.jinji.go.jp/toukei/taisyokukyuufu/taisyoku_h23.htm, (accessed 9-20-2013).

Pension Fund Association, "Annual Report 2011," http://www.pfa.or.jp/jigyo/tokei/shisanunyo/jittai/files/AnnualReport2011.pdf, (accessed 9-20-2013).

Pension Fund Association, "Financial Condition on Defined-Benefit Corporate Pension," http://www.pfa.or.jp/jigyo/tokei/zaisei/kakuteikyufu/index.html, (accessed 9-20-2013).

Pension Fund Association, "Financial Condition on Employees' Pension Fund," http://www.pfa.or.jp/jigyo/tokei/zaisei/koseinenkin/index/html, (accessed 9-20-2013).

Pension Fund Association, "Financial Condition on Tax-Qualified Pension Plan," http://www.pfa.or.jp/jigyo/tokei/zaisei/zaisei02.html, (accessed 9-20-2013).

Pension Fund Association, "Glossary," http://www.pfa.or.jp/yogoshu/yo/yo06.html, (accessed 9-20-2013).

Pension Fund Association, "Management Condition on Pension Assets," http://www.pfa.or.jp/jigyo/tokei/shisanunyo/shisanunyo01.html, (accessed 9-20-2013).

Pension Fund Association, "The Survey and Comment on Pension Asset Management," http://www.pfa.or.jp/jigyo/tokei/shisanunyo/jittai/index.html, (accessed 9-20-2013).

The Asahi Shimbun Company, "20 Toshiba Group Companies Introduced a Floating Interest Rate for a Part of Their Corporate Pension," http://www.asahi.com/money/pension/news/TKY200310180278.html (accessed 9-20-2013).

The National Association of Pension Funds, *Trends in Defined Benefit Asset Allocation: the Changing Shape of UK Pension Investment,* July 2013, http://www.napf.co.uk/PolicyandResearch/DocumentLibrary/~/media/Policy/Documents/0314_Trends_in_db_asset_allocation_changing_shape_UK_pension_investment_NAPF_research_paper_July_2013_DOCUMENT.ashx, (accessed 9-20-2013).

The Securities Analysts Association of Japan, "Comment Letter on Exposure Draft of Statement No.39: *Exposure Draft of Accounting Standard for Retirement Benefits,*" May 31, 2010, http://www.saa.or.jp/account/account/pdf/ikensho100531.pdf, (accessed 9-20-2013).

The Senate and House of Representatives of the United States of America in Congress, *Pension Protection Act of 2006*, http://www.gpo.gov/fdsys/pkg/PLAW-109publ280/pdf/PLAW-109publ280.pdf, August 17 2006, (accessed 9-20-2013).

United States Department of Labor, "Employee Retirement Income Security Act - ERISA," http://www.dol.gov/dol/topic/health-plans/erisa.htm, (accessed 9-20-2013).

Verrall, R. J., T. Sithole and S. Haberman, "Second International Comparative Study of Mortality Tables for Pension Fund Retirees," *Sessional Research Discussion Paper* of The Actuarial Profession, June 2011, http://www.actuaries.org.uk/research-and-resources/documents/second-international-comparative-study-mortality-tables-pension-fun, (accessed 9-20-2013).

Yoshii, Kazuhiro, "Review on Accounting Standard of Retirement Benefits," *Legal and Tax Report*, Daiwa Institute of Research, March 23, 2012, http://www.dir.co.jp/souken/research/report/law-research/accounting/12032301accounting.pdf, (accessed 9-20-2013).

著者略歴

笠岡恵理子（かさおか・えりこ）

1979 年：兵庫県に生まれる。
2001 年：流通科学大学商学部経営学科卒業　学士（経営学）
2003 年：関西学院大学大学院商学研究科博士課程前期課程修了　修士（商学）
2006 年：関西学院大学大学院商学研究科博士課程後期課程単位取得満期退学
2006 年：ゴールデンゲート大学会計学修士課程　M.Acc.
2013 年：関西学院大学大学院商学研究科博士課程後期課程修了　博士（商学）
2014 年 3 月現在：関西学院大学大学院商学研究科博士課程後期課程　研究員

Eriko Kasaoka

1979: Born in Hyogo, Japan.
2001: B.A. in Management, University of Marketing and Distribution Sciences, Japan.
2003: M.A. in Business Administration, Kwansei Gakuin University, Japan.
2006: Completed Ph.D. Program in Business Administration without Dissertation, Kwansei Gakuin University, Japan.
2006: M.A. in Accountancy, Golden Gate University, USA.
2013: Ph.D. in Business Administration, Kwansei Gakuin University, Japan.
As of March 2014: Post-Doctoral Fellow, Graduate School of Business Administration, Kwansei Gakuin University, Japan.

The Effect of Defined Benefit Liability on Firms' Valuations in Japan: Comparison of Japanese GAAP for Retirement Benefits with IAS19

2014 年 3 月 20 日初版第一刷発行

著　者　　笠岡恵理子

発行者
発行所　　関西学院大学出版会
所在地　　〒662-0891
　　　　　兵庫県西宮市上ケ原一番町 1-155
電　話　　0798-53-7002

印　刷　　協和印刷株式会社

©2014 Eriko Kasaoka
Printed in Japan by Kwansei Gakuin University Press
ISBN 978-4-86283-155-2
乱丁・落丁本はお取り替えいたします。
本書の全部または一部を無断で複写・複製することを禁じます。
http://www.kwansei.ac.jp/press